New York's
Great Lost Ballparks

New York's
Great Lost Ballparks

Bob Carlin

**EXCELSIOR
EDITIONS**

Cover: The "original" Yankee Stadium (I) as photographed by Carol Highsmith in the 1980s. From the Carol M. Highsmith Archive, at the Prints and Photographs Division, Library of Congress.

Published by State University of New York Press, Albany

© 2022 Bob Carlin

Excelsior Editions is an imprint of State University of New York Press

For information, contact State University of New York Press, Albany, NY
www.sunypress.edu

Library of Congress Cataloging-in-Publication Data

Name: Carlin, Bob, author.
Title: New York's great lost ballparks / Bob Carlin.
Description: Albany : State University of New York Press, 2022. | Series:
    Excelsior editions | Includes bibliographical references and index.
Identifiers: LCCN 2022006880 | ISBN 9781438490229 (pbk. : alk. paper) | ISBN
    9781438490236 (ebook)
Subjects: LCSH: Baseball—New York (State)—History. | Baseball fields—New
    York (State)—History.
Classification: LCC GV863.N7 C37 2022 | DDC 796.35706/809747—dc23/
    eng/20220509
LC record available at https://lccn.loc.gov/2022006880

10 9 8 7 6 5 4 3 2 1

Contents

Introduction

Welcome to the world of baseball parks. You see, unlike any other
arena, the diamond can be as much a part of the game as the teams
themselves. Where the game is played is often as important as how it
is played, as each ballpark plays a vital role in creating the atmosphere
and mystique of baseball.

—David Pietrusza, *Baseball's Canadian-American League*

Baseball: A (Very Quick) Historical Overview

During the second quarter of the 19th century, the American game of
baseball was born. Throughout the United States of that time (which
was primarily centered in the Northeast), various versions of what was
to become "the national pastime" began to be played. Setting aside the
folklore of Doubleday and Cooperstown (although not diminishing in
the least the Baseball Hall of Fame, a place that every fan of the game
should regularly visit), according to current scholarship, the amateur
game was actively germinating in many parts of the new republic. In the
greater New York City area, the sport of cricket, associated with England
(against whom the United States had just fought two wars), was gradually
giving way to the very American game of baseball. Likewise, the open
fields where cricket was pursued were usurped as the initial homes for the
game of "ball." Albany appears to have had an "organized" baseball club
by 1856, Troy in 1859, and Schenectady, Saratoga Springs, and Scotia by
1860, when the first "National Association" was formed.

According to early baseball historian Richard Hershberger:

Upstate New York was the first hotbed of modern baseball, the "New York Game," as it emerged from the incubation ground of Manhattan and its immediate environs. . . . The game spread quickly up the Hudson River to Albany, and from there westward along the Erie Canal corridor.[1]

By the time of the lead up to the Civil War, the New York game or "New York Rules" had come to dominate the nascent sport. Touring by professional teams, amateur in name only, spread the New York City structure and led to the emergence after the conflict for the first leagues of paid players. These excursions included trips by New York City based squads to other metropolitan areas throughout the state.

After 1865, baseball's growth continued unencumbered. Seeds for the first professional major baseball league, the National Association, were sown in Troy in 1871. The National League followed in 1876.

What's a Ballpark, Anyway?

Noun: A park or stadium in which ball games (such as baseball) are played.

—Merriam-Webster online

The coming of salaried players, of course, led to the original baseball "grounds" or fields (which were just that, without any of the amenities we've come to expect from our modern facilities) giving way to the ballparks and (eventually) stadiums of today. How do owners maintain facilities and teams pay their players? Charge admission! How are the spectators who bought tickets kept separate from nonpaying enthusiasts? By building walls and gates around the diamond. How do you keep the fans occupied during the lulls in the on-field action? Sell food and drink, along with scorecards and other swag. Hence, the promulgation, in the later part of the 1800s, of the enclosed ballpark.

With a few notable earlier exceptions, during the last two decades of the 19th century, the first of the facilities with seating and other conveniences opened. The largest of these wooden structures included the Polo

---

1. Richard Hershberger, "Upstate New York" introduction, in Morris et al., *Base Ball Pioneers, 1850–1870.*

Grounds, Washington Park, and Eastern Park in New York City; Buffalo's Olympic and Riverside Parks; Celoron Park in Celoron; Rochester's Culver and Riverside Parks; Star Park in Syracuse; Albany's Riverside Park; Donovan Field in Kingston; and Driving Park in Schenectady, among others. The original structures were almost designed to be disposable. They were built quickly, and often dismantled after a season or two. Sometimes, the buildings, stands, and fences were recycled, and moved to a different location. Consequently, it should come as no surprise that collapsing seating and fires were a common occurrence in the nascent "good old days" of baseball. Between the world wars of the 20th century, "modern" stadiums of steel and concrete replaced these wooden edifices. Author and baseball aficionado Stew Thornley labels 1909 through the Depression as "the classic period of ballparks."[2]

New York's Great Lost Ballparks covers all baseball venues (1) that have hosted (my very loose definition of) "professional" organizations that no longer exist and (2) have passed from use by teams that paid their players and charged admission. I've stretched this characterization somewhat to include those facilities utilized by the sport since it became a public spectacle. Included are the "grounds" of baseball's earliest version around the Civil War, the first wooden enclosed "fields" of major and minor league baseball during the late 19th and early 20th centuries, as well as the steel and concrete "stadiums" mostly erected through World War II. I've even thrown in a few modern spectacles costing millions of dollars to construct that have come and gone in New York's metropolitan centers.

Both the first grounds and enclosed fields generally sat on privately owned lots. Sometimes, they already included features such as grandstand seating used for the spectators of other sports, like horse and bicycle racing. Franchise holders would lease the land and bear the costs of any improvements needed to yield a functional ballpark. As baseball facilities became more complicated, owners spent larger and larger amounts on fields. The original Yankee Stadium of 1923 signaled the peak in owner-financed sporting palaces.

Eventually, as the budgets for stadium construction ran into the millions of dollars, the proprietors of baseball clubs looked to local municipalities to provide the means for them to play the game. Franchisees and city officials justified these taxpayer costs through the perceived direct and indirect

---

2. Thornley, *The Polo Grounds*.

economic benefits games would create for area businesses and tax bases alike.

My own enjoyment stems equally from the competition between the players, the food, team merchandise for sale, interactions with the other fans, and, importantly, the comfort, design, and construction of the ballpark. I'll freely admit a bias toward classic, old-style facilities. Give me a covered grandstand, mechanical scoreboard, and a misshapen field, and I'll be happy.

One primary function for the older ballparks is approximating a pastoral experience within an urban setting. Life slows down, the food evokes (as it often is) picnic fare, and everything is about observing, dissecting, and interpreting the play and the umpire's decisions. The grass is green, the sky is blue, or, for a night game, star filled or really black outside the reach of the lights.

New York's Great Lost Ballparks tells the story of how baseball shaped the history of the state, an area that was one of the most important incubators toward the development of the modern game. Within this volume, you'll find the playing grounds, ballparks, and stadiums of yesteryear. Laid out in a guidebook format, each listing includes, wherever possible, a photographic illustration of the field, along with data such as the name and geographic location of each park, size of the diamond, the years built and in operation (when dissimilar, separated by a /), seating and capacity (again, divided if different by a /), the names of the professional clubs and leagues that called it their home, and a "Fun Fact" or two that distinguished each locale from other fields. For the more famous ballparks, there is an expanded history, encompassing the architects and engineers responsible for their design and construction, select visiting squads that played there, and the importance of the field in the annals of the game. I've also indicated if the park still exists and, if not, what currently sits on the site. Each listing additionally includes various sources and weblinks for more information. Entries are arranged by region (the New York City area, the Southern Tier, Western New York State, the Northern Tier, and Eastern New York State) and therein alphabetically by city, with the stadiums inventoried chronologically by construction date. In some cases, where one team utilized a succession of fields at the same locale, I've grouped those parks together. Along with the many minor league and professional clubs that flourished over the decades, I've also made a special effort to highlight facilities that hosted Negro Leagues and all-women's teams.

Methodology and Acknowledgments

In researching this work on New York's baseball fields pre-2020, I have endeavored to be as thorough as possible. However, I often had to contend with contradictory conclusions and incongruities inside the cannon of baseball scholarship. Therefore, within these pages, I have either used my best judgment, supported by additional research in primary sources, or, in the most difficult cases that I simply couldn't unravel, presented the conflicting information for readers to make their own determinations.

To help those enthusiasts who would like to visit historic ballpark sites, we've included ten maps within major metropolitan areas. As some street names have changed or moved and some addresses are ambiguous, ballpark locations are only approximate. Unfortunately, due to space limitations or a lack of specific coordinates, we've been unable to map all listed fields.

To help right prior societal wrongs, one of my goals has been to include underrepresented African-American and women's teams wherever possible. This has meant featuring semiprofessional clubs whose skills were equivalent to (or above) area pro players. However, because the focus of this book is on residential squads, opportunities were limited to present the touring professional organizations that existed outside of major and minor league (i.e., white, male) baseball.

Once I began discovering New York's Black squads, questions were raised in my own mind about how to identify these teams. Not all readers would recognize organizations that weren't a member of an officially labeled "Negro League." The history of baseball and the media that described and promoted the sport, and, likewise, the society around it, has not always been kind in the terminology used for describing teams of non-white players. Nor, in fact, would the names used by the professional leagues and teams pass current tests of sensitivity and correctness. Therefore, I've utilized Negro Leagues (without the quotation marks) as a generic label for segregated groups of Black players. This term appears to be in current usage among baseball scholars and cultural institutions presenting the stories of these baseballers. For the few instances where I've mentioned Black and Native Americans organizations (such as the National Colored League), as well as the use of (sometimes offensive) baseball descriptors (for example, the Syracuse Chiefs) in the names for white players, I've kept those original historically correct terms.

Due to the limitations placed by the COVID pandemic, I was unable to physically travel to local archives and historical collections. Therefore, instead of my going to the library, the libraries had to come to me. By assembling a small collection of volumes on New York State baseball history here at home, I've consulted as many works by the real baseball authorities as I could. Additionally, I've taken advantage of the wealth of baseball websites and blogs, along with primary source materials from digitized period newspapers, available on the internet.

I'm not "the" expert (or even an expert) on any aspect of baseball, in New York State or elsewhere. Fortunately, I've had access to the research of many authorities on the sport. With the risk of leaving someone out, thanks goes to Priscilla Astifan at rochesterbaseballhistory.org; Gary Ashwill of agatetype.typepad.com and seamheads.com; Thomas Barthel; Michael Benson; Dick Beverage; Thomas M. Blair; William H. Brewster; Marietta Carr of Schenectady County Historical Society; Jerrold Casway; Gregory Christiano; Marvin A. Cohen; L. Robert Davids; James Delaney, Jr.; Mike Disotelle of Ilion Free Public Library; Rachel Dworkin, archivist for Chemung County Historical Society; David Dyte of brooklynballparks.com/covehurst.net; Dennis Evanosky; Scott Fiesthumel; Thomas W. Gilbert; Mike Hauser; Paul Healey of projectballpark.org; Brock Helander; Richard Hershberger; Miriam Hoffman of the Historical Society of the Nyacks; Chris Hunter of the Museum of Innovation and Science; Jerry Jackson; W. Lloyd Johnson; David Karpinski of the Parkhurst Field Foundation; Frank M. Keetz; Norm King; Tony Kissel of tonykisselbaseball.com; Eric J. Kos; Jeffrey Michael Laing; Bill Lamb; Paul Langendorfer; Roger L. Luther of Broome County Historical Society; Bob LeMoine; Dick Leyden; Stephen Loughman and Jennifer Lemak of the New York State Museum; Vern Luse; Rich MacAlpine; Jim Maggiore; Jim Mandelaro; Bob Mayer; Michael J. McCann; Bill McCarthy; Larry McCray of protoball.org; Jim McGreal; Brian Merzbach of ballparkreviews.com; Aaron W. Miller; Collin Miller of Mountain Athletic Club; Peter Morris; Timothy P. Murphy; Charlie O'Reilly of charliesballparks.com; Kim Reis of Imagn; James H. Overfield; Joseph Overfield; Jim Overmyer; John Pardon; John Pastier; Eric and Wendy Pastore of digitalballparks.com; David Pietrusza; Scott Pitoniak; Richard A. Puff; William J. Ryczek at SABR (Society for American Baseball Research); Samantha Saladino, Fulton County Historian; Ron Selter; David B. Stinson of deadballbaseball.com; John Thorn of ourgame.mlblogs.com; Stew Thornley; Anthony Violanti; Bernard G. Walsh; Dave Walsh; Steve West; Bob Whittemore; Richard Worth; John G. Zinn; and others too numerous to mention here. Specific sources are available in the For More Information section for each ballpark listing, with full bibliographic information contained in the References section after the listings. Although I don't mention them in the FMI sections, I've also made extensive use of Wikipedia, newspapers.com, nyshistoricnewspapers.org, ancestry.com, http://www.brooklynballparks.com, and digitalballparks.com. Because the FMI is meant as informational and not as a comprehensive listing of sources, I've also chosen to omit websites and links that have changed and are no longer functional.

I'll additionally give a shout out to my editor (who is also my brother), Richard Carlin, and all the others at Excelsior Editions/State University of New York Press including copy editor Gordon Marce and my production and design manager Ryan Morris for structural and grammatical guidance throughout the process of bringing this book to completion. Thanks, as well, to my "buds in baseball" Wil Scotten, John W. Miller, Elizabeth Loring, Tony Klassen, my late mother-in-law Jean Smith, Bill Evans, Gary Davidson, Bill Nowlin, Mark Simos, Jim Bollman, Alan Munde, Marc Fields, Wayne Rogers, Henry Sapoznik, Roy Bookbinder, and Wayne Henderson. Attending games as an adult all started with my son, Benjamin, who always loved the souvenirs and a good playground.

This book is dedicated to my grandfather, Morris Carlin, who played and loved the game. My father's father gave me my first major league experience by taking my brother and I to Yankee Stadium around 1960.

A note on terminology: before the current one-word term "baseball" came into usage, the game was labeled "base ball," broken into two words. Unless I'm directly quoting a source, I've standardized the term throughout as "baseball." I've taken the same approach to "ball park" and "ballpark."

The Ballparks

Building a baseball field is more work than you might imagine.

—W. P. Kinsella, *Shoeless Joe*

New York City Area

Godspeed the churches and ball clubs of our sister city.

—one Manhattanite's comment about Brooklyn

THE BRONX

CROTONA PARK

With one of the first enclosed grounds in baseball, the Union charged 25 cents for admission. The field lacked a grand stand, in favor of simple board seats. Shade trees and embanked railroad tracks surrounded the Union outfield. This unusual playing surface provided for tough obstacles for the outfielders, who had to climb the embankments in order to retrieve fly balls hit over them.

—Aaron W. Miller, "Union Base Ball Club of Morrisania," in Morris et al., *Base Ball Founders*

Location: 163rd Street, Morrisania, the Bronx

Dimensions: unknown

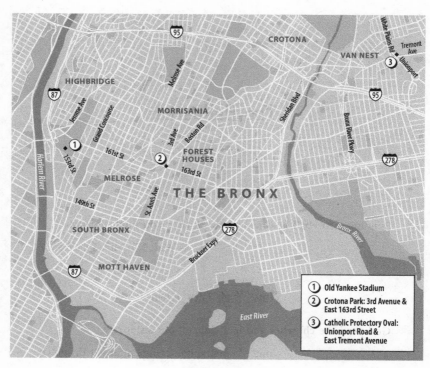

Map 1. The Bronx Ballparks.

Home Team(s): Union/National Association

Built/In Operation: late 1860s

Seats/Capacity: unknown

Fun Facts: This Union team built their ballpark on a property located 14 miles north of midtown New York City near Tremont, New York. At present, this location is part of the Crotona Park neighborhood in the Bronx.

FMI: Gilbert, *How Baseball Happened*; Aaron W. Miller, "Union Base Ball Club of Morrisania," in Morris et al., *Base Ball Founders*.

CATHOLIC PROTECTORY OVAL

One by one, New York's semi-pro baseball field[s] are disappearing. Last season [1938], Dyckman Oval, Recreation Park under the Queensboro Bridge and Catholic Protectory Oval went the way of all real estate. A street has already been cut through the Bay Ridge Oval and the site of Farmers' Stadium has been sold for building lots, leaving only Dexter Park, the Bay Parkways' home of Erasmus Field, and Queens Park, Woodside for the semi-pro lads.

—*Democrat and Chronicle*, January 10, 1939

Location: on the grounds of the Catholic orphanage, East Tremont Avenue and Unionport Road, the Bronx

Dimensions: left 180', center 292', right 180'

Home Team(s): New York Lincoln Giants/Eastern Colored League; American Negro Leagues; and Eastern Independent League

Built/In Operation: 1920/1920, and 1922 through 1930. Demolished in 1938 after the end of the baseball season, replaced by the Parkchester Apartments.

Seats/Capacity: 8,000/10,000

Fun Facts: In 1920, a grandstand and bleachers were moved here from **Olympic Field** for Sunday games. At the start of the 1925 season, some

The "original" Yankee Stadium (I) as photographed by Carol Highsmith in the 1980s. From the Carol M. Highsmith Archive, at the Prints and Photographs Division, Library of Congress.

large trees were eliminated from right field to make the player's job easier. During the 1930 season, the House of David baseball squad visited the Lincoln Giants (Negro Leagues), losing two games to the New Yorkers. For 1932–1938, the semipro white Carltons took up residency at the Oval. Along with other like-minded teams, they challenged Negro Leagues squads as well as other barnstormers, sometimes under lights.

FMI: Benson, *Ballparks of North America*; Ashwill, *Agate Type*, February 28, 2011; Leland, "Black Baseball"; "The Rise of the Cubans"; Robertson, "Harlem and Baseball in the 1920s"; Nielsen, "The Lincoln Giants (1911–1930)."

YANKEE STADIUM (I)

The first game I went to—May 30, 1956—we drove from Long Beach, Long Island to the Bronx. . . . And, as we came up into the Bronx and Jerome Avenue, my dad said, "There it is." And, you know, I'd seen games before, but on TV, on a Dumont. And there it was, and, it ate up the Bronx. It was the biggest thing I'd ever seen in my life. And, it had that great roof, that green copper roof. The breeze was just blowing all those pennants, telling you which way the wind was blowing. . . . And I sat in between third base and home plate, you know, REAL CLOSE. . . . You can't imagine what [the ballpark was] like. There was this green, the grass—it just went on forever. And the dirt of the infield was so brown and the bases were so white. And the scoreboard with all of that news—Ballentine Beer and what was happening in Detroit. . . . And it was 461 feet to the center field fence, and they had monuments and I thought [that] Babe Ruth was buried out there. There was a great deal of respect in that building for the past and for the game.

—Billy Crystal, speaking about Yankee Stadium (I)
in the introduction to part 7 of Ken Burns, *Baseball*

Location: 161st Street and River Avenue, the Bronx

Dimensions: left 281–318', center 408–90', right 296–314'

Home Team(s): New York Yankees/American League; and New York Black Yankees/Negro National League

Built/In Operation: 1923/1923 through 1973, and 1976 through 2008. Demolished between 2008 and 2010; now a public park.

Seats/Capacity: 57,545 to 67,224/82,000

Fun Facts: Arguably, the most "perfect" stadium of the steel-and-concrete era between the world wars was this version of the home to the New York Yankees. Team owner Jacob Ruppert had grown tired of sharing the **Polo Grounds (V)** with the domineering Giants manager John McGraw. With Babe Ruth drawing the fans, Ruppert began the land search for the Yankees own ballpark. In February of 1921, Ruppert spent $675,000 (almost $10 million today) to purchase land over the Harlem River in the Bronx. He hired the most famous designers of sports arenas for the period, the Osborn Engineering Corporation of Cleveland, Ohio.

Founded in 1892 by Frank Osborn, the firm eventually built around 100 stadiums, and is still in practice today. Frank was a son of privilege, born into a family of true American blue bloods, in North America since the 17th century. His father, among other accomplishments, was a physician and Michigan state senator. Frank Osborn trained as an engineer at the Rensselaer Polytechnic Institute. One of his classmates, who became his close friend and associate, was William Ferris, most famous for his namesake wheel premiered at the 1893 Chicago Exposition. While initially designing structural steel bridges, Osborn gained an expertise in reinforced concrete and applied his knowledge to the fabrication of facilities for sport.

Frank Osborn's son Kenneth would follow in his father's footsteps, attending engineering school at RPI and joining his father's firm in 1911. Kenneth Osborn spearheaded Osborn Engineering's expanding stadium architecture practice. In addition to Yankee Stadium (I), early Osborn-designed major league baseball parks included Forbes Field, Pittsburgh (1909); League Park, Cleveland (1910); Comiskey Park, Chicago (1910); Griffith/National Park, Washington, DC (1911); Fenway Park, Boston (1912); Tiger-Navin Field, Detroit (1912); and Braves Field, Boston (1915). Also engineered by Osborn's group, with Henry Herts as architect, was the 1911 **Polo Grounds (V)** in New York, the sixth concrete and steel stadium built for the majors.

Yankee Stadium (I), with its triple-decker grandstand, was fabricated from 20,000 cubic yards of concrete at a cost of around $2.5 million in 1920s dollars ($40 million today). Only a 16-minute subway ride from Times Square, the American's new home dwarfed all other major league facilities built up to that occasion in the new century.

"The House That Ruth Built" was altered many times before it became completely outdated, prompting New York City and the Yankees to erect their current ballpark next door. Notable changes over the years included an expanded grandstand in 1928, the addition of a public address system in the mid-1930s, and wooden bleachers replaced by concrete seating at the end of the 1930s. Lights for first night games were installed in 1946.

Since 1932, outfield/playing field monuments and plaques that were often mistaken for tombstones (as did a young Billy Crystal quoted above) honored manager Miller Huggins and players Lou Gehrig, Babe Ruth, Joe DiMaggio, and Mickey Mantle. At the end of 1953, the Yankee organization, which had owned the park since its inception, sold off the Stadium (I), but continued to play home games therein. The famous scoreboard advertising Ballantine Beer was in use until 1959.

Finally, Yankee Stadium (I) needed a complete rebuild. Originally budgeted at $100 million, it ended up costing New York State $160 million. Over the course of two seasons in the mid-1970s, the major alterations included support columns for the grandstands, the replacement of the stadium's roof, new escalators and ramps, new plastic seats replacing the original wooden ones, a new middle tier and upper concourse, and a wall blocking Gerard Avenue and the elevated subway platform above River Avenue. The side of the barrier facing the field was fitted with the first "instant replay" screen in baseball. All told, the Stadium (I) lost around 10,000 seats in that renovation.

To facilitate these changes, the diamond itself was altered. The field was lowered seven feet and moved slightly away from the original home plate. The right field line was lengthened and center field shortened. The outfield monuments were moved outside Yankee Stadium (I) to create what was named Monument Park. The coming years were to witness further alterations, including adjustments to the playing field in 1985 and 1988.

For the first game in this stadium, the New York–Boston rivalry was fanned with a game against the Red Sox, which the Yankees won 4–1. Former Soxer Babe Ruth homered during the third inning. Of course, this ballpark witnessed many teams of "Bronx Bombers." Besides the Babe, this included pitchers Don Larson and Whitey Ford, and hitters Joe DiMaggio, Mickey Mantle, and Lou Gehrig, the last of whom played his entire major league career in Yankee Stadium (I). In 1939, Gehrig, struck down by an incurable disease that later was named for him, used the Stadium (I) for his retirement speech, telling the assembled multitudes, "Today, I am the luckiest man in the world."

For the last game in the original Yankee Stadium (I), the visiting Baltimore Orioles lost to the Yankees by a score of 7–3. Jose Molina hit a home run in the fourth inning and Andy Petite was the winning pitcher.

FMI: O'Reilly, *Charlie's Big Baseball Parks Page*; Johnson, *Ballparks Database*; Walsh and Murphy, *The Fields of New York*; Evanosky and Kos, *Lost Ballparks*; Benson, *Ballparks of North America*; "Yankee Stadium," *ballparksofbaseball.com*; Weingardt, "Frank Osborn"; Hogan, "The Negro Leagues Discovered an Oasis at Yankee Stadium."

BROOKLYN

UNION STAR CRICKET CLUB GROUNDS

Location: opposite Sharp's Hotel, at the corner of Myrtle and Portland Avenues, in what became Fort Greene Park, Brooklyn

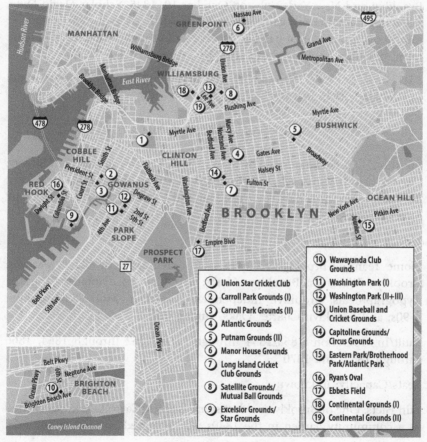

Map 2. Brooklyn Ballparks.

Dimensions: unknown

Home Team(s): Union Star Club

Built/In Operation: 1844/1845 through 1847, and 1860

Seats/Capacity: unknown

Fun Facts: The Union Star Cricket Club was formed in 1844 by Henry and William Russell, prior members of the St. George Cricket Club on Staten Island. The club was largely Jewish. (The stereotype of Jews being poor athletes just isn't true. Go ask Sandy Koufax, Hank Greenberg, Moe Berg, and their peers.) In later years, Union Star switched from cricket to baseball.

These grounds saw the earliest recorded game of organized baseball in Brooklyn, an eight against eight match between the members of the Brooklyn and New York clubs on October 10, 1845. Scholar David Dyte, when documenting this game, contextualizes the contest by citing the first informal appearances of baseball in the city/borough, albeit in its nascent form, during school matches dating back to the 1820s.

FMI: Ross and Dyte, "Brooklyn's Ancient Ball Fields"; Thorn, "Base Ball in Brooklyn, 1845 to 1870."

CARROLL PARK GROUNDS

Location: first field, bounded by Smith, Hoyt, Degraw, and Sackett Streets; second field, bounded by Smith, Hoyt, Carroll, and President Streets. The modern park is between President and Carroll Streets east of Court Street, Brooklyn.

Dimensions: unknown

Home Team(s): Brooklyn Excelsiors; Brooklyn Stars; Brooklyn Marions; Brooklyn Waverlys; Brooklyn Alerts; Brooklyn Esculapians; Brooklyn Typographicals; Brooklyn Independent; Brooklyn Mohawk; Brooklyn 4-90s; and Brooklyn Charter Oaks, among others

Built/In Operation: 1854/1854 through 1860, 1862 through 1864, 1866 through 1867, and 1870

Seats/Capacity: unknown

Fun Facts: One of Brooklyn's oldest sports spaces, Carroll Park was created as a community garden in the 1840s, and acquired by the city in 1856.

The Excelsiors, having been organized by the Jolly Young Bachelors social club, began their playing career here.

In 1862, on the southeast corner of the grounds, a clubhouse was constructed for the use by both the Excelsiors and Stars ballclubs. In the spring of 1866, it was announced that the Mohawk Baseball Club would share the grounds with the Star Club. The two "intend erecting a Club house for the use of the two clubs, to which will be attached a stand for their lady visitors" (*Brooklyn Daily Eagle*, May 9, 1866). This was despite the complaint by the Enterprise Club in June of 1865 that the field had become, as Waff, Ryczek, and Morris reported, "a vacant lot . . . a stony and sterile waste." Additionally, reporters from the Brooklyn papers protested that spectators at Carroll Park often got in the way of the action, impeding the movement of players and blocking the view from the scorers' table, where reporters often were located.

FMI: Ross and Dyte, "Brooklyn's Ancient Ball Fields"; Thorn, "Base Ball in Brooklyn, 1845 to 1870"; Gilbert, *How Baseball Happened*; Freyer and Rucker, *Peverelly's National Game*; Craig B. Waff, William J. Ryczek, and Peter Morris, "Star Base Ball Club," in Morris et al., *Base Ball Founders*.

ATLANTIC GROUNDS

Location: 800 Marcy Avenue between Putnam and Gates Avenues, near Wild's Hotel, Brooklyn

Dimensions: unknown

Home Team(s): Brooklyn Atlantics/National Association of Base Ball Players

Built/In Operation: 1855 through 1864

Seats/Capacity: 15,000

Fun Facts: The Atlantic Grounds was home to the Atlantic Club before their move to the **Capitoline Grounds** in 1864. This field saw many famous Atlantic victories during their first run of championships between 1859 and 1861. One of the smaller facilities of its time, the team and grounds were named for Brooklyn's Atlantic Avenue.

FMI: Atlantic Base Ball Club; Ross and Dyte, "Brooklyn's Ancient Ball Fields"; protoball.org, "Atlantic Grounds"; Nightingale, "The Unknowable Superstar."

PUTNAM GROUNDS (III)

The great disadvantage attached to the Ball Clubs—which every year is increasing—is that of procuring grounds. The vacant lots and unfenced fields in the suburban districts and the vicinity of the city are every year becoming in more demand, and the Ball Clubs have to make way for the giant of Time—improvement—and as he makes rapid strikes, are deprived of their grounds.

—"The Incoming Baseball Season,"
Brooklyn Daily Eagle, April 7, 1962

Location: Broadway between Lafayette and Greene/Gates Avenues, Brooklyn

Dimensions: unknown

Home Team(s): Putnams; Constellation Club; the second incarnation of the Harmony Club; Orientals of Bedford; and Roanokes

Built/In Operation: 1855/1857 through 1862. The field continued to be used for industrial and amateur contests as well as junior clubs until at least 1872.

Seats/Capacity: 15,000

Fun Facts: Poet Walt Whitman, evidently a fan of the sport, attended a game between the Putnams and the Atlantics, either here or at the **Continental Grounds**. Whitman reported the play-by-play of the 1858 contest within the pages of the *Brooklyn Daily Times*, calling the match "one of the finest and most exciting games we ever witnessed."

FMI: Ross and Dyte, "Brooklyn's Ancient Ball Fields"; Gilbert, *How Baseball Happened*; protoball.org, "Putnam Grounds"; Thorn, "Walt Whitman, Baseball Reporter"; Morris et al., *Base Ball Founders*.

MANOR HOUSE GROUNDS/
ECKFORD GROUNDS/GREENPOINT GROUNDS

After looking all over Manhattan Island for a ball ground, and none suitable being found, the Williamsburg members . . . suggested that the [Eckford] club move across the river, as they had an option on a large field in the upper section of the Fifteenth Ward. This field was on the Calvary Cemetery road, near the old manor house of the Backus family.

—*Times Union*, July 30, 1903

Location: Nassau and Driggs Avenues, and Russell and Monitor Streets, Brooklyn, or very near to there. The Manor House Grounds are probably now within McGolrick Park, Greenpoint.

Dimensions: unknown

Home Team(s): Eckford Club; Satellite Club; Wayne Club; and National Association

Built/In Operation: 1855 through 1862, and 1870 through 1872

Seats/Capacity: 6,000 to 10,000

Fun Facts: In the spring of 1857, the Eckford baseball club built a small building on this field in Brooklyn. Because the club did not charge admission, the lot was never fenced. However, by 1860, the area, which had been idyllic and undeveloped when the first games were staged, had begun to be settled. Between then and the 1862 season, the Eckfords found a new home at the **Union Baseball Grounds**.

FMI: Ross and Dyte, "Brooklyn's Ancient Ball Fields"; John Pardon and Jerry Jackson, "New York State Ball Clubs," in Puff, *The Empire State of Base Ball*; protoball.org, "Manor House Grounds"; Morris et al., *Base Ball Founders*.

CONTINENTAL GROUNDS/WHEAT HILL GROUNDS/ PUTNAM GROUNDS (I+II)

Location: Lee and Bedford Avenues, Ross and Hewes Streets, Brooklyn

Dimensions: unknown

Home Team(s): Continentals and Putnams

Built/In Operation: 1856 through 1862

Seats/Capacity: unknown

Fun Facts: An unidentified writer, recalling games of yesteryear in the *Times Union* newspaper, contended that "the Putnams had been forced uptown by the building of St. John's Church" ("Bit of Baseball History," July 22, 1903). The first Putnam Grounds was located at Division and Lee Streets, Brooklyn. The second grounds sat one hundred yards from Wheat Hill.

FMI: Ross and Dyte, "Brooklyn's Ancient Ball Fields"; Morris et al., *Base Ball Founders*.

LONG ISLAND CRICKET CLUB GROUNDS

The locality of the grounds of the Pastime Club are unquestionably the best in Brooklyn. Ample shade is afforded, and a fine green turf renders the field peculiarly attractive to the players, and far superior to the dusty grounds of a majority of the clubs.

—*Spirit of the Times*, 1858

Location: the terminus of the Fulton Avenue Railroad in Bedford, at the corner of Nostrand and Fulton Avenues, Brooklyn

Dimensions: unknown

Home Team(s): Atlantic Club and Pastime Club

Built/In Operation: 1856 through 1859

Seats/Capacity: 1,000

Fun Facts: unknown

FMI: Ross and Dyte, "Brooklyn's Ancient Ball Fields"; Craig B. Waff, William J. Ryczek, and Peter Morris, "Star Base Ball Club," in Morris et al., *Base Ball Founders*.

SATELLITE GROUNDS/MUTUAL BALL GROUNDS

Location: Broadway, Harrison Avenue, Rutledge and Lynch Streets, Brooklyn, across Harrison Avenue from the **Union Baseball and Cricket Grounds**

Dimensions: unknown

Home Team(s): Satellites; Fulton Club; Resolute Club; Eckfords; Uniques; and Mutuals

Built/In Operation: 1856, 1860, and 1866 through 1869. Traveling shows continued to use the lot into the early 1870s. Currently, part of the space is occupied by a police station.

Seats/Capacity: unknown

Fun Facts: The Satellite Grounds was the location for one of the many wintertime skating ponds hosting the ever popular "baseball on ice." Circuses as well would utilize the lot, taking over the grounds in the off-season after baseball's departure. Most notably, the Satellite Grounds was the site of many early contests between Black baseball squads. These included the 1867 championship of Brooklyn between the Monitors and the Uniques, won by a score of 49–17 by the former team.

FMI: Ross and Dyte, "Brooklyn's Ancient Ball Fields"; protoball.org, "Satellite Association Grounds"; Kaplan, "10 Black Baseball Sites in NYC."

EXCELSIOR GROUNDS/STAR GROUNDS

Location: the foot of Court Street, between Hamilton Avenue and the mouth of the Gowanus Canal, Brooklyn. Now a soccer field within the Red Hook Recreational Area.

Dimensions: unknown

Home Team(s): Excelsior Club; Star Club; and Mohawk Club

Built/In Operation: 1857 through 1865

Seats/Capacity: 7,000 to 8,000

Fun Facts: The Excelsiors were a prominent New York City area baseball team. The club supposedly originated the hat structure upon which

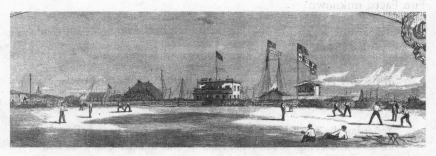

Illustration depicting a championship game between the Excelsiors and Atlantics of Brooklyn, at the Excelsior Grounds on July 19, 1860. The Excelsiors beat the under-performing Atlantics that day by a score of 10 to 8. From *The New-York Illustrated News*.

"modern" ballcaps were designed. In 1860, the Excelsiors took one of the earliest road trips up the Hudson to play against local baseball aggregations.

Evanosky and Kos contend that historian Tom Shieber identifies this as the first walled purpose-built ballpark, "apparently erect[ing] an enclosure to keep out the local riffraff who were considered 'undesirables' at gentlemanly baseball games."

During the 1865 season, the *Brooklyn Eagle* (June 26, 1865) described the Star Club's field as a vacant lot bordered on three sides by cobblestone streets and in a deteriorated condition. However, the reporter admitted that "this [was] the best ground[s] that South Brooklyn affords," and, therefore, players just had to adjust to its idiosyncrasies.

FMI: Ross and Dyte, "Brooklyn's Ancient Ball Fields"; Gilbert, *How Baseball Happened*; Evanosky and Kos, *Lost Ballparks*; Craig B. Waff, William J. Ryczek, and Peter Morris, "Star Base Ball Club," in Morris et al., *Base Ball Founders*; protoball.org, "Excelsior Grounds near Carroll Park."

WAWAYANDA CLUB GROUNDS

Location: southeast of Ocean Parkway and Neptune Avenue, Duck Hill, Coney Island, Brooklyn

Dimensions: unknown

Home Team(s): Wawayanda Club

Built/In Operation: 1859 through 1860

Seats/Capacity: unknown

Fun Facts: unknown

FMI: Ross and Dyte, "Brooklyn's Ancient Ball Fields"; protoball.org, "Wawayanda Grounds."

WASHINGTON PARK (I)/FIFTH AVENUE GROUNDS/WASHINGTON POND/ LITCHFIELD'S POND/WASHINGTON PARADE GROUNDS

> Yesterday the hazardous feat of playing a match of base ball upon skates was accomplished by the Atlantic and Charter Oak Base Ball Clubs. What next?
>
> —*Brooklyn Daily Eagle*, February 5, 1861

Location: between Third and Fifth Streets, and Fourth and Fifth Avenues, Park Slope, Brooklyn

Dimensions: unknown

Home Team(s): Ironsides; Albions; Atlantics; Brooklyn Atlantics; Brooklyn Grays/Interstate League and American Association; and Brooklyn Bridegrooms/National League

Built/In Operation: 1861/1861 through 1891

Seats/Capacity: 4,500 to 8,000/10,000 to 20,000

Fun Facts: This location for Brooklyn sport started life as a simple pond. Although initially a site for skating, Washington Pond was also used for baseball. As well as the "regular" game played on dirt and grass, in the later part of the 19th century, "baseball on ice" had achieved some modicum of popularity. Especially in a northern state such as New York, "ice ball" allowed for players to stay active in the winter months. As indicated by the above quote, the resident Atlantics practiced the art of baseball on skates, with their base paths delineated by lines of red paint.

Washington Park (I)'s baseball diamond was built around a structure from 1699, the Old Stone House, which still stands in a much-restored form. Utilized by George Washington for his headquarters during the Revolutionary War, the building was incorporated into the original ballfield as a facility for female fans, as well as for storage.

Construction began in February 1883 of structures for a proper ballpark. These included a 2,500-seat grandstand, 2,000-person "free" stand, and carriage facilities, plus a 13-foot-high fence around the enclosure. Construction costs have been stated as low as $13,000 and as high as $30,000 ($357,000–$832,000 in today's dollars), invested by the Brooklyn baseball association. For the team's second home game on May 12, Washington Park (I) was ready for 6,000 spectators. After a gala opening ceremony, the Brooklyns defeated Trenton 13–6.

The ballpark experienced two fires: one in 1886 and the second, which burned the original double-decker wooden grandstand completely to the ground, in 1889. Improvements following the 1886 blaze included a new grandstand seating 3,000 patrons and free seats along the Third and Fifth Street fences. The stands that survived the fire were elevated to afford those seated a better view.

For the later improvements, eventual team owner Charlie Ebbets supervised the reconstruction, completing the work in time for the start of the season on May 30, 1889. In a strangely prescient move, Ebbets requested that the grandstand be "portable," so that the seating could be more easily removed and reconstructed in another location, if necessary. This wasn't as strange as one might think, because these were the days when teams leased the land that their parks sat upon. Property owners could be counted on selling when better offers came along. And, especially in urban areas, neighborhoods were expanding quickly into any available open spaces. The demand for housing was great, and that fed the hunger for the acreage commanded by the ballparks.

There was one more set of improvements for Washington Park (I) in 1890, the most notable of which was sidewalk pavers on Fifth Avenue, framing the entrance with the words "Brooklyn Base Ball Club."

But, still, Charlie Ebbets was dissatisfied with Washington Park (I). Therefore, after the 1890 schedule concluded, Ebbets and the Brooklyns decamped for **Eastern Park**. Their move was completed when, in the spring of 1892, the portable grandstand at Washington was taken apart and moved to the Grooms' new facility.

FMI: Johnson, "Washington Park III," *Ballparks Database*; Evanosky and Kos, *Lost Ballparks*; Johnson, "Washington Park IV," *Ballparks Database*; Ross and Dyte, "The Washington Park Wall"; Ross and Dyte, "Washington Park"; Richard A. Puff, "The First to Take It on the Road," in *The Empire State of Base Ball*; "Zachary Taylor Davis"; Benson, *Ballparks of North America*; Los Angeles Dodgers, "Ballparks: 1862–Present"; LeMoine, "February 4, 1861: Brooklyn Atlantics Win a Baseball Game on Ice"; Lippman, *List of New York's Baseball Sites*; Friedlander and Reising, *Chasing Moonlight*.

WASHINGTON PARK (II)

Location: just across from **Washington Park (I)**, between First and Third Streets and Third and Fourth Avenues, Park Slope, Brooklyn

Dimensions: left 335', center 500', right 295'

Home Team(s): Brooklyn Superbas, Robins, Nationals, and Trolley Dodgers/National League

Built/In Operation: 1898/1898 through 1912

Seats/Capacity: 12,000 to 20,900/25,000

Washington Park (II) after the 1908 renovation.

Fun Facts: Ebbets's move of Brooklyn's National League member to **Eastern Park** ultimately didn't work out. Eastern was too far from their legion of fans and possibly dissatisfying in other ways as well. Charlie felt that building a new ballpark was his only choice. And so, on March 24, 1898, hard on the upcoming spring start to the season, construction was begun back across from **Washington Park (I)**, with daughter Maie Ebbets turning the first shovel full of dirt.

Luckily, the costs for the move and the new facility, around $100,000 (about $3 million today), were partially covered by the Nassau and Brooklyn L railroad companies. Both rail lines serviced the area and stood to see gains in their ridership with the return of the Trolley Dodgers.

Because of the rush for completion by opening day, the incomplete facility received several "tweaks" over the course of the season. To improve sightlines for both the players and fans, seats were raised and moved around. Field drainage was also upgraded to improve play and prevent rain delays.

These renovations continued for years to come. Seating was enhanced through bleachers being moved and extensions built onto the grandstand. In 1908, thousands of "cheap" bleacher seats were added along the side backing onto Third Avenue. Dugouts, a new innovation for the protection of the players, made their appearance, along with state-of-the-art club-houses behind the left field flagpole.

The following year, Charlie Ebbets, always frustrated with the capacity of his ballparks, hit on a scheme to yet again expand seating at Washington Park (II). By moving the front of the grandstand forward 15 feet, almost 1,000 additional seats could be added. This had the unfortunate effect of shortening the distance between home plate and the pitcher's mound. Luckily, that dimension at Washington still exceeded the smallest major league parks.

Nonpaying spectators outside of the grounds were a constant issue for owners struggling to make ends meet during these nascent years for our "national game." Ebbets attempted to limit these occurrences, first by blocking views with canvas stretched between poles, and, for the 1907 season, raising the fence along First Street by several feet.

The temporal nature of ballpark structures was brought home to Ebbets when a surprise inspection by Brooklyn's Department of Buildings revealed rotten grandstand supports and aisles violating local codes. Round-the-clock emergency repairs corrected these issues in time for the 1911 home opener. Summer fires that year luckily only took out parts of the fencing.

Before Sunday baseball was legalized by New York State in 1919, owners had few options open to them. Because most fans worked a six-day week, and night games had yet to become standard, Sundays were baseball's best drawing day despite the objections by religious leaders. Rather than lose that Sunday income, team owners came up with several subterfuges. The first was to move, as the Dodgers had attempted, further away from urban authorities to less populated and regulated areas. However, it wasn't enough to be "out of sight, out of the minds" of authorities. Additional measures needed to be taken to promote the appearance that these were games for fun rather than of profit. As an example, during 1904, Ebbets avoided prosecution by charging fans for programs rather than admission. Two years later, the Dodgers took donations through boxes placed near stadium entrances. For 1910, Ebbets formed an amateur nine, the Washington Park Athletic Club, that played on Sunday. Unfortunately, as the athletes were the same pros that populated the Superbas, the powers that be figured the scam out and stopped their play.

One notable event at Washington Park (II) was a late-in-the-game appearance by Archibald "Moonlight" Graham. On June 29, 1905, Giants manager John McGraw subbed minor leaguer Archie Graham in for a few minutes of uneventful play against the Brooklyn aggregation. Graham was a real baseball player who served as the inspiration for a fictional character in the book *Shoeless Joe* and the resulting movie adaptation, *Field of Dreams*.

By the second decade of the 20th century, Charlie Ebbets was once again looking discontentedly at his ballpark. He briefly toyed with the idea of a steel and concrete rebuild at the current location. Nevertheless, Ebbets quickly decided that a larger, brand-new park would more completely fulfill the needs of the Brooklyn Dodgers.

At the end of 1912, the wooden grandstands and clubhouse at Washington Park (II) were torn down. The turnstiles were moved to the newly commissioned **Ebbets Field**, and other metal work was recycled into area ballparks and structures.

However, baseball wasn't yet finished with the Washington Park site. There would be one more hurrah for Brooklyn baseball in Park Slope.

FMI: Johnson, "Washington Park III," *Ballparks Database*; Evanosky and Kos, *Lost Ballparks*; Johnson, "Washington Park IV," *Ballparks Database*; Ross and Dyte, "The Washington Park Wall"; Ross and Dyte, "Washington Park"; Richard A. Puff, "The First to Take It on the Road," in *The Empire State of Base Ball*; "Zachary Taylor Davis"; Benson, *Ballparks of North America*; Los Angeles Dodgers, "Ballparks: 1862–Present"; LeMoine, "February 4, 1861: Brooklyn Atlantics Win a Baseball Game on Ice"; Lippman, *List of New York's Baseball Sites*; Friedlander and Reising, *Chasing Moonlight*.

WASHINGTON PARK (III)

> Base Ball Players are all human, and therefore love applause. If you want a winning team, root for them, speak well of them to your friends, and while we are here let us all be clean of speech—so that the ladies may find it pleasant to come often.
>
> —sign on the right field wall of Washington Park (III)

Location: the same as **Washington Park (II)**

Built/In Operation: 1914/1914 through 1915. Demolished in 1926, the property is now owned by Consolidated Edison. A section of the left wall from the ballpark is still standing at the corner of Third Avenue and First Street.

Dimensions: left 335', center 500', right 295'

Home Team(s): Brooklyn Tip Tops/Federal League

Seats/Capacity: 12,000 to 16,000/18,000

Fun Facts: After the Dodgers left for Ebbets Field, the Tip Tops of the Federal League leased the land where the previous Washington Park (II) was located. The Feds' owners were wealthy baseball outsiders that had been blocked from National and American League ownership by the powers controlling the professional game. The individuals that formed the outlaw Federal League had decided to go head-to-head with pro teams in major metropolitan areas such as New York and Chicago to attract the attention of the two existing leagues. Their end goal wasn't to establish a third organization, but to gain ownership shares in the established game.

Ultimately, these individual Federal League owners were willing to lose money to make their case.

There is some evidence that the Brooklyn franchise was originally held by the father and son team of Ambrose William Hussey, Sr. and Jr., administrators of the semiprofessional Ridgewoods. In 1912 and 1913, after proprietorship in two different (and unsuccessfully launched) outlaw United States Leagues, the Hussey's committed to the Brooklyn team in the Federal League. When Ambrose Hussey, Sr., took ill, dying two weeks later, his son abandoned a chance at league ownership. Instead, the Brooklyn franchise went to the Ward family, whose Ward Baking Company produced Tip-Top bread (hence the team's name). You might also know them as the firm that later took Wonder Bread, which was the first mass-produced bread sliced in the factory, and Hostess Brand baked goods (Twinkies, HoHos, and DingDongs, among others) nationwide.

The patriarch of Ward Baking was James Ward, who, with his son Hugh, opened a "one-oven" store on Manhattan's Broome Street in 1849. Hugh and his children Robert and George moved their base of operations to Pittsburgh after the Civil War. The Wards eventually opened what was then (reportedly) the largest bread factory in the United States, labeled the first totally mechanized "modern, sanitary bakery." By the time of the Federal League, members of the Ward family controlled bakeries in (among other cities) Brooklyn, Buffalo, and Rochester through their headquarters back in the New York City area. Company head Robert B. Ward had been a baseball fan since his time in Pittsburgh, and eagerly embraced the chance in 1914 to buy into the Federal League.

For their new stadium, the Brooklyn Feds' owners originally requested an exact copy of Chicago's Weeghman Park (now, with great modification, Wrigley Field). Charles A. Weeghman owned the Federal League franchise in the windy city, and had built his ballpark from a design by architect Zachary Taylor Davis. Davis, a protégé of Louis Sullivan, was also responsible (along with Osborn Engineering—see the **Polo Grounds [V]** and **Yankee Stadium [I]**) for the Chicago White Sox's original Comiskey Park. Because of his active role in stadium design and his origins alongside Frank Lloyd Wright in the Chicago architecture practice of Adler and Sullivan, Davis was sometimes known as the "Frank Lloyd Wright of baseball." In late February of 1914, Zachary Taylor Davis was brought to New York City to consult on the plans for the new ballpark. However, at that time, it was revealed that the true architect and engineering supervisor for the project would be C. B. Comstock.

Corry Benjamin Comstock was born in western Pennsylvania in 1874. He began his career in Pittsburgh as an architect and refrigeration engineer by early in the first decade of the 20th century. My best guess is it was while Comstock was based in Pittsburgh that he became acquainted and began working with the Ward baking family. Comstock followed the Wards back to New York City, designing their Brooklyn factory, billed as "the [first] snow-white temple of bread-making cleanliness," in 1910–1911. By the time of the Brooklyn Feds baseball team, Comstock had been responsible for all new Ward facilities, including those in Baltimore, Maryland, Washington, DC, and Buffalo, New York. Therefore, it made perfect sense for Robert Ward to bring Comstock along into the Federal Baseball League as his architect of choice. Local newspapers speculated that the concrete, brick, and steel stadium would cost between $125,000 and $200,000 (a bit over $3–5 million today) to bring Comstock's vision to fruition.

With Comstock on board, and his plans available at the end of February 1914, construction began a month later. Snow hampered the progress, as did predictable labor troubles. Because the stadium workers belonged to a construction union, but the workers in the Ward factories were nonunion, the various trades sometimes viewed working on the stadium as synonymous with scabbing. Against all odds, Washington Park (III) was ready for opening day on May 11, 1914.

This final version of what was known as Washington Park (III), besides being the smallest of the three, contained several curious elements. The scoreboard, located in center field, was in fair territory, and could easily interfere with play. The flagpole had come from the sailboat *Reliance*, the winner of the 1903 America's Cup. Still in place after professional baseball had evacuated the grounds, it was struck by lightning in 1921.

Comstock's connection with the Ward family and the engineer's work on Washington Park (III) led to his being designated as the "official architect" for the Federal League. In 1915, he was credited with designing the new facilities for the Newark, New Jersey, team, which had been moved before the start of the season from Indianapolis. By the end of the 1915 schedule, the league projected introducing night baseball into all their ballparks for 1916. Toward that end, Comstock erected 75-foot-high light towers at Washington Park (III) to test out the idea. Cost estimates of $20,000 were published for the fall experiment, when semiprofessionals stood in for the Brookfeds players. Furthermore, as a kind of "last hurrah," the league projected going "head-to-head" with the New York Giants and Yankees in

1916. Comstock's planned baseball palace would be constructed on Lenox Avenue between 142nd and 145th Streets in Manhattan, less than a mile away from the **Polo Grounds (V)**. Intended was a steel and concrete park with a double decker grandstand and covered bleachers, seating around a total of 55,000 patrons, equivalent to the Coogan's Hollow's field.

For his troubles, the Federal League partially compensated Comstock with a seat on the board of their Pittsburgh franchise. Comstock also chose to invest in his "hometown" club, the Stogies, sometime after his appointment.

Tragically, the Tip Tops and Washington Park (III) owner, Robert Ward, died suddenly of a heart attack at the end of the ultimate 1915 season. After his brief flirtation with baseball, Comstock continued working for the Ward company. When the Great Depression hit, his architecture business failed. On October 25, 1932, the *New York Times* reported that a despondent Comstock had shot himself in his office, taking his own life.

In 1926, this last iteration of Washington Park (III) was demolished. Part of the 13-foot enclosing clubhouse wall survives. As I write these words in the spring of 2021, you can still see this remnant on the east side of Third Avenue, south of First Street in the Gowanus section of Brooklyn.

FMI: Johnson, "Washington Park III," *Ballparks Database*; Evanosky and Kos, *Lost Ballparks*; Johnson, "Washington Park IV," *Ballparks Database*; Ross and Dyte, "The Washington Park Wall"; Ross and Dyte, "Washington Park"; Richard A. Puff, "The First to Take It on the Road," in *The Empire State of Base Ball*; "Zachary Taylor Davis"; Benson, *Ballparks of North America*; Los Angeles Dodgers, "Ballparks: 1862–Present"; LeMoine, "February 4, 1861: Brooklyn Atlantics Win a Baseball Game on Ice"; Lippman, *List of New York's Baseball Sites*; Spellen, "The Ward Bakery Company, the Snow-White Temple of Cleanliness"; "Brooklyn Feds Preparing Plans For Washington Park Stadium," *Brooklyn Eagle*, February 24, 1914; Pousson, "Ward Baking Company Building"; "Comstock, C. B. (1874–1932): Projects"; "Landmarking: Wonder Bread Factory"; "Pittsburgh Rebels," Wikipedia; *Outlaw League Executives* (photo).

YUKATAN GROUNDS

Location: Yukatan Pond, Bedford, Brooklyn

Dimensions: unknown

Home Team(s): unknown

Built/In Operation: 1862

Seats/Capacity: unknown

Fun Facts: On October 16, 1862, a *Brooklyn Eagle* reporter, probably pioneering baseball journalist Henry Chadwick, reported a "match" in progress at this locale between the Unknown and Monitor Clubs: "This is the first match to our knowledge that has been played in this city between players of African descent."
    Yukatan was a popular public skating spot come winter.

FMI: Ross and Dyte, "Brooklyn's Ancient Ball Fields."

UNION BASEBALL AND CRICKET GROUNDS/ UNION SKATING RINK-POND

These grounds, if managed properly—and there is little doubt but that they will be—could be made not only to prove very profitable, but a credit to the section in which they are located.

—*The Standard*, April 19, 1869

Location: the corner of Marcy Avenue and Rutledge Street, Wheat Hill, Williamsburg, Brooklyn

Dimensions: unknown

Home Team(s): Union Club; Brooklyn Mutuals/National Association and National League; Brooklyn Atlantics/National Association; Brooklyn Eckfords/National Association of Base Ball Players and National Association; Grays; Braves; Olympics; White Stockings; Resolutes; Dark Blues, Hartfords/National League; Putnams; and Constellations

Built/In Operation: 1862/1862 through 1882. Demolished in 1883. Heyward Street now runs through the site, which has also hosted a school and an armory.

Seats/Capacity: 1500/10,000

Fun Facts: After the all-star game contested on the **Fashion Race Course** in 1858, Brooklyn leather merchant William Cammeyer was inspired to construct his own (hopefully money-making) baseball field. Cammeyer purchased this piece of Brooklyn land in 1861, first flooding it for winter use as an ice-skating rink to generate some immediate financial return. After the spring thaw of 1862, William Cammeyer drained the property and constructed a baseball diamond.

The first game of ball here occurred on May 15, 1862, when the Union Grounds hosted a baseball competition between all-stars chosen from the three resident squads: the Eckfords, Putnams, and Constellation clubs. However, there wasn't an admission charge for that event.

One entered the Union Grounds from Rutledge Street. The *Brooklyn Eagle* further described the park on its opening day in an article headlined "Inauguration of the Union Base Ball and Cricket Grounds—Grand Opening Game—2,000 to 3,000 Spectators present":

> The buildings occupied last winter [including a three-story pagoda in deep center field that lit up and decorated the winter skating pond] are left standing, used pretty much for the same purposes as them [*sic*]. Near these a long wooden shed [grandstand] has been erected, capable of accommodating several hundred persons, and benches provided for the convenience of the fair sex. . . . Several acres more have been added to the enclosure, which is fenced in with a board fence six or seven feet in height. On the southeast corner a large and commodious club house has been erected, containing accommodations for three clubs. The field is now almost a perfect level, covering at least some six acres of ground, all of which is well drained, rolled, and in a few weeks will be in splendid condition. . . . Several flagstaffs have been put up, from which floated the banners of the clubs o'er shadowed by the nations' ensign. (May 16, 1862)

Like the later **Polo Grounds**, because the field of the Union Grounds was built around home plate (writes John Pastier), it mimics the shape (as dubbed by baseball scribes) of a "bathtub."

More than one historian has labeled the Union Grounds as the first purpose-built baseball park in the New York City area. The **Excelsior Grounds/Star Grounds** has also been cited as the primary enclosed arena. Another "first" attributed to Union, according to scholar Thomas W. Gilbert, was charging spectators a fee to attend games, with the ball clubs taking a cut of the door. Some sources cite an all-star contest held in April of 1869 as the first game in this facility with paid entry. Brooklyn baseball expert David Dyte adds that the cost was in lieu of Cammeyer assessing the clubs for use of his facility.

Notable games held here included two visits by the Cincinnati Red Stockings. In June of 1869, the Reds contested with both the Brooklyn Atlantics at the **Capitoline Grounds** and the Mutuals and Eckfords at the Union Baseball Grounds. Supposedly, the official scorekeeper on that day was Henry Chadwick, journalist and inventor of the box score. Cincinnati won 4–2. For their return the following season, the Red Stockings increased their lead to 16–3. In the fall of 1871, the National Association championship game between Philadelphia and Chicago (which Chicago won) was held here because the White Stockings' stadium had been destroyed in the Great Chicago Fire.

FMI: Johnson, *Ballparks Database*; Gilbert, *How Baseball Happened*; Evanosky and Kos, *Lost Ballparks*; John Pastier, "Polo Grounds Seating, Dimensions and Design," in Thornley, *The Polo Grounds*; Healey, "Union Grounds"; "Union Grounds," *Bullpen*; Ryczek, "Baseball's First Enclosed Field"; Casway, "July 24, 1860: The First Enclosed Ballpark"; Benson, *Ballparks of North America*; Thorn, "Base Ball in Brooklyn, 1845 to 1870"; Morris et al., *Base Ball Founders*; Gershman, *Diamonds*; Seymour, *Baseball*.

CAPITOLINE GROUNDS/CIRCUS GROUNDS

Location: Nostrand Avenue and Halsey Street, Putnam Avenue, Bedford-Stuyvesant, Brooklyn

Dimensions: unknown

Home Team(s): Brooklyn Atlantics/National Association; Brooklyn Enterprise; Brooklyn Excelsior; Brooklyn Chelseas/League Alliance; New York Metropolitans; Star Club; and Brooklyn Powhatans

The Cincinnati Red Stockings playing the Brooklyn Atlantics, at the Capitoline Grounds, on June 14, 1870, as drawn by C. S. Reinhart.

Built/In Operation: 1863/1863 through 1876, 1878, and 1880. Demolished in 1880, when subdivided by new roads and residential development.

Seats/Capacity: 5000/20,000

Fun Facts: The Capitoline Grounds was built by Hamilton Weed and Reuben Decker on farmland inherited from Decker's grandfather. Named for one of the hills in ancient Rome, this is the next-known enclosed ballpark built after the **Union Baseball and Cricket Grounds**.

The facility boasted two sets of bleachers, "sitting rooms" for female attendees, clubhouses, and a circular brick outhouse in right field. Like the **Union Baseball and Cricket Grounds** and other period ballfields, Capitoline was flooded during the winter for ice skating. During January of 1865, the Atlantics took advantage of Capitoline's ice rink to play the New York Gothams on skates for multiple baseball games, winning two of the three contests.

For the 1867 season, to become competitive with other area facilities, the field was split in two. The lower diamond was designated a practice area, while the upper was utilized for contests.

In June of 1870, the Brooklyn Atlantics played the Cincinnati Red Stockings at Capitoline. The Red Stockings were known as the best squad in baseball. However, the Atlantics were no slouches, having gone undefeated for the three seasons between 1863 and 1865, and taking the championship in 1869. On June 14, the Atlantics and Reds met in Brooklyn, with nine innings of baseball ending in a tie. Instead of calling the contest, the Stockings elected to play extra innings. Although Cincinnati was in front during the first half of the eleventh, Brooklyn pulled ahead in the bottom part, winning the competition by a score of 8–7. This was the first game that the Red Stockings had lost in two years. Four days later, while still in town, it appears that Cincinnati also took on the Star baseball club. This time, the Reds, after a hard-fought contest, broke a sixth inning tie to win by a score of 16–11. Later that season, the Atlantics and Stars both took on the visiting Chicago White Stockings. As against Cincinnati, the Atlantics triumphed and the Stars were defeated.

For some of 1880 (its last year as a ballfield), Capitoline served as the headquarters for the New York Metropolitans. The Mets played here before moving across the river to Manhattan's **Polo Grounds (I)** in the fall of 1880.

FMI: Ross and Dyte, "The Capitoline Grounds"; Gilbert, *How Baseball Happened*; Helander, "The League Alliance"; Atlantic Base Ball Club; Casway, "July 24, 1860: The First Enclosed Ballpark"; Benson, *Ballparks of North*

America; Craig B. Waff, William J. Ryczek, and Peter Morris, "Star Base Ball Club," in Morris et al., *Base Ball Founders*; *The Bat and Ball*, May 1, 1867.

EASTERN PARK/BROTHERHOOD PARK/ATLANTIC PARK

Location: bordered by Eastern Parkway (now Pitkin Avenue), Vesta (now Van Sinderen) Avenue, Powell Street and Sutter Avenue, Brownsville, Brooklyn

Dimensions: left 260–315'

Home Team(s): Brooklyn Ward's Wonders/Players' League; and Brooklyn Bridegrooms, Superbas and Trolley Dodgers/National League

Built/In Operation: 1890/1890 and 1897. Demolished after the end of 1897 season.

Seats/Capacity: 12,000

Fun Facts: After the Brooklyn National League club's initial pass on the site, Players' League owner Monte Ward leased the property from the Ridgewood Land and Improvement Company of investors. Walter Coutts designed the 433-foot curved grandstand, built at the price of $24,950 (around $750,000 today). The proposed name of "Atlantic Park" was in honor of the pioneering Brooklyn baseball franchise.

As with many other teams and locales, the facility was barely ready for play at the season's onset. Besides the muddy conditions, many visiting players complained of the great distances to the fences, unhittable in that era of the "dead ball." When the Wonders left on a May road trip, a second floor was added to the grandstand, locker rooms were plumbed, and a permanent ticket office was built. With the disbandment of the Players'/Brotherhood organization after one season, the Wonders merged with the soon-to-be Dodgers, who moved from **Washington Park (I)** and took over the lease of the stadium. Because of the preponderance of rail and trolley lines around the new ballpark, the team nickname applied by fans in 1895 was the "Trolley Dodgers," which soon shortened to just "Dodgers." There were also bicycling and football competitions at the park.

Improvements continued during the 1891 and 1892 seasons. In 1891, attempts to enhance sight lines from the grandstands moved the diamond 25 more feet out. The field was also rotated clockwise to increase the left field line from 260 to 315 feet. Of course, now the bleachers were in fair territory, so, those too were moved to the left side. Lastly, a ladies' waiting room and a new press box were added. For the next season, a pavilion opposite first base was repurposed from the **Washington Park (I)** grand-stand. Bleacher seats were inserted and elevated to better see play. In a strange presaging of **Ebbets Field**, a sign advertising the *Brooklyn Eagle* stood in the outfield. A player hitting a baseball into the placard would earn $10 from the newspaper.

Because of the location of Eastern Park (too far east from the Brooklyn fans), the Dodgers returned in 1898 to **Washington Park (III)**.

FMI: "Brooklyn Dodgers Team History"; Johnson, *Ballparks Database*; Ross and Dyte, "Eastern Park"; Benson, *Ballparks of North America*.

RYAN'S OVAL

Location: Columbia and Pioneer Streets, Red Hook, Brooklyn

Dimensions: unknown

Home Team(s): Brooklyn Edisons/Atlantic League; and Brooklyn Pioneers (semiprofessional)

Built/In Operation: 1906/1907, and 1910 through 1920

Seats/Capacity: unknown

Fun Facts: Used for amateur baseball as early as 1906.

FMI: Benson, *Ballparks of North America*.

EBBETS FIELD

Ebbets Field, one of the finest baseball parks in the country, stands as a lasting tribute to the national game in this borough.

—*Brooklyn Eagle*, October 26, 1916

Location: 55 Sullivan Place, Flatbush, Brooklyn

Dimensions: left 419–343', center 466–384', right 301–292'

Home Team(s): Brooklyn Robins, Trolley Dodgers, and Dodgers/National League; Brooklyn (Negro Leagues) Eagles; Brooklyn Brown Dodgers; and Bacharach Giants/Eastern Colored League

Built/In Operation: 1913/1913 through 1957. Demolished in 1960.

Seats/Capacity: 18,000 to 32,000

Ray Caldwell of the New York American League team, pitching in an exhibition game that opened Ebbets Field. April 5, 1913. Bain News Service, George Grantham Bain Collection, Library of Congress.

Fun Facts: Since 1884, when the franchise that became the Brooklyn Dodgers was founded, the team had played on the various fields known as **Washington Park**, situated in the Park Slope neighborhood (**I+II**), as well as at **Eastern Park**, located in Brownsville, all within the confines of the Brooklyn borough. By the end of the first decade of the 20th century, club owner Charlie Ebbets was faced with the reality that his Dodgers had outgrown these home diamonds. Because of the massive amount of work and money required to upgrade **Washington Park (II)**, it made more sense for Ebbets to start anew with a modern facility.

Toward this end, as early as 1908, the Brooklyn owner began buying up concurrent building lots in a slum called Pigtown. Located between the Flatbush and Crown Heights neighborhoods, the area Ebbets had quietly chosen for his new stadium was formerly a garbage dump (there's a pattern here!). By the end of 1911, enough land had been obtained for an adequate site, and Ebbets approached architect Clarence Randall Van Buskirk to commission what Charlie hoped would be a grand monument to Brooklyn baseball. Van Buskirk had satisfactorily drawn up proposed alterations and improvements for **Washington Park (II)**, which gave Ebbets the confidence to move ahead with the architect's proposed design for his new stadium.

Van Buskirk was the oldest son of a Brooklyn minister; his training in engineering and architecture came from New York University. Since 1895, Van Buskirk had worked as an assistant engineer in the City of Brooklyn

Works Department. However, in 1907, a bribery scandal within the department involving his boss resulted in Van Buskirk's dismissal from his city job. Without the taint of formal charges against him, Clarence Van Buskirk was able to successfully enter private practice, where he designed buildings for the rapidly expanding city. In the run-up to conceiving Ebbets Field, Van Buskirk toured other existing major league stadiums to evaluate the types of features to incorporate (and to exclude) from Brooklyn's newest ballfield. His enhanced plans further thrilled Charlie Ebbets.

On March 4, 1912, an audience of 500 spectators gathered on the future site of the Dodgers' new home to witness the groundbreaking. Borough president Alfred Steers spoke about his early experiences with America's game, and Ebbets—utilizing a silver spade presented him by the Castle Brothers, the contractors for the actual construction—turned the first ground. Because the final cost topped $750,000 (around $22 million today), the only way Charlie Ebbets could afford the construction was to sell a half-interest in his team.

The stadium was ready in time for the 1913 season. Fittingly, the home season pre-opener was an exhibition contest with Brooklyn's cross-river archrival, the New York Highlanders, soon to be renamed the Yankees. This modern ballpark of concrete, brick, and steel originally held 18,000 spectators. It was an immediate success with the public.

In a time before the standardization of ballparks, Ebbets's playing field was a bit off-balance. Although it was 401 feet along the left field foul line to the fence, right field measured only 298 feet. I suppose, because right-handed batters, who generally hit to the left side of the stadium, predominated, the architect was stingy with right field. Strangely, the design of the right field wall tended to favor left-handers, and Ebbets became known as a hitter's park.

Unfortunately, the year the stadium opened, its architect saw his world collapse. Van Buskirk's spouse, catching him sharing time with another woman claiming to be his wife, divorced him. At the same moment, his business partner went public with the assertion that he, not Clarence, had designed Ebbets's stadium.

Over the years that Ebbets Field was open, spectators turned out in droves. This necessitated several renovations. A press box, neglected in the original design, was added in 1929. The next major redo occurred in 1931, when the left and center field stands were expanded, increasing capacity to 32,000. Another alteration came in 1947, changing the dimensions of the field when 850 new box seats were added. Lights came to Ebbets in June of 1938, when the visiting Cincinnati Reds shut out the Dodgers in the first major league night game. The Cincinnati squad was back in August of the following year for the premiere televised professional baseball contest.

A famous feature of Ebbets Field was its signage. In 1930, a new scoreboard prominently showcased Schaefer Beer. Beside functioning as a beverage advertisement, the letters in "Schaefer" were variously illuminated to denote action on the field: when there was a "hit," the "h" lit up; an "error" was signaled with a brightened "e." The long-standing advertisement at the bottom of the scoreboard for clothier Abe Stark appealed to batters, reading, "Hit sign, win suit." Originally located in a much more hittable location on the right field wall, it appears the post-1931 scoreboard position about three feet above the ground was only struck once. Stark did reward outfielder Carl Furillo for shielding his ad (and pocketbook) from fly balls. Another scoreboard feature was its oversized clock by Bulova. In May of 1946, visiting Braves hitter "Bama" Rowell sent a baseball right into the timepiece's glass front, covering Brooklyn's outfielder "Dixie" Walker in glass. Rowell should have gotten a free watch, but the Bulova company was slow in delivering on their promise. Supposedly, a similar scene in the baseball movie *The Natural* was inspired by that event.

Over the years, the Dodgers won the National League pennant nine times at Ebbets: in 1916, 1920, 1941, 1947, 1949, 1952, 1953, 1955, and, finally, before moving to Los Angeles, in 1956. However, for the rest of the approximately 45 years in Pigtown, the Dodgers were regarded as also-rans. Called the "Daffiness Boys" in the 1920s by the press and "Dem Bums" by their fans, the Brooklyn club was great at almost winning games for most of its existence.

One of New York City's greatest baseball rivalries involved its three professional teams. Many contests were waged between the Yankees of the American League and the Giants and Dodgers of the National League. The aptly named "subway" series (because teams and fans alike could supposedly travel by mass transit among ballparks) between the Yanks and Dodgers began with the 1941 championship, which Brooklyn conceded in four games. World Series loses to the Bronx Bombers continued in 1947, 1952, 1953, and 1956. After another ascendance to the top of the league in 1955, it took the Brooklyn Bums seven games to beat the New York Yankees at **Yankee Stadium (I)** and take the World Series championship. This was a first in its history for the Dodger franchise and the last for the Brooklyn team before its move.

As the Yanks famously had the Dodgers' number, so went their regular season face-offs as well with the New York Giants. Most famously, in 1951, the season ended with the Dodgers and Giants tied for first place in the National League. A three-game playoff was initiated, with each team taking a win. In the deciding game 3 at the **Polo Grounds (V)**, home of the Giants, the Dodgers were up by a score of 4–2. In the bottom of the ninth inning, Bobby Thompson hit a home run to drive in two players for the Giants' win. Thompson's blast became known as the "shot heard around the world." "Maybe next year," cried the long-suffering Brooklyn fans, "there's always next year."

Along with their losses, Ebbets Field was also witness to many moments of joy. On August 31, 1950, Dodger Gil Hodges joined an extremely exclusive club by hitting four home runs within one nine-inning game. Hodges entered the record books as the first player in the National Association to achieve that mark, and the second in all major league baseball history (American Leaguer Lou Gehrig was the first in 1932). Four different pitchers for the opposing Boston Braves each gave up one of Gil's "out of here" hits.

The most important moment in the annals of the Dodgers (and, possibly, all major league baseball) occurred in 1947. Five days earlier, Jackie Robinson had signed his major league contract with Brooklyn, leading to his debut on April 15 at Ebbets Field. Robinson broke the unspoken color barrier that day, leading to the eventual integration for professional baseball and an end to the separate Negro Leagues.

Eventually, the ballpark, designed for the days of the trolley car and, therefore, lacking adequate parking, became a liability. With most fans fleeing to the suburbs, spectators now expected to drive to see "Da Bums." Additionally, the stadium suffered from 40 years of use, driving current owner Walter O'Malley to focus on moving the franchise. When Los Angeles made the Dodgers an offer they couldn't refuse, the Brooklyn ball club pulled up stakes and made the relocation to the West Coast. The last game at Ebbets Field occurred on September 24, 1957, and fittingly saw the Brooklyn Dodgers defeat the Pittsburgh Pirates by a score of 2–0.

Other baseball clubs that used Ebbets included the Brooklyn Eagles (1935) as well as the Brooklyn Brown Dodgers (1945–1946), both of the Negro Leagues. Roy Campanella's Brooklyn Stars, a conglomeration of local Black players, took on the Kansas City Monarchs after the Brooklyn Dodgers had decamped for LA. Football was even occasionally attempted over the years during baseball's off-season.

On February 23, 1960, a wrecking ball painted to resemble a baseball began the task of dismantling Ebbets Field. It was replaced by apartments, and then by a shopping center. Nothing remains of the original park on the site; a plaque marks the location for visiting baseball fans.

FMI: Ross and Dyte, "Ebbets Field"; "1955 World Series," *Baseball Reference*; "1955 World Series," Wikipedia; Anapolis, "Robinson Debuts Five Days after Signing with Dodgers"; Schwartz, "Hodges Sets NL Record with Four Home Runs"; "Brooklyn Dodgers," *Bullpen*; "Ebbets Field," *ballparksofbaseball.com*; Spellen, "The Architect, the Baseball Stadium and a Really Bad Couple of Years"; James, "Ballparks, Scoreboards and Signage"; Lippman, *List of New York's Baseball Sites*; Bennett, "Charlie Ebbets's Field"; "Ebbets Field," *Ballparks, by Munsey and Suppes*; "Ebbets Field Scoreboard."

MANHATTAN

MADISON SQUARE PARK

Map 3. Manhattan South Ballparks.

Map 4. Manhattan North Ballparks.

Dimensions: unknown

Home Team(s): New York Knickerbockers

Built/In Operation: 1845

Seats/Capacity: unknown

Fun Facts: Reportedly the first field used by the Knickerbockers club. The team went on to play at Fifth Avenue and 23rd Street, as well as at the Murray Hill Grounds located at 34th Street and Park Avenue.

FMI: "Madison Square Park: Where Baseball Was Born"; Morris et al., *Base Ball Founders*.

POLO GROUNDS (I+II)

Location: 110th Street between Fifth and Sixth Avenues, Manhattan, at the northeast corner of Central Park

Dimensions: unknown

Home Team(s): New York Gothams/National Colored League; New York Gothams, Giants/National League; and New York Metropolitans/American Association

Built/In Operation: 1880/1880 through 1888. Demolished/burnt down during 1888 and 1889.

Seats/Capacity: 12,000 to 20,709

Schedule of home games for the New York Ball Club from 1887 showing an illustration of their ballpark, the Polo Grounds (I+II). From the Library of Congress.

Fun Facts: The Polo Grounds (I+II) began life as (wait for it) a polo field owned by James Gordon Bennett, publisher of the *New York Herald* newspaper. Ironically, Bennett's interests, gained from his travels abroad, included the very British (especially during that time) and upper crust game of polo. Luckily for his sporting cronies, James Bennett's myriad of real estate holdings included a vacant lot on 110th Street. This proved the perfect locale for their Westchester Polo Club practice field. The land once again became vacant when Bennett and his cohorts from the Polo Club moved their playground closer to home base.

With the lot's availability, cigar magnate and New York Metropolitans' owner John B. Day had the perfect Manhattan locale for his newly formed team. Day relocated the Mets from their temporary homes in Brooklyn and New Jersey to the first Polo Grounds.

With a flagpole inconveniently dividing center field, the original baseball diamond sat on the southeastern part of the leased property. This earliest version of the Polo Grounds (I+II) opened to spectators in September of 1880. The first grandstand seated 12,000, and was expanded for the upcoming 1883 season with an added second level. According to Ron Selter, this format of the grounds may have been the first two-tiered stadium in baseball.

John B. Day had become interested in the pastime as a youth, when he pitched for various amateur aggregations. Day's love of the sport carried into his adulthood, when he not only owned the Metropolitans of the American Association, but also the National League Gothams (later called the Giants). So, it wasn't surprising that the two teams shared the grounds, albeit in a unique way.

In the spring of 1883, Day had a second diamond added on the southwest portion of the Polo Grounds (I+II). However, since that diamond was built atop a former dump, both teams preferred the original field. This was only an issue when both squads were at home. For some of the years when both the Gothams and the Metropolitans utilized the Polo Grounds (I+II), they alternated games on the original field. At other times, play ran concurrently on both diamonds. When both basepaths were in use, the teams were separated by a 10-foot-high canvas fence. Baseballs rolling under the fence were "in play," forcing outfielders to crawl under the barrier and somehow get the ball over the canvas and back to their infielders on the other side. In 1886, the first permanent outfield fences were added to the grounds.

The one-two punch that spelled extinction for the original Polo Grounds (I+II) was New York City's planned street expansion, running pavement through part of the facility. The coup de grâce was a fire at the park in the spring of 1889.

FMI: Johnson, *Ballparks Database*; Jim Overmyer, "City of Diamond Heros," in Puff, *Troy's Baseball Heritage*; Ron Selter, "By the Numbers: The Five Polo Grounds Ballparks," in Thornley, *The Polo Grounds*.

POLO GROUNDS (III)/MANHATTAN FIELD

Location: Coogan's Hollow, around 155th Street and Eighth Avenue, Manhattan

Dimensions: left 345–75', center 315–46', right 320–36'

Home Team(s): New York Giants/National League; and Brooklyn Gladiators/American Association

Built/In Operation: 1889/1889 through 1890. Remnants demolished in 1948.

Seats/Capacity: 15,000

Fun Facts: After the loss of the Giants original **Polo Grounds (I+II)**, the National Leaguers moved further uptown. Their new park was completed partway through the 1889 season. After starting their home games at the **St. George Cricket Grounds** on Staten Island and at Oakdale Park in Jersey City, New Jersey, the team was relocated to the Polo Grounds (III) in early July.

The Giants new facility was below an outcropping named for Manhattan borough president James T. Coogan. Coogan's Bluff, a large, steep embankment that surrounded right and center fields, overlooked the third base side of the ballfield. It was diminished between the 1889 and 1890 seasons, allowing the center and left field fences to retreat around 40 feet.

Besides a 5,000-seat grandstand behind the infield, bleachers filled in from first and third base along the outfield, as well as behind the outfield line. Additionally, some uncovered stands occupied fair territory in left field. A 20-foot-high wooden fence covered with advertisements enclosed the outfield bleachers, while right and left field were surrounded by 6-foot poles with canvas stretched between them that ran from the bleachers to the foul lines. A clubhouse of two stories occupied the right field corner.

In 1904, parts of this facility were disassembled, moved, and reassembled at **Polo Grounds (IV)**.

FMI: Ron Selter, "By the Numbers: The Five Polo Grounds Ballparks," in Thornley, *The Polo Grounds*; Bill Lamb, "The Polo Grounds Owners and Overlords," in Thornley, *The Polo Grounds*.

POLO GROUNDS (IV)/BROTHERHOOD PARK

Location: 157th Street Alley, behind center field of the **Polo Grounds (III)**

Dimensions: left 335–277' feet, center 400–500', right 335–258'

Built/In Operation: 1890/1890 through 1911. Partially destroyed by fire and rebuilt as **Polo Grounds (V)**.

Home Team(s): New York Giants/Players' League; and New York Giants/National League

Seats/Capacity: 22,000 to 28,500

In this print, titled *A Baseball Match*, the New York Giants take on the Baltimore Orioles in 1894 at the Polo Grounds (IV). Photogravure after Henry Sandham. Printed by Boussod, Valadon and Company, Paris, ca. 1896. From the Prints and Photographs Division, Library of Congress.

Fun Facts: For the 1890 baseball schedule, there were two New York Giants. The original, National League team played at **Polo Grounds (III)** next to a new ballfield constructed for the other Giants. Named Brotherhood Park for the Players' League, whose official name was "the Brotherhood of Professional Baseball Players," this upstart association, although lasting only one season, greatly damaged National League teams by stealing their best players and fans. With the demise of the Players' League in 1891, their National League neighbors and namesakes moved operations over two blocks, and rechristened Brotherhood Park as Polo Grounds (IV).

The original "short" foul lines of Brotherhood and the Polo Grounds (IV) were a remnant of the "dead ball" era, when the weight of the baseball limited the distance a hitter could propel the sphere. Seating included a double-decker wooden grandstand and four sets of bleachers, one along each foul line and one each in left and right fields located in fair territory. During the life of the Polo Grounds (IV), seating areas were modified and rebuilt.

Originally, the team facilities stood in left field, with the scoreboard on the opposite side. However, in between the 1903 and 1904 seasons, the clubhouse from the **Polo Grounds (III)** was moved to behind the ropes in right-center field.

Some of the "fences" were just posts with cords between them. Consequently, carriages could park outside center field to view the games. Another unintended outcome of the "ropes for fences" setup was a variety of "Blocked Ball Rule" controversies. In short, "Blocked Balls," which cleared the park boundaries in fair territory but touched by member(s) of the crowd, had to be returned to the pitcher before the runner was stopped and play concluded. To simplify the game, the "Blocked Ball Rule" was modified several times during the 1896 and 1897 seasons.

On April 14, two games into the 1911 season, fire swept the wooden structures of the Polo Grounds (IV). Destroyed were the grandstand and part of the right field bleachers. At approximately the same location would emerge **Polo Grounds (V)**, the most renowned of all the Giants' New York ballparks.

FMI: Ron Selter, "By the Numbers: The Five Polo Grounds Ballparks," in Thornley, *The Polo Grounds*; "Dachshunds, Dog Wagons and Other Important Elements of Hot Dog History"; Johnson, *Ballparks Database*.

POLO GROUNDS (V)/BRUSH STADIUM

Location: Coogan's Hollow around the corner of Eighth Avenue and 159th Street, Manhattan, on the Harlem River, along the border between Harlem and Washington Heights

The Polo Grounds (V) during the 1913 World Series. George Grantham Bain Collection, Library of Congress.

Dimensions: left 277', center 430–505', right 258'

Home Team(s): New York Giants/National League; New York Yankees/ American League; and New York Mets/National League

Built/In Operation: 1911/1911 through 1957, and 1962 through 1963. Demolished in 1964.

Seats/Capacity: 34,000/56,000

Fun Facts: After the 1911 fire (see **Polo Grounds [IV]**), current Giants owner John T. Brush hired theatrical architect Henry B. Herts and his firm of Herts and Tallant, along with Cleveland's Osborn Engineering, to rebuild the park. Herts and Tallant had designed the New Amsterdam, the Gaiety, and the Brooklyn Academy of Music, among other showplaces. Frank Osborn was familiar with structural work, as well as having experience fireproofing ballparks. Some baseball stadiums built by Osborn Engineering during the same period as the Polo Grounds (V) include Cleveland's League Park, Griffith Stadium in Washington, DC, and Tiger Stadium in Detroit.

As speed was the order of the day, Herts's role was unfortunately limited to a bit of decoration on top of the bones installed by Osborn (for more information on Frank Osborn and Osborn Engineering, see **Yankee Stadium [I]**). This "icing on the cake," if you will, included stucco bas relief ornamentation, as well as sculptures of eagles on the grandstand. An ornate Italian marble facade around the upper deck featured the coat of arms for each National League city. The result was substandard to Henry Herts' usual theatrical level, and the parts of the crumbling facade still evident were eliminated in a park redo during 1922–1923.

In a rush toward reopening, the Giants' owners retained some of the outdated features from the previous structures, such as the surviving wooden bleachers and the "bathtub" shape of the field. These joined the newly designed and built steel and concrete horseshoe-shaped grandstand holding 34,000. The actual playing ground featured a deep center and short right field line. The incomplete Polo Grounds (V) opened at the end of the 1911 season.

Between 1922 and 1923, ballpark improvements included expanded seating areas, with a new clubhouse and bullpens. In 1940, lights were added, allowing for night games. Advertisements on the outfield walls vanished in 1948 when the Giants' sponsorship went exclusively to Chesterfield Cigarettes. Through all the updates to the seating and structures, the shape of the playing field stayed about the same as before the 1911 fire.

Three of New York City's major league teams played their home games at this version of the Polo Grounds. The Giants were in residence from 1911 to 1957, before abandoning New York City for the West Coast. Prior to the building of **Yankee Stadium (I)**, the Bronx Bombers had a 10-year stretch (1912–1922) at the Upper West Side facility. Even the initially sorry replacement for the Giants, the New York Mets, spent their premiere seasons in this ballpark.

Sunday baseball came to the Polo Grounds (and other New York ballparks) early in the 1919 season, when New York State officially legalized play on the Sabbath. It was an immediate success, increasing attendance and, therefore, financial support for the teams.

Many other notable events in baseball happened on this field. On June 28, 1911, Christy Mathewson powered the Giants to a 3-0 shutout of the Rustlers (Braves) to launch the last iteration of Polo Grounds (V).

In 1951, Bobby Thompson hit his "shot heard around the world" here (see **Ebbets Field**). And the inimitable Mets lost their last game in 1963 to the Phillies at the Polo Grounds (V) before moving to **Shea Stadium**.

Today, the site houses apartment buildings named "Polo Grounds Towers," as well as the "Coogan's Bluff Playground." The only other remnant of the Polo Grounds besides the names are the Bushman Steps, which led fans from the subway station to the ballpark.

Although initially named for the Giants' owner John T. Brush, the moniker never caught on. For the fans of New York baseball, it will forever be the Polo Grounds.

FMI: Johnson, *Ballparks Database*; Walsh and Murphy, *The Fields of New York*; Evanosky and Kos, *Lost Ballparks*; Ron Selter, "By the Numbers: The Five Polo Grounds Ballparks," in Thornley, *The Polo Grounds*.

METROPOLITAN PARK/EAST RIVER BALL PARK

Location: East 107th Street and First Avenue, East Harlem, Manhattan

Dimensions: unknown

Home Team(s): New York Metropolitans/American Association

Built/In Operation: 1884. Dismantled several years later. Now a high-rise apartment building.

Seats/Capacity: 5000 to 10,000

Fun Facts: For 1883, the adjoining diamonds of the Metropolitans and the Gothams (later the Giants) at the **Polo Grounds (I+II)** had proved unsatisfactory for the mutually owned ball teams. Therefore, for a part of the 1884 season, the Mets moved 10 blocks from their shared home at the **Polo Grounds (I+II)** east to this wooden ballpark in an industrial area built on—as it became known by fans, players and sports writers alike—"The Dump." (The Metropolitans' management seemed to favor playing the team on top of garbage! As John B. Day also owned the more important National League franchise, was this a not-so-subtle message to the Mets?)

A single-level grandstand seating 5,000 was projected to be joined by 5,000 bleachers seats along the first and third base lines. When finished, the grounds was enclosed by a 14-foot outer wall.

Located on the East River, this solution for avoiding conflicting home games with the Gothams proved unacceptable, and the Metropolitans returned to their old park for the end of their 1884 schedule.

FMI: Johnson, *Ballparks Database*; Ron Selter, "By the Numbers: The Five Polo Grounds Ballparks," in Thornley, *The Polo Grounds*; Lamb, "Metropolitan Park (New York)."

HILLTOP PARK/AMERICAN LEAGUE PARK

Location: Broadway between 165th and 168th streets, Washington Heights, Manhattan

Dimensions: left 300–85', center 370–542', right 400'

Home Team(s): New York Highlanders and Yankees/American League; and New York Giants/National League

Built/In Operation: 1903/1903 through 1912. Demolished in 1914.

Seats/Capacity: 16,000/28,584

Fun Facts: For their new ballpark, the New York American League team signed a 10-year lease for an undeveloped property owned by the New York Institute for the Blind. The Highlanders latest wooden home was hastily built at a cost of $275,000 (about $825,000 in today's money), with most of that amount going toward preparing the unimproved lot. Not surprisingly, Hilltop Park opened in poor condition, with a swamp in right field, and a scoreboard that stood in a center field devoid of grass. The clubhouse was located behind the outfield fence, forcing players to arrive for games already dressed. When finally finished, the covered grandstand was all on one level and supplemented with further uncovered seating along the foul lines. Named Hilltop because the park sat on high ground, the stadium's one saving grace were the majestic views from the seats of the Hudson River and the Palisades on the New Jersey side. The lot was quite large compared to other ballparks, leaving ample space for carriage and automobile parking.

Hilltop Park, ca. June 1910, as photographed by the Pictorial News Company. From the Library of Congress.

In 1909, the emblematic sign advertising Bull Durham tobacco made its debut. In 1910, an agreement with the Giants saw the American Leaguers transfer some of their "home" games to the **Polo Grounds (IV)**. When the Giants stadium burned at the beginning of the 1911 season, the Highlanders invited the Nationals to play at Hilltop Park. During the period when both teams held home games in the same stadium, covered center field bleachers costing an additional $75,000 were added at Hilltop.

Over the 10 seasons the Highlanders played at Hilltop Park, the management attempted to improve sight lines and limit home runs. Towards this end, the outfield fences were constantly being modified and moved. Unable to assemble a consistently strong team, the Highlanders best seasons at Hilltop saw second place finishes (in 1904, 1906, and 1910).

Probably one of the most infamous incidents occurring at Hilltop Park transpired during its last season in use. On May 15, 1912, the Detroit Tigers' combative outfielder Ty Cobb climbed into the stands to reach a spectator who had been mercilessly heckling him. Although the Highlanders' fan turned out to be physically impaired, Cobb still beat him severely. This led to Ty's suspension by American League president Ban Johnson, in turn causing a walkout by Ty Cobb's Detroit teammates.

As the lease on the property was about to expire, the New York Highlanders' management began building a new park in the Bronx. The site appears to have been inappropriate, and the Highlanders' organization was never able to make much progress toward a completed stadium. That would have to wait until 1923 (see **Yankee Stadium [I]**).

Instead, after the 1912 season, the Highlanders vacated Hilltop Park, following the Giants to the newly reconstructed **Polo Grounds (V)**. The Hilltop site now contains New York-Presbyterian and Columbia University Irving Medical Center. Within the medical center is a plaque donated by the New York Yankees in the shape of home plate commemorating the 10 years that the American Leaguers called this their home.

FMI: Ron Selter, "By the Numbers: The Five Polo Grounds Ballparks," in Thornley, *The Polo Grounds*; "Hilltop Park," *ballparksofbaseball.com*; "Hilltop Park Historical Analysis"; Lamb, "Hilltop Park (New York)"; "Hilltop Park," *Ballparks, by Munsey and Suppes*; Bennett, "Hilltop Park and the Church of Baseball."

OLYMPIC FIELD

Location: East 138th Street and Madison Avenue, Manhattan. Not to be confused with Olympia Field, an earlier park located one long block away from this location.

Dimensions: unknown

Home Team(s): New York Lincoln Giants/Eastern Independent Colored League; and Negro American League

Built/In Operation: 1904/1911 through 1919. Demolished at the end of 1919 season. Currently the Riverton Apartments.

Seats/Capacity: 10,000

Fun Facts: Constructed in 1904 as a soccer facility, Olympic Field was converted the following year for the Olympic Athletic Club by the McMahon brothers (see **Lenox Oval**) for semiprofessional baseball. The McMahons, then owners of the Lincoln (Negro Leagues) Giants, lost the team after the 1913 season. From 1914, Charles Harvey took over the Giants and Olympic. When the field was demolished in 1920, the bleachers were moved to a facility at the **Catholic Protectory Oval**.

FMI: Benson, *Ballparks of North America*; Ashwill, *Agate Type*, February 28, 2011; Johnson, *Ballparks Database*; "The Rise of the Cubans"; Ashwill, *Agate Type*, October 23, 2012; Robertson, "Harlem and Baseball in the 1920s."

LENOX OVAL

Location: Lenox Avenue and 145th Street, Manhattan

Dimensions: "short right field fence"

Home Team(s): New York Lincoln Stars/Eastern Independent Colored League

Built/Built/In Operation: 1911/1911, and 1914 through 1916

Seats/Capacity: 1500 to 2000

Fun Facts: An article in the *Buffalo Commercial* about the "outlaw" United States (Baseball) League mentions the Lenox Oval as being a semiprofessional facility that had been considered and rejected by several major league teams, including the Giants and (what became) the Yankees, as well as the projected local United States League team. The 1911 New York Highlanders/Yankees played some games here during Hal Chase's management, taking on Negro Leaguers such as the Newark Stars, all-star squads of professional players such as one led by Ty Cobb, and the semipro New York Metropolitans. Even the Giants engaged in some exhibition contests here.

By the time of the 1912 season by the Mets, the Lenox Oval had gained a covered grandstand. The dressing rooms/clubhouse was located under the seating.

From 1914 to 1916, the McMahon Brothers, formerly promoters of a semiprofessional white team, having lost control of the Lincoln (Negro Leagues) Giants, sponsored the Lincoln (Negro Leagues) Stars, leasing the oval for Sunday baseball. Several times during the 1914 season, the Stars were challenged by Frank Wickware and the Mohawk (Negro Leagues) Giants of Schenectady (see **Island Park**).

For 1915, the Federal League designated Lenox Oval as the home park for the New York Americans. Unfortunately, the Americans never played any games, neither at the oval or anywhere else.

There are several reported instances of attempted prosecution for Sunday contests. On one occasion in 1912, the New York Giants were cited for an exhibition game. During another the following year by the Female Giants, which included a mixture of female athletes and male players from the regular team, police witnessed the players selling programs. The officers shut the contest down, arresting some of the participants in the process. A judge later threw out the case.

The Lenox Oval was also utilized by high school, college, amateur, and semiprofessional athletes for soccer, cricket, track and field, and winter ice skating. It should not be confused with the similarly named facility in Brooklyn.

FMI: Ashwill, *Agate Type*, February 28, 2011; "The Famous Lenox Oval in Harlem NY 1911–1930's"; "And Now, the New York Female Giants"; Johnson, *Ballparks Database*; Robertson, "Harlem and Baseball in the 1920s"; "Jordan and Ryan May Join Outlaws," *Buffalo Commercial*, January 24, 1912; "Stopped the Games," *Buffalo Morning Express*, November 5, 1912; "Play Ball, Judge!" *Evening World*, October 21, 1912.

A view of the corner at Nagle Avenue and Academy Streets in Manhattan. The photograph shows the Dyckman Oval, when hosting the New York Cubans in the mid-1930s. Irma and Paul Milstein Division of United States History, Local History, and Genealogy, the New York Public Library. From the New York Public Library Digital Collections.

Location: 204th Street and Nagle Avenue between the Harlem and Hudson Rivers, Manhattan

Dimensions: unknown

Home Team(s): Kingsbridge Athletics; Treat 'Em Rough-Tesreau Bears; New York Cuban Stars, and Stars West/Negro National League and Negro East-West League; New York Cuban Stars East/Eastern Colored League and Negro American League; Bacharach Giants/Eastern Colored League; and New York Black Yankees/Negro National League

Built/In Operation: 1915/1917 through 1930, and 1932 through 1937. Demolished in 1938 by New York City and remade as a parking lot, then as the Dyckman Houses apartment buildings.

Seats/Capacity: 4500 to 10,000/5000 to 10,000

Fun Facts: Because of its location in Harlem, New York's primary African-American neighborhood, the Dyckman Oval hosted many Negro Leagues and unaffiliated Black teams throughout the period between the world wars. Additionally, countless local major league players were more than happy to keep their spikes on to pick up some additional income at the oval after their regular season had ended.

For the 1917 baseball season, the field was fenced in and a grandstand with seating was erected. The home team for 1917 and 1918 was the Kingsbridge Athletics, who sound from surviving descriptions like a semipro team that included former big leaguers. It should be said that, like their crosstown brethren the Brooklyn Bushwicks, the Kingsbridge squad (and their successors, the Treat 'Em Rough ballclub) featured professional-level players and competition. The Athletics played other semipros, Negro Leagues teams, and barnstorming professionals alike.

By 1919, the stands had been covered, turf added to the field, and other improvements made. For the years following, the ownership of the facility was in contention. Because litigation clouded the issue of who held the rights to program the oval, scheduling baseball became difficult if not impossible.

This problem of ownership was alleviated by the 1930s. In 1935, Alessandro Pompez, the owner of the Cuban Stars (Negro Leagues), leased the Dyckman Oval for three years. Pompez built fireproof stands and added a clubhouse and a beer garden. Under his watch, the playing field was expanded by moving the outfield fences. The addition of lights added the possibility of night games at the oval.

Pompez had made his money in the Harlem numbers racket, investing his ill-gotten gains in the baseball facility to the tune of $60,000, after the notorious "Dutch Schultz" had elbowed the Cuban gangster out of gambling. Unfortunately, Pompez had not completely left crime behind, leading to his arrest in 1937, and the end for baseball at Dyckman Oval.

FMI: Benson, *Ballparks of North America*; "The Dyckman Oval," *My Inwood*; Costello, "Dyckman Oval (New York)."

JASPER OVAL/HEBREW ORPHAN ASYLUM OVAL

Location: West 138th and Covent Avenue, Manhattan. Now on the campus of the City College of New York.

Dimensions: unknown

Home Team(s): Bacharach Giants/Eastern Colored League

Built/In Operation: 1922

Seats/Capacity: unknown

Fun Facts: unknown

FMI: Benson, *Ballparks of North America*; Ross and Dyte, "Brooklyn's Semipro Fields."

JOHN J. DOWNING STADIUM/TRIBOROUGH STADIUM/ RANDALL'S ISLAND STADIUM

Location: Eastern Parkway and Sutter Avenue, Randall's Island, East River, Manhattan

Dimensions: unknown

Home Team(s): New York Black Yankees/Negro National League; and Pittsburgh Crawfords/Negro National League

Built/In Operation: 1935–1936/1938 through 1939. Demolished 2002, replaced with Icahn Stadium.

Seats/Capacity: 22,000

Fun Facts: Randall's Island Stadium was a WPA project built for $1 million (almost $20 million today). Owned by New York City and attributed to Robert Moses, the planner who began reshaping the city in the 1930s, the stadium replaced the existing poor house and various asylums previously located on the island. The first game played here was on Sunday, August 7, 1938, a doubleheader with the Black Yankees versus the Nashville Elite Giants and the Pittsburgh Crawfords versus the Philadelphia Stars (all Negro Leagues).

Later, Randall's Island was utilized for Olympic trials, professional soccer, and football, as well as musical events. The facility's light towers came from **Ebbets Field** after its demolition in 1960.

FMI: "Randall's Island Park," New York City Department of Parks and Recreation; Johnson, *Ballparks Database*; "New York Cubans," *Bullpen*.

59TH STREET SANDLOT/RECREATION PARK

One by one, New York's semi-pro baseball field [*sic*] are disappearing. Last season [1938], Dyckman Oval, Recreation Park under the Queensboro Bridge and Catholic Protectory Oval went the way of all real estate. A street has already been cut through the Bay Ridge Oval and the site of Farmers' Stadium has been sold for building lots, leaving only Dexter Park, the Bay Parkways' home of Erasmus Field, and Queens Park, Woodside for the semi-pro lads.

—*Democrat and Chronicle*, January 10, 1939

Location: East 59th Street and First Avenue, Manhattan, under the ramps for the 59th Street/Queensboro Bridge

Dimensions: unknown

Home Team(s): New York Cubans/Negro National League

Built/In Operation: 1939

Seats/Capacity: unknown

Fun Facts: unknown

FMI: Benson, *Ballparks of North America*.

PORT CHESTER

EMPIRE STADIUM/SAVIN FIELD

Location: Boston Post Road between Olivia and South Regent Streets, Port Chester, on Savin Hill

Dimensions: unknown

Home Team(s): Port Chester Clippers/Colonial League

Built/In Operation: 1947/1947 through 1948. No longer standing.

Seats/Capacity: 3000 to 3500

Fun Facts: Empire Stadium was part of the temporary post–World War II baseball boom in the wake of the return to prosperity. Constructed in 1947 on property associated with the Empire Brush Works, the Clippers were granted free use of the facility with an option to purchase the land. In preparation for the upcoming season, semipermanent grandstands were erected and the playing area enclosed. However, the stadium was not ready for the opening of the season, and so the team began its schedule on the road. When the Colonial League squad finally played its first home game on June 13, the stadium lights were still not fully functional for another week.

After the inaugural season, the team sold shares to raise the funds needed for further stadium improvements. The 1948 pennant winners were eventually affiliated with the St. Louis Browns. In 1949, after a few games at the beginning of the season, the Port Chester Clippers moved to Bristol, Connecticut.

FMI: *digitalballparks.com* on the Colonial League; "Professional Baseball in Port Chester, New York: Historical Records"; *Stats Crew*, "Empire Stadium"; McGreal, "Colonial League a Trail Blazer in 1947 Debut"; "Port Chester League Team Secures Field," *Daily Item*, May 1, 1947; Steven J. Stark, "Field Days," *Daily Item*, April 5, 1993.

QUEENS

FASHION RACE COURSE/NATIONAL RACE COURSE

Location: 37th Avenue and 103rd Street, Corona, Queens

Dimensions: unknown

Home Team(s): Brooklyn vs. New York

Built/In Operation: 1853/June 20, 1858. The racetrack closed in 1866.

Seats/Capacity: 4,000 to 10,000/50,000

Fun Facts: The first all-star game between the best players from the two, what were then, neighboring municipalities occurred on June 20, 1858. For the championship between Brooklyn and New York City, a baseball

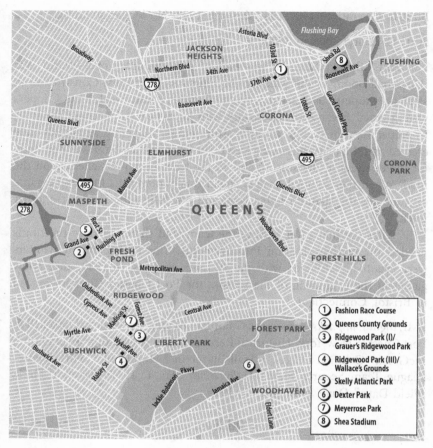

Map 5. Queens Ballparks.

diamond was laid out on the Fashion Race Course in front of the track's grandstands within what we would today call the "infield." June's contest was the first of a three-game series; the others were played on August 17 and September 10. New York took the first round, Brooklyn the second, but, even though heavily favored, Brooklyn lost the third to New York City.

According to Thomas Gilbert:

The first baseball game that anyone ever paid to see. Admission was 10 cents, plus 20 cents more for parking a one-horse vehicle and 40 cents more for a two-horse vehicle. The announced

An all-star baseball contest between Brooklyn and New York was held at the Fashion Race Course on July 20, 1858. From *The New York Clipper*, July 24, 1858.

reason for charging admission was to pay grounds keeping costs. Any profit over expenses was to be donated to the Widows and Orphans Funds of the fire departments of [Brooklyn and New York. After the series, the two funds split $71.10.]

This race course was named for a former champion thoroughbred named Fashion. Although totally purpose-built ballparks would come later, Fashion was an enclosed facility, making it the first fenced field utilized for baseball.

FMI: Gilbert, *How Baseball Happened*; Thorn, "The All-Star Game You Don't Know"; Zinn, "Summer 1858."

QUEENS COUNTY GROUNDS

Location: the south side of Grand Street (now Grand Avenue), Maspeth, Queens, immediately west of where 54th Street, Brooklyn now exists.

Dimensions: unknown

Home Team(s): Atlantic Base Ball Club of Brooklyn (not *the* Atlantic Club)/Eastern League

Built/In Operation: 1884/1886. Demolished.

Seats/Capacity: unknown

Fun Facts: Close by the **Long Island Grounds** was the Queens County Grounds. Two different Atlantics clubs played here. NEITHER was the famous Brooklyn Atlantics.

FMI: John Pardon and Jerry Jackson, "New York State Ball Clubs," in Puff, *The Empire State of Base Ball*; Ross and Dyte, "The Parks of Maspeth"; Schlapp, "Past Ballparks of New York City."

RIDGEWOOD PARK (I)/GRAUER'S RIDGEWOOD PARK/ LONG ISLAND ATHLETIC CLUB GROUNDS

Location: between Cypress Avenue, Myrtle Avenue, Seneca Avenue, and Decatur Street, Queens

Dimensions: unknown

Home Team(s): Brooklyn Grays/American Association

Built/In Operation: 1885/1886. Grauer's existed at least until 1907 as an events ground. Divided into building lots and sold off in 1911.

Seats/Capacity: 3,000/10,000

Fun Facts: At the beginning of 1885, brewer George Grauer acquired ten acres adjacent to his Ridgewood event site on the Queens-Brooklyn border. It's hard to know one 150 years later if Grauer was aware of the need for Sunday facilities by professional Brooklyn baseball teams away from the prying eyes of local authorities. As has been stated in other listings, New York prohibited Sabbath ball until 1919, influencing pro squads to play in alternative venues on that day.

For the premier year of Grauer's new park, the diamond was strictly used by local amateur teams. The resident Long Island Athletic Club continued using the field, which in some reports had their name attached, for contests such as against the Cuban Giants (Negro Leagues) of Trenton, New Jersey. However, for 1886, the Brooklyn Grays successfully played their Sunday games at Ridgewood. Some reporters attributed the "hands off" by local law enforcement to lavish bribes provided to officials.

Regardless, this successful relationship between the Grays and George Grauer only lasted for one season. While attendance and the lack of police harassment had kept the Brooklyn pros at Ridgewood (I), other factors ended this agreement. First off, the diamond had many drawbacks. It was poorly maintained, and the short distance to the outfield fences made many hits unplayable, therefore benefiting the team at the plate. Secondly, the Grays' management expressed their resentment toward what they saw as unreasonably high fees charged by Grauer, which severely affected their bottom line. Therefore, Grauer came to believe, possibly mistakenly, that the use of his property for social events would yield more than the Brooklyn's were willing to pay. Luckily for Brooklyn baseball, the solution lay just next door at **Ridgewood Park (III)**.

FMI: Johnson, *Ballparks Database*; Dereszewski, "The Bushwick Ridgewood Border Was Once Home to a Majorly Important Baseball Field"; Lamb, "Ridgewood Park (New York)"; Barthel, *Baseball's Peerless Semipros*; "Passing of the Picnic Parks," *The Chat*, March 4, 1911.

RIDGEWOOD PARK (III)/WALLACE'S GROUNDS

Location: between Wyckoff Avenue, Covert Street, Halsey Street, and Irving Avenue, Ridgewood, Queens

Dimensions: unknown

Home Team(s): Brooklyn Grays-Bridegrooms/American Association; Brooklyn Gladiators/American Association; Brooklyn Bushwicks (semiprofessional); Brooklyn Ridgewoods (semiprofessional); Brooklyn Royal-Cuban Giants/International League of Colored Baseball Clubs; Jersey City Jerseys/Eastern League; Newark Trunkmakers/Central League; Jersey City Skeeters/Central League; and Newark Little Giants/Atlantic Association

Built/In Operation: 1885/1885 through 1917 (semipro after that date). Demolished in 1928, and roads built through the site.

Seats/Capacity: 10,000/16,000

Fun Facts: When the Brooklyn Grays grew disenchanted with George Grauer, an alternative for Sunday baseball was located just a stone's throw away. Around the same time the **Grauer's Ridgewood Park** baseball diamond was completed, William Willock Wallace, representing the Ridgewood Athletic Association, leased the site of an old horse market about two blocks south of George Grauer's grove. A diamond was added and the first amateur game, with the association's squad taking on the Brooklyn Atlantic Club, occurred in April of 1885. The next season, Wallace formed an investment group to buy and improve the facility. When the Grays agreement was completed, William Wallace constructed a covered wooden grandstand as well as unroofed bleacher seats along the baselines.

By the 1888 season, the large crowds attracted by the games had incurred the wrath of local clergy, necessitating an attempt at selling scorecards instead of charging admission. As arrests never came, that scam was abandoned and the gate charges reinstated. Problems arose again the following season, leading to William Wallace and his partners being officially charged with "blue law" violations. Sunday baseball might also have been the engine for the government of the borough deciding to run Halsey Street through left field of Ridgewood Park (III). To overcome this problem, home plate was relocated back 75 feet and a new grandstand holding 3,500 seats built. The finished facility was then enclosed with a picket fence around the outfield.

By 1890, the Grays (now the Brooklyn Bridegrooms of the National League) stopped playing Sunday baseball. Their new League prohibited games on the Sabbath, and so Brooklyn had no use for the Ridgewood (III) field. The Bridegrooms replacement in both the American Association and Wallace's ballpark was the newly formed Brooklyn Gladiators.

However, this was only a temporary solution for the problems of William Wallace. By early June, the failing Gladiators had decamped for the **Polo Grounds (III)**, eventually moving to Baltimore in August. Wallace and company were finally tried in July of 1890 and convicted of violating prohibitions against Sunday play. They were fined $500 and threatened with jail if they continued their infractions.

Improvements continued to be made to Ridgewood Park (III) in hopes of continuing to lure baseball to the facility. From 1891 until 1917, a mixture of amateur, semiprofessional, and professional teams called Ridgewood (III) home. For the 1912 season, Ambrose Hussey, owner of the semipro Ridgewoods, moved his squad here from **Meyerrose Park**, adding additional seating to accommodate their fans.

After a fire in September of 1917 consumed the grandstand and most of the bleachers, Wallace built a smaller ballpark elsewhere on the site. In 1928, those structures also were razed.

FMI: Johnson, *Ballparks Database*; Dereszewski, "The Bushwick Ridgewood Border Was Once Home to a Majorly Important Baseball Field"; Lamb, "Ridgewood Park (New York)"; Barthel, *Baseball's Peerless Semipros*; *Daily News*, July 26, 1966.

Location: Johnson and Gardiner Avenues, Queens, just across Grand Street from the **Queens County Grounds**, where Grand Avenue and 57th Street now meet

Dimensions: unknown

Home Team(s): Long Island Club/Eastern League; and Cuban Giants (Negro Leagues)

Built/In Operation: 1885/1886 through 1893

Seats/Capacity: 5,000

Fun Facts: These Grounds were utilized for exhibition games between the National League and the American Association, as well as by the resident amateur organization. After one season by the Long Island Club, the Cuban Giants played their Sunday games here from at least 1886 until 1893. In 1887, a special grandstand was constructed exclusively for the ladies in attendance. In 1890, the field was leased by the Greenpoint Athletic Club, who provided a complete overhaul. Seating and new drainage was added, and additional diamonds for amateur clubs were completed. Also in 1890, the Brooklyn Gladiators of the American Association were briefly based here as well. In September of 1901, the Brooklyn Ladies Club matched wits with a team of prize fighters. Baseball exhibition and amateur contests continued at least until 1911, and included games by the locals with the Newark Royal, Baltimore, and New York Colored Giants squads. During the summer of that year, the facility changed hands, and was renamed Arctic Baseball Park. Cigar magnate Max Rosner, who managed and sponsored the semipro Brooklyn Paramounts, moved his team here in 1909. Supposedly, Max also (jokingly, I assume) renamed the facility "Schaefer's Pigs Knuckles Park" after his fans' favorite snack. Rosner eventually ran the Bushwicks, Brooklyn's most famous semiprofessional ball club (see **Dexter Park**).

FMI: Ross and Dyte, "The Parks of Maspeth"; Barthel, *Baseball's Peerless Semipros*; "Walker Park," New York City Department of Parks and Recreation; Staten Island Cricket Club, "A Brief History."

DEXTER PARK

Don't kill the umpire—Maybe it's your eyes.
　　　　　　　　　—advertisement on the outfield wall of Dexter Park

Location: near Eldert Lane and Jamaica Avenue, Woodhaven, Queens

Dimensions: left 418', center 431', right 304'

Home Team(s): Brooklyn Cyprus Hills, Dexters, and Bushwicks (semi-professional); Brooklyn Royal Giants/Eastern Colored League; New York Cubans/Negro National League; and New York Black Yankees

Built/In Operation: 1889/1905 through 1951. Demolished in 1957, now a parking lot. Since the fall of 2000, there is a plaque commemorating Dexter Park near the original site.

Seats/Capacity: 2,000 to 8,850/20,000

Fun Facts: As Brooklyn began developing after the Civil War, large open spaces remained unimproved in the borough to the north and west. Around 1880, this area of Queens became a park with a racetrack; it gained acclaim as an amateur baseball grounds by the end of the nineteenth century. When the racetrack was replaced by this ballfield, the owner's name (Charles Dexter) was attached to the new field. In 1901, the William Ulmer Brewery purchased the property, constructing in the first decade of the 20th century a pleasure garden with a dance pavilion, picnic grounds, a carousel, and a new field for baseball.

Because Dexter Park sat just over the Brooklyn line in Queens, away from the prying eyes of Brooklyn's clergy and police, its original rurality marked it as ideal for Sunday professional and semipro games. This is probably what attracted a local cigar maker and Brooklyn Bushwicks baseball team owner Max Rosner. Rosner added seating to the wooden ballpark in 1913 in preparation for home contests by his squad.

As this arrangement proved successful, Max Rosner and his partner Nat Strong purchased the property/ballpark in 1922 from Ulmer for $200,000 (a hair over $3 million today). Strong was active as a "booking agent" who acted as a middleman between barnstorming ball clubs without home fields and ballparks and other teams. Nat particularly arranged games for the Black professional teams that traveled the country.

Once he procured ownership, Max Rosner didn't waste any time making further improvements to Dexter. Between the 1922 and 1923 seasons, a 6,000-seat steel-frame and concrete grandstand with 650 box seats was installed. Two sections of wooden bleachers, seating 2,000 apiece, flanked each side of the grandstand. Along with the ballfield, the Dexter Park complex included a restaurant featuring music and dancing. Other events held at Dexter comprised professional boxing, amateur sporting, and school and social events. "It was a miniature Coney Island," remembered Rosner's son Lenny, who was quoted in Thomas Bartel's book on Max Rosner and the Bushwicks (see FMI).

Along with other semiprofessional squads, many of the area's major leaguers played against the Brooklyn/Queens aggregation, including Babe Ruth and Lou Gehrig of the Yankees, members of the New York Giants, and the best of the Negro Leagues. Although money and not the hometown talent brought these opponents to ballparks, the Bushwicks boasted some outstanding teams. Throughout their history, because the semipros only played a few days a week (and, therefore, fewer games than the professionals), Rosner was able to utilize some exceptional talent. The Bushwicks comprised gifted former major and minor league athletes at the end of their careers, professional ballplayers who had finished their regular seasons, and those area athletes working another full-time job.

Although other night baseball contests had been previously held utilizing portable illumination, Dexter Park boasted the first permanent baseball lighting rig in New York City. Thirty thousand dollars' worth of stadium lights were introduced at Dexter on July 23, 1930 (they were updated in 1931). In comparison, major league baseball didn't promote their first game under fixed lights for another five years.

Rosner continued upgrades to the ballpark facility in 1937. The wooden bleachers were replaced with a steel-frame structure, and grandstand seating was increased to 7,500. In 1940, Max Rosner surprisingly decided to install a rock garden in deep center field. In the same area as the flagpole, three groupings of rocks spelled out "Bushwick B. B. C.," "God Bless America," and "Dexter Park." In 1941, the infield was raised two feet to better facilitate drainage. During World War II, due to an understandable drop in attendance, the left field bleachers at Dexter were replaced with income-producing billboards. At the same time, the scoreboard was moved from center to left-center field.

In 1949, the year the facility was shared with the amateur ball team from St. John's University, the outfield fence advertised Kist soda, Gallagher and Burton's liquor, Columbia Savings, and Abe Stark, whose famous **Ebbets Field** advert promised free goods for whichever hitter sent one down the right field line into his sign. In 1950, to bolster further declining revenues due to drops in attendance, local television broadcasts of games were initiated.

Unfortunately, none of these efforts could save the Bushwicks: exit semiprofessional baseball, and enter roller derby and stock car racing. After the death in 1953 of Max Rosner, Dexter Park was sold. Developers took over in 1955, demolishing the ballpark midway through 1957, and covering the site with homes and retail businesses.

FMI: King, "May 24, 1935: Reds Fans See the Lights in First Night Game in MLB History"; Dereszewski, "The Bushwick Ridgewood Border Was Once Home to a Majorly Important Baseball Field"; "The Lost Baseball Stadium That Became a Supermarket Parking Lot"; Ross and Dyte, "Dexter Park"; "The Brooklyn Bushwicks and Dexter Park"; Benson, *Ballparks of North America*; "The Rise of the Cubans"; Barthel, *Baseball's Peerless Semipros*; Lippman, *List of New York's Baseball Sites*; Revel, *Early Pioneers of the Negro Leagues: Nat Strong*.

MEYERROSE PARK/RIDGEWOOD PARK (II)

Those who hunger for baseball will doubtless take the long journey to Ridgewood to see the harum-scarum article supplied by the semipros that make up the outlaw outfit. A bundle of errors, a few hits, and there you are. Not much different from what has been seen at Washington Park, except that the team at Ridgewood wins a bit oftener. But it isn't the same kind of baseball.

—*The Brooklyn Eagle*, quoted by
Ross and Dyte, "The Brooklyn Bandits"

Location: the corner of Onderdunk Avenue and Madison Street between Covert (Seneca) Avenue and Woodward Avenue near the Covert Avenue "L" station, Ridgewood, Queens

Dimensions: unknown

Home Team(s): Brooklyn Atlantics, Edisons, Senors, and Invaders/Atlantic League and Union League; and Brooklyn Ridgewoods (semiprofessional)

Built/In Operation: 1907/1907 through 1911. Structures demolished in 1912.

Seats/Capacity: 2,500 to 10,000

Fun Facts: Meyerrose Park was located on what had been a farmstead belonging to the family of former sheriff Joseph Meyerrose. A well-known activist in local Democratic politics, Meyerrose was president for the 1907 and 1908 professional Brooklyn franchises as well as the semipro Ridgewoods. An unknown reporter from the *Brooklyn Citizen* stated that the sheriff was "practically" the owner of the ballclub and grounds (see FMI).

When the Atlantic League was formed, Meyerrose asked Ambrose Hussey and his son, who owned and managed the Ridgewoods, to look after the new Brooklyn professional squad as well. An immigrant from Ireland, Ambrose William Hussey, Sr., had controlled the semiprofessional Brooklyn Ridgewoods since 1902. Interestingly, if the news media is to be believed, many of Hussey's semipros also populated the Atlantics team. Just a change of uniform and, "viola!," an Atlantic took the field as a Ridgewood and vice versa. Around the time that Hussey senior added the Brooklyn Atlantics to his responsibilities, his son Ambrose, Jr., began helping with the family's baseball business.

The Atlantic League was the brainstorm of ex-player Alfred Lawson, later the inventor of the portable lighting rigs used for night games and founder of the religious/philosophical movement Lawsonomy. Control of the Atlantic League came in handy when the 1907 season ended with contested record keeping. The Brooklyns claimed the championship, but the pennant was eventually awarded to Lawson's Reading, Pennsylvania, franchise instead of to the Brooklyn boys.

For 1908, Brooklyn, without any change of management, moved over to the Union League. Team and League president Joseph Meyerrose green lighted improvements to Meyerrose Park. To prepare for the upcoming spring season, the field, used for wintertime ice skating, needed to have several dams eliminated. Seating was added to center field, and individual chairs replaced some of the benches in the grandstand. Hussey's boys officially became the Invaders after a contest in the *Brooklyn Eagle* declared that the winning name.

Alfred Lawson was again behind the new league. However, this time, things quickly went wrong. By the first days in June, the Brooklyn Invaders as well as the Union League had folded. Although attempts were made the following season to tempt Brooklyn back into the Atlantic League, Meyerrose lacked the interest in fooling again with professional baseball. Ambrose Hussey, Jr., was then able to focus all his energy and players on the Ridgewoods.

From the rest of the 1908 season through 1911, the semipros held forth at Meyerrose Park. Some notable occasions included yearly fall visits after the end of the professional season by their neighbors across the river, the National League New York Giants. In 1908, Giants' pitcher Christy Mathewson and fielder Fred Merkle, among others, beat the Ridgewoods in extra innings. In the spring of 1911, the Ridgewoods took on the Cuban Stars of the Negro Leagues. Also that spring, the Brooklyn Farmers stood in for the Ridgewoods to play the barnstorming Western Bloomer Girls, owned, managed, and led from the mound by Maud Nelson. And, during the fall of that year, the notorious Detroit player Ty Cobb brought his team of all-stars to Meyerrose Park.

Even though Meyerrose had been specifically chosen as the location for the Atlantic League because of its distance from the heart of Brooklyn, Hussey and his squad faced disruption by the same Sunday "blue laws" that had hounded baseball throughout its history. In mid-May of 1907, during the first week of season, law enforcement blocked games held on the Sabbath. By the end of June, Ambrose Hussey had probably grown concerned about the drop in income from the lack of Sunday play. After restarting contests on the Sabbath, police arrested several Atlantics players, leading Hussey to obtain an "injunction" for the resumption of contests on Sundays. On July 22, 1907, the *Brooklyn Citizen* newspaper reported that Ambrose Hussey attempted to "game" the system by billing Sunday's contest as an "exhibition" game. The home team sold grandstand "membership" tickets in advance and at the train stop closest to the ballpark. Everyone else got in free to stand uncovered on the field. The police attempted, unsuccessfully, to shut down the train station transactions, and the game went on as scheduled. Sunday baseball continued under these conditions for the rest of the 1907.

Unfortunately, this harassment by local officials continued into 1908. For a July game between the (Negro Leagues) Royal Giants and Cuban Stars, the membership scam was again employed. This time, three players were plucked off the field by law enforcement and, along with the two employees on the gate, were arrested mid-game. Strangely, play proceeded after the five were taken away. Charges were later dismissed on a technicality, and, as in 1907, Sunday games continued. Even after professional baseball had "left the field" at the end of May 1908, owner Joseph Meyerrose was brought into court early in the 1911 season to answer charges of baseball on the Sabbath. However, there was insufficient evidence that an admission fee had been requested for attendees, and the case was once again dismissed.

Area development finally caught up to Meyerrose Park. With large profits to be made, Joseph Meyerrose sold off his homestead, which was quickly divided into building sites. Under the guidance of Ambrose, Jr., the Ridgewoods left after the 1911 season for **Wallace's Grounds**. Ambrose W. Hussey, Sr., died in 1914, having divested himself of his Ridgewoods a year or two before. At the beginning of 1912, the stands and fences were removed and sold off for their lumber. Although a few amateur games were staged in 1912 on the remaining diamond, the extension of surrounding streets through the property ended its usefulness even for nonpros.

FMI: Benson, *Ballparks of North America*; *Brooklyn Eagle*, June 7, 1907; Ross and Dyte, "The Brooklyn Bandits"; Johnson, *Ballparks Database*; Johnson, *Ballparks Database*; Barthel, *Baseball's Peerless Semipros*; "Union League Busy Here," *Brooklyn Citizen*, February 5, 1908; *Brooklyn Daily Eagle*, March 30, 1908.

SHEA STADIUM

Nobody has ever called Shea Stadium a cathedral.

—George Vecsey, *New York Times*, quoted in
Costello, "Shea Stadium (New York)"

Location: Flushing Meadows Corona Park, Queens

Dimensions: left 341', center 410', right 341'

Home Team(s): New York Mets/National League; and New York Yankees/American League

Built/In Operation: 1961 through 1964/1964 through 2008. Demolished 2008 through 2009.

Seats/Capacity: 55,300/57,175

Fun Facts: In 1961, New York City commissioned the team of architects and engineers at Praeger, Kavanagh, and Waterbury to design a "modern" sporting arena that could accommodate both baseball and football. Partner John Waterbury led the designers who later, ironically, blueprinted Dodger Stadium in Los Angeles. The original concept, including a domed roof and additional seating, was hailed as "futuristic," although these features were never added after Shea opened. Delayed by bad weather and labor problems, Shea Stadium eventually debuted in time for, and on the site of, the 1964 New York World's Fair. What was built at the final cost of $28.5 million included escalators to every seating level, sight lines unobstructed by support columns, and stands that moved on tracks to change the seating configuration of the stadium between the two sports. It was named for William Shea, a New York attorney and politician instrumental in bringing National League baseball back to the city after the abandonment by the Dodgers and Giants.

Some distinctive physical features that Shea was known for over the years included its seven stories high scoreboard, which showed pictures and data from around the league, state-of-the-art in 1964. Topped with a panoramic outline of the New York City skyline, the board now resides on the roof of the new Citi Field Shake Shack. In 1967, clear plexiglass was added to the fronts of the bullpens so pitchers warming up could be viewed by the fans. For 1980, a supersized color instant replay screen was added behind the left field fence and plastic seats replaced the wooden ones. That year also marked the debut for the "home run apple," a cheap plywood sign that appeared from out of a top hat whenever the team delivered a home run. It was fabricated by one of the concerns that provided floats to the Macy's Thanksgiving Day Parade. The apple now lives in the parking lot for Citi Field.

In the mid-1980s, the outside walls of the stadium were painted what was labeled "Mets' blue." In 1988, a neon "art work," an abstract depicting a pitcher in his windup viewable from the number 7 subway train, was added to the outside of the stadium. Also that year, a new scoreboard was designed and built by the White Way Sign Company, and the wooden outfield fence replaced with a padded wall.

Notable events during Shea's history included concerts by the Beatles in 1965 and 1966. Because of the screaming fans, coupled with the use of the house PA, not a note was heard by anyone in attendance, including the band, as is revealed in the resulting recordings and film. Various other rock concerts with more appropriate (and louder, judging from complaints by the neighbors) amplification systems followed these appearances by the Fab Four.

For the 1972–1973 seasons, Willie Mays returned to New York as a Met. He retired from the team in 1973 at the age of 42. And, finally, as **Yankee Stadium (I)** was being rehabbed during 1974 and 1975 seasons, the New York Yanks played their home games at Shea.

The bad news about Shea Stadium was that the home of the New York Mets represented all that was faulty about the new era of "concrete donut" multipurpose stadiums. Games could be cold and windy, seating was cramped, the upper deck was steep, frequent airplanes coming and going from LaGuardia Airport were noisy, and stairways and tunnels were dark and damp. From a player's point of view, the outfield was always swampy, dangerously so, as it injured some and shortened one player's career, Yankee Elliot Maddox.

The good news was that, eventually, it didn't matter. The great thing about Shea was, when the Mets fielded good players, it was only a special express subway ride from mid-town Manhattan to the ballpark. Going to Shea Stadium was more about feelings than realities. The experience managed to transcend the stadium's lack of functionality and form. The team and the stadium drew well, despite (or maybe because of) their losing inaugural seasons. In spirit, the New York Mets was appropriately more like the wacky Brooklyn Dodgers of old than the dependable but staid (and winning) Yankees.

Because it was owned by New York City, when Shea Stadium was being dismantled, much of its infrastructure was reused in other city facilities.

FMI: Alberts, "Remembering New York's Historic Baseball Stadiums, in Photos"; O'Reilly, *Charlie's Big Baseball Parks Page*; Johnson, *Ballparks Database*; Evanosky and Kos, *Lost Ballparks*; Benson, *Ballparks of North America*; Costello, "Shea Stadium (New York)"; New York Mets, "Citi Field"; Lippman, *List of New York's Baseball Sites*; Bennett, "Shea Stadium's Ghost in the Shadow of Citi Field."

STATEN ISLAND

Color print by the Hatch Litho. Co., 49, 51, and 53 Lafayette Place, New York City, showing the St. George Cricket Grounds around 1886. From the Library of Congress.

[A] luxurious wooden palace.

—Dennis Evanosky and Eric J. Kos, *Lost Ballparks*

Location: Wall Street and Saint Mark's Place, St. George, Staten Island. Now the location (or damn near it) for Richmond County Bank ballpark, home until 2019 of the Staten Island Yankees

Dimensions: unknown

Home Team(s): New York Metropolitans/American Association; and New York Giants/National League

Built/In Operation: 1886/1886 through 1887, and 1889

Seats/Capacity: 4,400

Fun Facts: Not to be confused with the St. George Cricket Grounds in Hoboken, New Jersey, which was home to the original cricket club. The amateur Staten Island Cricket and Base Ball Club moved here in 1886 when their location was taken by commercial development and the Baltimore and Ohio Railroad. The Staten Island locale, on the site of the Delafield homestead, cost $40,000. The club's facility featured a double-decked grandstand and an on-site restaurant with a view of the baseball action.

Walker Park was used for a game by the New York Knickerbockers in 1853. During the 1886 season, fans attending a contest by the New York Metropolitans were afforded views of the erection of the Statue of Liberty. Michael Benson (see FMI) claims that the Mets additionally played some games at the Wild West Grounds, also on Staten Island. Finally, the Giants played the first part of their 1889 season here as the **Polo Grounds (III)** was being built. It's from those last two franchises that the cricket grounds gained the moniker, "Mutrie's Dump" after the manager for both the Mets and Giants. In 1925, the property passed from the hands of the cricket club, eventually finding its way to ownership by the New York City Parks Department.

FMI: Alberts, "Remembering New York's Historic Baseball Stadiums, in Photos"; Johnson, *Ballparks Database*; Evanosky and Kos, *Lost Ballparks*; Ron Selter, "By the Numbers: The Five Polo Grounds Ballparks," in Thornley, *The Polo Grounds*; Mele, "Staten Island Memories: When the Mets Called the Island Home"; Benson, *Ballparks of North America*; Healey, "St. George Cricket Grounds"; Staten Island Cricket Club, "A Brief History"; Berowski, "Baseball on Staten Island"; "Walker Park," New York City Department of Parks and Recreation.

YONKERS

EASTERN FIELD

Location: unknown

Dimensions: unknown

Home Team(s): Yonkers/Eastern League; and Yonkers/Hudson River League

Built/In Operation: 1888, 1894 and 1895

Seats/Capacity: unknown

Fun Facts: Yonkers fielded a team for the Hudson River League from May 15 until early June 1888, although it's unknown if and where they played their home games. In 1894, Yonkers joined the Eastern League, although the team played in Allentown, not Yonkers. For 1895, the team did move to Yonkers, but played instead back in the Hudson River League.

FMI: Steven J. Stark, "Field Days," *Daily Item*, April 5, 1993; "The Hudson River League," *New York Times*, May 11, 1888.

LEAGUE PARK (I)

Location: the west side of Central Avenue, 200' north of Yonkers Avenue

Dimensions: unknown

Home Team(s): Yonkers/Hudson River League

Built/In Operation: 1905

Seats/Capacity: 1,700

Fun Facts: In 1905, the Yonkers baseball franchise hired city engineer William Henry Baldwin (not to be confused with his namesake, the president of the Long Island Railroad) to layout the playing diamond for League Park (I). Originally, the club hoped that the Rosendale property at the corner of Jerome and McClean Avenues, "an ideal place for a baseball park," as reported in the *Yonkers Herald*, would be available. Construction on the ballpark was projected to begin the third week in March, with its opening a month later for an exhibition contest scheduled between the New York Giants and the New York Highlanders (Yankees). When an agreement couldn't be reached with the owners of that property, the field was moved to the old Valentine Estate at the corner of Yonkers and Central Avenues, accessible by trolley from Yonkers, Mt. Vernon, and New York City. The six-acre plot included a 75 by 30-foot grandstand holding 700 hundred seats, with bleachers holding 1,000 more. These were scaled down from the original site plan seating 3,500.

For the opening contest against Peekskill on May 11, the grandstand was incomplete. After three weeks, players complained that they weren't being paid. After the Peekskill club disbanded at the end of May, Yonkers also called it quits. Several years later, the park was still at least partially standing.

FMI: Morin, "William Henry Baldwin"; "Yonkers League Baseball," *Yonkers Herald*, March 9, 1905; "League Baseball for Yonkers Now Assured," *Yonkers Herald*, April 19, 1905; *Yonkers Herald*, May 5, 1905; *Yonkers Herald*, May 12, 1905; *Yonkers Herald*, June 1, 1905; "Yonkers League Ball Team Is Disbanded," *Yonkers Herald*, June 3, 1905; *Yonkers Herald*, June 9, 1905; *Yonkers Herald*, August 30, 1907.

LEAGUE PARK (II)/CENTRAL OVAL

Location: Saw Mill River Road

Dimensions: unknown

Home Team(s): Yonkers/Hudson River League

Built/In Operation: 1905 through 1906/1907

Seats/Capacity: 1,700/6,000

Fun Facts: In 1906, the New York Central Railroad took over the former grounds of the St. Aloysius Baseball Club, moving their amateur team as well as grandstands and fencing to this location. The railroad renamed the facility Central Oval. When the Hudson River League moved in the following year, the Yonkers squad renamed it League Park (II).

The ill-fated Yonkers nine and their League opened the season on May 15 against Kingston. Two clubs left the Hudson River League early in the 1907 season, reducing the number of teams to four. The second week of June, players on both the home Yonkers squad and visiting Newburgh nine, along with the stadium's gate keepers, were arrested and charged with "playing for pay" on the Sabbath. As the monies collected were deemed "voluntary contributions," the players et al. were later acquitted by a jury. Unfortunately, 10 days later, the league disbanded, as did the Yonkers team.

FMI: John Pardon and Jerry Jackson, "New York State Ball Clubs," in Puff, *The Empire State of Base Ball*; *Yonkers Herald*, March 5, 1906; *Yonkers Statesman*, May 15, 1907; *Yonkers Statesman*, May 14, 1907; "Police Stop Baseball Game," *New-York Tribune*, June 10, 1907; *Post-Star*, June 17, 1907; "Hudson River League Disbands," *Buffalo Evening News*, June 20, 1907; *Yonkers Statesman*, July 25, 1907; *Yonkers Herald*, February 14, 1908.

JAMES J. FLEMING FIELD/PRESCOTT FIELD

Location: Prescott Street at Garfield Street

Dimensions: left 320', center 400', right-center 340'

Home Team(s): Yonkers Hoot Owls/Northeast League

Built/In Operation: 1933/1995

Seats/Capacity: 1,500 to 1,800

Fun Facts: Fleming/Prescott Field is regarded by many online fan sites as possibly the worst stadium ever utilized for baseball in the history of the professional game. Since its acquisition by the City of Yonkers in 1937, the facility has been the home to primarily amateur and semiprofessional ball. Its original moniker came from the diamond's geographical location.

During the postwar period, the semipro Yonkers Indians, among others, held forth at Prescott, hosting the barnstorming Homestead Grays, Washington (DC) Colored All-Stars, and the Atlanta Black Crackers (all Negro Leagues) in 1947. These contests introduced nighttime baseball to the area. During that same year, the Brooklyn Dodgers began sending their rookies, often from the Dodgers farm system, to play the locals. With the Brooklyn Bums departure for the West Coast, this tradition was continued by the New York Yankees, at least until 1961. In 1953, Prescott Field was renamed to honor James J. Fleming, a local politician, public safety commissioner, and postmaster.

Lights were added by the mid-1950s, although the cost for their usage, charged by the city, were deemed prohibitive by most amateur and semiprofessional baseball organizations. These systems were repaired in both 1959 and again in the late 1960s. Concrete bleachers were a feature by 1994.

Considering the competition from two major league as well as several affiliated and unaffiliated minor league teams in the area, it seemed ill-advised that literary agent Adele Leone would invest in a Yonkers professional franchise. Or that Fleming Field would be the proper location for the independent minor league Hoot Owls.

When the season began in July of 1995, Fleming lacked the most basic player amenities. Missing locker rooms, the Yonkers nine changed into their uniforms in the adjacent woods. Uncommonly, there wasn't grass in the infield, a dugout to sit in, or, permanent lighting, the last installed by Leone herself during the season. The press, lacking a box, sat with the fans on concrete risers. All had to bring their own refreshments and park on the street. As one unknown Wikipedia contributor commented, professional baseball had no business at such a lowly facility.

With poor attendance caused, in part, by a horrific losing record of 12 and 52, the Yonkers Hoot Owls folded up their tent at the end of the season and rode off into the sunset. Professional baseball was gone, and only amateur teams remained at Fleming Field.

FMI: O'Reilly, *Charlie's Big Baseball Parks Page*; Danny Lopriore, "Chasing a Dream," *Herald Statesman*, June 15, 1995; "Yonkers Police Historical Notes"; *Herald Statesman*, February 15, 1986; Jennie Tritten, "Park Always Busy," *Herald Statesman*, August 22, 1974; Marv Schneider, "From 300 Sunday Players," *Herald Statesman*, September 10, 1952; Kelley Quinn, *Elmira Star-Gazette*, December 22, 1995.

THE SOUTHERN TIER

ADDISON

UNKNOWN NAME

Location: unknown

Dimensions: unknown

Home Team(s): Addison White Sox, and Addison and Wellsville Tobacco Strippers/Southern Tier League

Built/In Operation: 1903 through 1905

Seats/Capacity: unknown

Fun Facts: One newspaper reporter called their original field "a strange diamond" that was a "home-run diamond." The recommended remedy was "a new baseball park [that] will be built across the road from the place where the old one stood. The diamond will be turned around so the sun will not be in the faces of the players as it was last season" (see FMI).

In 1905, the Tobacco Strippers started the season in Addison, but joined with Wellsville by the end of June/early July. However, it appears that games continued to be played in Addison. The Southern Tier League possibly lost teams and fell apart by the third week of August.

FMI: *Star-Gazette*, August 25, 1903; "Addison Beat Oil Drillers," *Star-Gazette*, July 12, 1904; "Addison Alright," *Star-Gazette*, April 14, 1905.

BATH

UNKNOWN NAME

Location: unknown

Dimensions: unknown

Home Team(s): Bath Bathers/Western New York League

Built/In Operation: 1890

Seats/Capacity: unknown

Fun Facts: The season lasted less than a month in September of 1890.

FMI: John Pardon and Jerry Jackson, "New York State Ball Clubs," in *The Empire State of Base Ball*; *Stats Crew*, "1890 Western New York League."

BINGHAMTON/JOHNSON CITY/LESTERSHIRE/ENDICOTT

MORGAN'S FLATS

Location: between Wall Street and the Chenango River to the west, Court Street to the south, and Water Street to the east, Binghamton

Dimensions: unknown

Home Team(s): Binghamton Nationals; and Binghamton Crickets

Built/In Operation: 1865 through 1871

Seats/Capacity: 4,500

Fun Facts: This circus grounds and town dump was in the flood plain of the Chenango River. According to the *Press and Sun-Bulletin* newspaper, the Nationals played at least one 1865 game here. In 1871, the locals were called the Crickets, named not for the insect but instead for the game (the insinuation by writers being that this team grew out of a cricket club).

FMI: "Binghamton's Baseball History Dates Back to Crickets," *Press and Sun-Bulletin*, April 11, 1929; *Press and Sun-Bulletin*, January 10, 1908; "Morgan's Flats Scene of Exciting Game of Baseball Back in 1865," *Press and Sun-Bulletin*, October 21, 1913.

STOW FLATS PARK/RIVERSIDE PARK/ BINGHAMTON EXPOSITION GROUNDS

Location: the current locale of the State/Binghamton Plaza Shopping Center, Binghamton

Dimensions: unknown

Home Team(s): Binghamton Crickets/League Alliance and International Association; Binghamton Bingos and Lunatics/New York State League, International League, Central League, and Eastern League

Built/In Operation: 1871/1877 through 1878, 1884 through 1888, 1892 through 1895, 1899 through 1903, and 1905 through 1912

Seats/Capacity: 1,400/3,000

Fun Facts: North of **Morgan's Flats** along the Chenango River was Stow Flats. The Park, with a horse track, was located as well on the flood plain. Many community events occurred at Stow Flats Park, including early county fairs, traveling shows, and even Ku Klux Klan rallies complete with cross burnings. Two of Binghamton's earliest professional teams disbanded early: the Crickets folded up their wings on July 8 of the 1878 season, while the 1885 New York State League franchise closed with the league's collapse in early July.

Probably the most infamous occurrence in the early history of professional baseball in the Triple Cities grew out of the acquiring, by the Binghamton Bingos in 1887, of African-American player John "Bud" Fowler. Born John W. Jackson on March 16, 1858, in Fort Plain, New York, this barber's son grew up in Cooperstown. Fowler's professional baseball career began sometime between 1873 and 1878. Before signing with the Bingos, Bud Fowler bounced between teams in Massachusetts, Canada, Minnesota, Indiana, Iowa, Colorado, and Kansas. Interestingly, while with Binghamton, the club played two home exhibition games against the independent Cuban (Negro Leagues) Giants. Local newspaper coverage was slanted toward racist pronouncements, which should have clued Fowler into what was coming next.

Unfortunately, his teammates, in an all too familiar story, refused to play with Bud Fowler, hastening his exit before the conclusion of the season. The league as well, in response to organization-wide prejudice among white baseballers, decided mid-July in their "finite" wisdom to ban the incorporation of any additional black players into their association. The only positive outcome from Fowler's time in Binghamton occurred on August 9, 1887, when local newspapers reported that, "the players of the Binghamton Baseball club were yesterday fined $50 each by the directors because six weeks ago they refused to go on the field unless Fowler, the colored second baseman, was removed."

In 1892, the Binghamton Bingos, featuring future Hall of Famer "Wee" Willie Keeler, won the championship of the International League. Credited with the adage "Keep your eye on the ball, and hit 'em where they ain't," third baseman Keeler went on to play for, among others, the

New York Giants and Highlanders, as well as the Baltimore Orioles. The Bingos were again champs in 1902, this time as a member of the New York State League. Their 1904 State League squad played the season at **Suburban Park**.

FMI: Fiesthumel, *"Pent-Ups"*; Cohen and McCann, *Baseball in Broome County*; Maggiore and McCann, *Celebrating 100 Years of Baseball in Greater Binghamton*; baseball coverage, *Press and Sun-Bulletin*, 1905–1912; L. Robert Davids, "Bud Fowler: Black Baseball Star," in Puff, *The Empire State of Base Ball*; John Pardon and Jerry Jackson, "New York State Ball Clubs," in Puff, *The Empire State of Base Ball*; Brewster, *The Workingman's Game*; Delaney, "The 1887 Binghamton Bingos"; *Buffalo Commercial*, November 26, 1878; "Lestershire Will Probably Have an Independent Team," January 20, 1904; "Lestershire Will Have a Ball Team," *Press and Sun-Bulletin*, March 10, 1905; "Binghamton's Baseball History Dates Back to Crickets," *Press and Sun-Bulletin*, April 11, 1929; *Press and Sun-Bulletin*, January 10, 1908; "Real Novelty for Saturday," *Star-Gazette*, July 20, 1908; *Press and Sun-Bulletin*, July 25, 1908; *Press and Sun-Bulletin*, July 28, 1908.

SUBURBAN PARK/RECREATION PARK

Location: 70 Court Street, corner of North Brockton and Broad Street, Johnson City

Home Team(s): Binghamton Bingos/New York State League

Dimensions: unknown

Built/In Operation: 1904. Dismantled in the fall of 1912.

Seats/Capacity: unknown

Fun Facts: In 1904, the State League team from Binghamton played in Lestershire/Johnson City at Suburban Park. Sunday baseball was always an issue at Suburban Park, with games being blocked or cancelled in 1904 and 1910. This may have precipitated the exit by the professionals. After the Bingos returned to Binghamton proper in 1905, amateur and semi-professional squads utilized Suburban until the ballpark was dismantled in the fall of 1912 in anticipation of a new stadium.

In 1908 and 1909, the local nine hosted several touring teams. These included a collection of barnstorming Black squads: the Cuban Giants, the Brooklyn-Philadelphia Colored Giants, and Binghamton's Royal Cuban Giants. A highlight for 1908 was the visit in August by a traveling team of "Cherokee Indians." During this road trip, the "Indians" also played in Elmira, Waverly, and Oneonta. The Cherokee brought along female pitcher Maud Nelson (who was white; see **Ridgewood Park [II]**) and their own lights. The Cherokee had been touring New York State as early as 1905, when the *Chateaugay Record and Franklin County Democrat* described their portable ballpark:

> The Indians are traveling through the country in their own Pullman car and carry with them a canvas fence 1,200 feet long and ten feet high, also a portable grand stand with a seating capacity of 2,000. They also carry lighting apparatus with which to light the ball field at night, giving two games at each place they stop—one in the afternoon and one at night. (July 14, 1905)

Initially, Suburban was under the control of the local Athletic Association. However, by the end of 1905, owner of the property (and the local team; see **Johnson Field**), George Johnson, purchased the structures after the association was disbanded. At the end of July 1909, Johnson decided that the village needed a public park. While keeping the diamond and grandstands, which were improved with painting and grading, the wooden board fence and bleachers were removed, and landscaping added. Ultimately, Johnson spent several thousand dollars on the changes.

FMI: "Lestershire Will Probably Have an Independent Team," *Press and Sun-Bulletin*, January 20, 1904; "Lestershire Will Have a Ball Team," March 10, 1905; "Suburban Park Will Be Sold," *Press and Sun-Bulletin*, November 22, 1905; *Press and Sun-Bulletin*, January 10, 1908; "Real Novelty for Saturday," *Star-Gazette*, July 20, 1908; *Press and Sun-Bulletin*, July 25, 1908; *Press and Sun-Bulletin*, July 28, 1908; "Start Work on New Park," *Press and Sun-Bulletin*, July 30–31, 1909; "G. F. Johnson Will Give Village Recreation Spot" and "Sunday Games to Be Stopped," *Press and Sun-Bulletin*, June 8, 1910.

This view shows the exterior of Johnson Field as seen from the parking lot behind the grandstand. Courtesy of the Broome County Historical Society.

Location: 70 Court Street, corner of North Brockton and Broad Street, Johnson City

Home Team(s): Binghamton Bingos and Brooms/New York State League and International League; and Binghamton Triplets/Eastern League and New York-Penn League

Dimensions: center 318–42', right 383–25'

Built/In Operation: 1912 through 1913/1913 through 1919, and 1923 through 1968. Demolished in 1968 to facilitate the expansion of Route 17.

Seats/Capacity: 2000 to 5500/10,000

Fun Facts: Constructed on the former site of **Suburban Park, Johnson Field** was named for the president of Endicott-Johnson, George F. Johnson. Part owner of the Binghamton professional team since 1899, the construction of this new home for the Bingos in "Shoetown" followed Johnson's attaining full team ownership in 1912. Financed to the tune of $40,000 (about a million of today's dollars), George hired his brother Charles Fred Johnson to supervise the new steel and concrete facility. Period photographs depict a covered grandstand, with bleachers along both foul lines.

Because the stadium had to fit in between existing structures, its contours were a bit odd. Another quirk was attributable to George Johnson's dislike of advertising (especially for businesses other than his own!). Johnson believed that the ads usually found on outfield walls detracted from a fan's enjoyment of the game, and, therefore, accepted none for his ballpark.

In 1920, Johnson had grown tired of the "business" of baseball (mostly, the lack of it) and, so, allowed the franchise to lapse. Three years later, the local American Legion, with George Johnson's support, revived the team. Because of the joint ownership between Legion chapters in Binghamton, Johnson City and Endicott, the team became known as the "Triple Cities" or, simply, the "Triplets." Their first league championships followed in 1929 and 1935.

In 1932, George Johnson persuaded the New York Yankees to finance the Binghamton Triplets. One of the perks Johnson offered were the new lights that he funded in the spring of that year. For the next thirty years, the local team developed players for the major league Yankees. During that period, the Yanks would play an annual contest with their farm club in Binghamton, bringing along fan favorites such as Lou Gehrig, Babe Ruth, Joe DiMaggio and Mickey Mantle.

After their initial affiliation with the Yankees concluded, the Trips supplied talent to the Kansas City Athletics and the Milwaukee Braves before renewing their association with New York. After the American Leaguers left for a second time following the 1961 season, dropping their ownership stake in the process, the now community-financed team began its rapid decline. 1968 was the Triplets last season; twenty-four years would pass before a new stadium and professional baseball returned to the Binghamton area.

FMI: digitalballparks.com on Johnson Field; https://dhprojects.binghamton. edu/s/BingBiz/page/1968Triplets; *Stats Crew*, "Johnson Field"; Cohen and McCann, *Baseball in Broome County*; Maggiore, Jim and McCann, Michael J. *Celebrating 100 Years of Baseball in Greater Binghamton*. Self-Published, 2014; Evanosky and Kos, *Lost Ballparks*; "First-year titles not new," *Press and Sun-Bulletin*, April 16, 1992.

CANISTEO

UNKNOWN NAME

Location: unknown

Dimensions: unknown

Home Team(s): Canisteo/Western New York-Penn League

Built/In Operation: 1890

Seats/Capacity: unknown

Fun Facts: For a season lasting less than a month in September of 1890, Canisteo played teams from Bath, Wellsville, and Hornellsville. It came in first place, having won the most games.

FMI: John Pardon and Jerry Jackson, "New York State Ball Clubs," in Puff, *The Empire State of Base Ball*; *Stats Crew*, "Canisteo Franchise History (1890)"; *Democrat and Chronicle*, September 10, 1890; *Dunkirk Evening Observer*, October 17, 1890.

CORNING

UNKNOWN NAME

Location: unknown

Dimensions: unknown

Home Team(s): Corning Monitors

Built/In Operation: 1860s

Seats/Capacity: unknown

Fun Facts: unknown

FMI: Morris et al., *Base Ball Pioneers, 1850–1870*.

EAST SIDE PARK DIAMOND

There will be a number of new phases in base ball attendance this year for the general benefit of the attendants at the grounds at East Side Park. No boys will be tolerated on top of the grand stand, no men or boys will be allowed anywhere near the players as a rope will be drawn as a guard to keep them away, and those trespassing will be arrested. No carriages will be allowed to enter or depart from the main entrance of the ball grounds.

—Star-Gazette, May 16, 1895

Location: unknown

Dimensions: unknown

Home Team(s): Corning White Ponies and Glassblowers/Southern Tier League

Built/In Operation: 1893/1893 through 1896, and 1903 through 1905. Bought by Corning in 1906 for a public park, which kept the diamond.

Seats/Capacity: 1,000/2,000

Fun Facts: East Side Park was in use for baseball by 1893, when the Corning team was visited by the Cuban (Negro Leagues) Giants. The Cubans continued playing at Corning, sometimes multiple times within a season, at least until 1896. The 1894 professional squad contested with the semipro Brooklyn Murray Hills in mid-May and, in 1896, lost to the Cleveland Spiders of the National League. It's hard to determine the professional status of Corning's teams during these last years of the 19th century, as the Corning nine moved between amateur, semiprofessional, and professional status during this time.

East Side Park was enlarged and remodeled before the 1896 season. After Corning fielded a Southern Tier League team for three years of the new century, in 1906, the city bought the property for use as a public park. Corning would lack professional baseball for the next 45 years.

FMI: "Corning Beat Wellsville Nine," *Star-Gazette*, September 12, 1903; *Star-Gazette*, May 31, 1895; *Star-Gazette*, August 2, 1893; *Star-Gazette*, May 11, 1894; *Democrat and Chronicle*, May 15, 1896; *Star-Gazette*, May 15, 1896; *Star-Gazette*, May 26, 1896; *Star-Gazette*, September 7, 1895; *Star-Gazette*, May 9, 1896; *Star-Gazette*, August 25, 1903.

CORNING (WAR) MEMORIAL STADIUM

Location: Craumer Drive at Jacoby Boulevard

Dimensions: unknown

Home Team(s): Corning Athletics, Independents, Red Sox, Corsox, and Royals/PONY League and New York-Penn League

Built/In Operation: 1948/1951 through 1960, and 1968 through 1969

Seats/Capacity: 3,000 to 4,800/8,000

Fun Facts: The original PONY League franchise was purchased by Corning from Lockport, who then sold it for one dollar to the Philadelphia Athletics. The sale included some players and the team bus. The Athletics then leased Memorial Stadium from Corning for the 1951 season. Baseball was brought in to replace auto racing at the facility to generate more income.

In 1954, Corning's PONY League team changed affiliation from the Athletics to the Boston Red Sox. With the influx of Sox contenders, the Corning Red Sox went from a last place finish in 1953 to capturing the pennant in 1954. Unfortunately, that was the high point of Corning's relationship with Boston. At the end of the 1960 season, the Red Sox moved their team to Olean.

After the loss of professional ball, the city, citing the high cost of maintaining War Memorial Stadium, passed ownership to the local board of education. By the end of 1961, a new high school had begun construction next to the stadium. About a year and a half later, the school building was completed.

During the 1962 season, the Elmira Pioneers of the Eastern League borrowed Memorial Stadium for one of their "home" games. Corning was to be without professional baseball until 1968, when the expansion Kansas City team brought Royals players to the Crystal City. After two more seasons, professional baseball once again left Corning.

Today, Corning Memorial Stadium has seen its share of high school football, amateur boxing, pro wrestling, country and western concerts, and stock car and midget auto racing. The dugouts and stands are still intact, along with the facility's lights, exterior features, imposing all brick facade, and grandstands with a press box on top.

FMI: O'Reilly, *Charlie's Big Baseball Parks Page*; digitalballparks.com on Corning Memorial Stadium; Walsh and Murphy, *The Fields of New York*; *Stats Crew*, "War Memorial Stadium"; "Philadelphia A's to Run Corning Baseball Club," *Star-Gazette*, December 22, 1950; "Study Stadium Costs in School Site Plan," *Star-Gazette*, February 26, 1961; " 'Home' Game Away from Home," *Elmira Advertiser*, April 17, 1962.

ELMIRA

MAPLE AVENUE (DRIVING) PARK/INTERSTATE FAIR GROUNDS

In very few cities are such accommodations for seeing the game offered as are to be found at the Maple Avenue Park, for visiting teams have said that no finer park exists in the state. If one delights in nature the view of valley and hill from the grand stand presents a scene of unsurpassed loveliness. There is no spot you can go to that will more quickly free your mind from care and will electrify drooping spirits than this same Maple Avenue Park and if you had to travel fifty miles instead of one to get to it you would appreciate it more fully too.

—"Playing in Owego Today," *Star-Gazette*, July 13, 1904

Location: Maple Avenue and Luce Street

Dimensions: unknown

Home Team(s): Elmira Colonels/New York State League and Central League; Elmira Elmiras; Elmira Gladiators/Western New York-Penn League and Eastern League; Elmira Pioneers/New York State League; Oswego Grays, Indians, and Elmira Pioneers/Atlantic League and New York State League; Elmira Father Mathew Temperance Society/Central League, New York State League, and Southern Tier League; and Gloversville and Johnstown JAGS, Elmira Rams, and Colonels/New York State League

Built/In Operation: 1885/1885 through 1895, 1898 through 1900, 1903 through 1905, and 1908 through 1910. Still in use for amateur sports in 1941.

Seats/Capacity: 1,500/7,000

Fun Facts: In the summer of 1885, the Maple Avenue Driving Park Association completed a horse racing track on a farm belonging to former New York governor Lucius Robinson. That same summer, the Elmira Colonels inaugurated Central League baseball at the facility. This was the first local use of the "Colonels" name in honor of attorney and baseball fan "Colonel" Joe Eustace (the title was an honorary one). For the next 25 years, a variety of amateur, semipro, and professional teams called Maple Avenue home.

However, there had been baseball in Elmira before this time. Local historians date the organized sport's arrival in town to the end of the Civil War, with the initially amateur Alerts and Unions. Unfortunately, I've been unable to determine where exactly these squads played. Interestingly, the ex-governor's son, Colonel David C. Robinson (his real, earned military rank), had been an umpire during the 1865 season for the Elmira Alerts, as well as having an involvement with the anniversary meet up of the Alerts and Unions twenty years later. Colonel Robinson was also involved with the companies controlling professional baseball in Elmira for another 15 years after that contest.

Author William Brewster reports that several celebrities frequented local ball games. One was the author and humorist Samuel "Mark Twain" Clements, who summered nearby. Clements was often in the company of a second baseball enthusiast, the Congregationalist Reverend Thomas K. Beecher, brother to Harriet Beecher Stowe, the author of the best-selling *Uncle Tom's Cabin*. During the summer of 1887, Colonel Robinson and other fans recruited Twain and Beecher to help Robinson umpire what we would now call a "vintage," "old-timey," "re-creation," or "old-fashioned" baseball contest. Period accounts depict Clements as being more interested in entertaining with his public persona those assembled fans than in the actual officiating or score keeping. Even so, the game went off without any major incidents.

In June of 1889, the year structures such as a grandstand and clubhouse were added, the park flooded, necessitating draining and reprepping of the playing field. Flooding was among the long-term problems leading to the poor condition of this facility. In July of 1891, the diamond was shrunken to facilitate easier infield play. During the 1892 season, the Eastern League revoked Elmira's franchise, ending the Maple Park season on July 19. Professional baseball returned in 1894. On August 9, Emancipation was celebrated with a baseball contest between the Casinos and the Cuban (Negro Leagues) Giants/Stars (called both in the newspaper coverage).

Unfortunately, professional baseball continued on an uncertain path in Elmira. During 1895, the State League organization ended their season (and Elmira's) in early July. Baseball was even crazier in 1900. That year, the Atlantic League squad began their schedule by getting arrested for attempting to play baseball on a Sunday. Next, the league lost several teams and stopped contests in May, without resuming reported games until the end of July. At that time, the Maple Avenue Railroad Company purchased the New York State League franchise from Oswego, moving the organization to Elmira and starting league games in August. Further complicating Elmira baseball in 1900 was the threat by the team's owners of moving home games to Rorick's Glen.

In 1899, the Elmira Water, Light, and Railroad Company, which controlled the Maple Avenue Railroad Company, that, in turn, owned the 1900 New York State League franchise in Elmira, had purchased Rorick's Glen. By Memorial Day the following year, Elmira Water had built what they hoped would become a recreational destination, a 125-acre park with a theater and a ballfield. Toward the goal of increased ridership for their street cars and trolleys, the utility kept swearing to move the baseball team from Maple Avenue Park to Rorick's Glen Park. The added stress couldn't have helped the franchise settle into Elmira.

During 1901, the "Ladies Champion Base Ball Club of the World" Bloomer Girls played Elmira, and in 1902, the Cuban (Negro Leagues) Giants came to town to challenge the amateur Father Mathew team. From 1903 to 1905, the Father Mathew Temperance Society decided to go pro. This Catholic organization, based on total abstinence from drinking alcohol, came to Elmira in 1890. One of their methods was to promote temperance through athletics. For the three seasons that the Father Mathew organization ran the professional team, it played exhibition games against visiting major leaguers like the New York Giants. Also under their watch was the first Elmira night baseball contest under portable lights against the barnstorming "Sioux Indians."

In 1906, with an opportunity caused by the lack of a local professional squad, attorney Walter Heffernan moved to town to run a group of semiprofessionals. Heffernan had played at Williams College and Syracuse University, continuing after graduation as a manager/pitcher for Addison of the Southern Tier League. The semipro Heff's Tigers of Elmira featured Heffernan on the mound, and played Black barnstormers such as the Brooklyn Royals and the Philadelphia Giants. However, their season was marred by a prohibition against Sunday games promoted through a local federation of ministers. Although the Tigers ended their schedule with the outstanding record of approximately 90 and 10, the team lost money, causing them to disband at the end of the year.

The New York State League was back for 1908, 1909, and 1910. A highlight for 1908 was the visit in August by a traveling team of "Cherokee Indians." During this road trip, the "Indians" also played in Oneonta, Waverly, and Lestershire. The Cherokee brought along female pitcher Maud Nelson (who was white; see **Ridgewood Park (II)**) and their own lights.

Much needed repairs to Maple Avenue Park undertaken during these years included these modifications:

> The diamond is to be moved in toward the grand stand, putting the game at closer range for the spectators. . . . New bleachers are to be built on both sides of the diamond [this didn't happen, only along first base line] . . . and portable fences will be built to cross the track from the bleachers to the grand stand fence. More fences will be built at the other ends of the bleachers extending parallel with the foul lines.
>
> Club house quarters for the players will be fixed up, probably under the grand stand, so the men will have a place they may call their own besides the ten foot bench. ("Elmira's Ball Team for 1909 Will Be Best in State League," *Star-Gazette*, November 17, 1908)

Also during this season, a new entrance was constructed off of Luce Street and vehicles were banned from the outfield.

Several weeks before the opening of the 1909 season, a wind storm blew the roof off the grandstand and damaged its supports. This occurred again, along with the flooding of the grounds, in January of 1910. At that time, there was a movement to relocate baseball to a newly purpose-built ballpark. However, the season would be started at Maple Avenue.

FMI: Walsh and Murphy, *The Fields of New York*; Brewster, *The Work-ingman's Game*; Morris et al., *Base Ball Pioneers, 1850–1870*; Chemung County Historical Society, "Baseball"; "Trotting at Elmira," *Poughkeepsie Eagle-News*, August 25, 1885; Pitoniak, "Vintage Baseball League Evokes the 19th-Century Game"; "Mark Twain and the Rev. T. K. Beecher to Umpire a Ball Game," *Sun*, July 1, 1887; "Elmira's Great Ball Game," *Sun*, July 3, 1887; "Shuffled Out," *Buffalo Morning Express*, July 21, 1892; "Ball Players Arrested," *Buffalo Evening News*, April 23, 1900; "Elmira Team Playing Well," *Star-Gazette*, July 26 and August 1, 1900; James Hare, "Elmira History: 'Demon of the Skies' Wowed Elmirans"; Jim Hare, "When Rorick's Glen Was the Place to Be," *Star-Gazette*, October 7, 2018; "Elmira in League," *Star-Gazette*, December 18, 1899; *Star-Gazette*, August 25, 1903; "To Play Baseball by Electric Light," *Star-Gazette*, June 11, 1903; "Death Takes Attorney Heffernan," *Star-Gazette*, July 23, 1940; "Report of Treasurer Goff Shows Deficit of over $804," *Star-Gazette*, September 27,

1906; "Real Novelty for Saturday," *Star-Gazette*, July 20, 1908; *Press and Sun-Bulletin*, July 25, 1908; *Press and Sun-Bulletin*, July 28, 1908; *Press and Sun-Bulletin*, July 28, 1908.

DUNN FIELD (I)/RECREATION BASEBALL PARK

Photograph of the grandstands from the field, Dunn Field (I), also known as Recreation Baseball Park, in the *Star-Gazette* newspaper, June 24, 1910.

Location: 546 Luce Street, Southport (now Elmira)

Dimensions: left 317', center 445', right 312'

Home Team(s): Elmira Colonels/New York State League; Elmira Pioneers and Red Jackets/New York State League and New York-Penn League; Elmira Red Birds and Red Wings/New York-Penn League and Eastern League; Elmira Pioneers/New York State League, New York-Penn League, and Eastern League

Built/In Use: 1910/1910 through 1917, 1923 through 1938

Seats/Capacity: 4,800/7,800

Fun Facts: With Elmira's State League franchise either on the road or at **Maple Avenue (Driving) Park**, new grounds began to be built on property located by the Chemung River. According to local reports, the new facility was modeled after one in Jersey City, New Jersey (possibly West Side Park, now called Lincoln Park).

Initially, the plan was for a steel substructure. However, fearful that the time needed for acquiring of the metal might delay construction, the builders went ahead with a wooden park. The resulting V-shaped grandstand featured "opera" chairs arranged in sixteen rows, with private boxes at the front. The grandstand itself sat low to the ground on the field side, rising twenty feet in the back to accommodate the clubhouse underneath. Once patrons parked along a high fence on the river side of the diamond, they entered the stand via a rear ramp. When the Colonels played their first game in their new park on June 27, 1910, it had been named through a reader's contest conducted by the *Star-Gazette* newspaper Recreation Baseball Park.

The next month, with a Sunday game against Binghamton on the schedule but local law enforcement threatening to stop contests on the Sabbath, Elmira decided on a private meetup. The park's gates were locked, no fans invited in and those few that did attend were immediately ejected. The sheriff interceded anyway, arresting two of Elmira's players for violating local "blue laws." This appears to have been part of a broader struggle during 1910 between New York's governor on the side of baseball and local officials, under pressure by religious groups, aligning with the ministers' association to stop games. The Royal (Negro Leagues) Giants, barnstorming the area, visited in 1913, and Elmira took the New York State League pennant in a nail-biting season finish the following year.

During the five-year break from professional baseball that followed the 1917 season, Recreation Park was acquired by local businessman/bank president Edward Joseph Dunn. In 1920, while still housing amateur and semiprofessional baseball, Dunn made a big show about donating Recreation to Elmira. The city reciprocated by renaming the facility Dunn Field. For the 1920 season, members of the local amateur Arctic League repaired the structures and field, building benches for the grandstand and restoring its roof.

Professional ball returned in 1923 with the Elmira Pioneers of the New York State League. During the Pioneers' tenure, both the team and the league underwent name changes. Elmira became the Red Jackets after a Seneca Native American chief. New wooden stands were built in 1929, and, in 1931, the franchise was sold to the St. Louis Cardinals. The team reverted to the Pioneers name when purchased in early 1937 by the Brooklyn Dodgers.

FMI: John Pardon and Jerry Jackson, "New York State Ball Clubs," in Puff, *The Empire State of Base Ball*; Walsh and Murphy, *The Fields of New York*; *Stats Crew*, "Elmira Pioneers Franchise History (1895–2005)"; *Stats Crew*, "Sports in Elmira, New York"; "Next Saturday Will Be Celebrated as 'Lee Breese Day' at Recreation," *Star-Gazette*, July 21, 1915; *Elmira Advertiser*, February 27, 1958; "F. Lee Breese Dead," *Star-Gazette*, September 5, 1928; "Begin at Once Baseball Park," *Star-Gazette*, May 2, 1910; "Grand Stand Appointments to Be Entirely Up-to-Date," *Star-Gazette*, May 18, 1910; "Will Open New Park June 27th," *Star-Gazette*, June 17, 1910; "More

Baseball Players Arrested, Private Game Is Attempted," *Star-Gazette*, July 25, 1910; "Appoint Big Committee to Perfect Plans for 'Dunn Appreciation Day' Celebration," *Star-Gazette*, April 22, 1920; "Artic League Makes Dunn Field Appear like a New Baseball Park," *Star-Gazette*, April 26, 1920; *Star-Gazette*, January 7, 1937.

DUNN FIELD (II)

Location: 546 Luce Street

Dimensions: left 325', center 384–400', right 325'

Home Team(s): Elmira Pioneers, Red Sox, Pioneer Red Sox, Suns, and Royals/Eastern League, Can-Am League, Northeast League, Northern League, PONY League, and New York-Penn League

Built/In Operation: 1938 through 1939/1939 through 1955, 1957 through 1970, and 1972 through 2005

Seats/Capacity: 4,020 to 5,100

Fun Facts: In January of 1937, the architecture firm of Haskell and Considine began drawing up plans for a brand-new stadium. Besides being an architect, Harry Myron Haskell was the director of the Elmira Community Baseball Club. Haskell's plans included a 5,000-seat grandstand of reinforced steel, concrete, and brick that would cost $100,000 to build (almost $2 million today). The work was to be accomplished by the Public Works Administration, a part of the Federal government's "New Deal," and would occur around the existing structures so that play wouldn't be interrupted. This would obviously result in a shift in the diamond as well.

Construction began at the conclusion of the 1938 season, when the old wooden seating was dismantled to be used for new bleachers. The modern structures included a covered grandstand topped by a press box and bleachers along the right field line. Parking was improved and expanded after the 1939 schedule, and lights made their first appearance as well.

In 1991, Elmira was informed that major league baseball was requiring all minor league affiliates to meet certain facility standards. For Dunn (II) to match American and National League prerequisites, the stadium would need around $700,000 worth of updates. The following year, "Dollars for Dunn" raised almost $200,000 for stadium improvements. Projected for 1993 were new dugouts, press box, and wheelchair ramp.

Eventually, professional baseball left Elmira. Luckily, Dunn Field (II) is still in use for collegiate summer "wooden bat" baseball. Dunn (II) retains its imposing classic 1930s entranceway and design, with Edward Dunn's bust greeting visitors entering through the front facade.

FMI: *digitalballparks.com* on Dunn Field (II); John Pardon and Jerry Jackson, "New York State Ball Clubs," in Puff, *The Empire State of Base Ball*; Walsh and Murphy, *The Fields of New York*; Keetz, *They, Too, Were "Boys of Summer"*; Benson, *Ballparks of North America*; Stats Crew, "Sports in Elmira, New York"; Hall, "Dunn Field Municipal Stadium—Elmira, New York"; *Star-Gazette*, January 7, 1937; *Star-Gazette*, September 28, 1938; "Pioneers Unveil Changes," *Star-Gazette*, December 11, 1992.

HORNELLSVILLE (Now HORNELL)

UNKNOWN NAME

Location: unknown

Dimensions: unknown

Home Team(s): Hornellsville Hornells/International Association

Built/In Operation: 1878

Seats/Capacity: unknown

Fun Facts: Team disbanded August 15, 1878.

FMI: *Buffalo Commercial*, November 26, 1878.

EXPOSITION GROUNDS

Location: unknown

Dimensions: unknown

Home Team(s): Hornellsville Hornells/Western New York League

Built/In Operation: 1890

Seats/Capacity: unknown

Fun Facts: The season lasted less than a month in September 1890.

FMI: *Hornellsville Weekly Tribune*, August 8, 1890.

MAPLE CITY PARK

Location: Seneca Street

Dimensions: unknown

Home Team(s): Hornellsville Maple Cities, Bluebirds, and Hornells/Southern Tier League; Hornell Pigmies, Green Sox, and Maple Leafs/Interstate League; Hornell Maples, Maple Leafs, and Dodgers/PONY League; and Hornell Redlegs/New York-Penn League

Built/In Operation: 1891/1903 through 1906, 1914 through 1915, and 1942 through 1957. Torn down in the 1960s. Replaced by the new Maple City Stadium.

Seats/Capacity: 2,200/2,500

Fun Facts: Maple City Park has been used over the years for fireworks displays, circuses like Barnum and Bailey, horse and automobile racing, amateur baseball, high school baseball, and semiprofessional football. The Brooklyn Royal Giants (Negro Leagues) visited in 1923.

When the PONY League came to town, it was preceded by a fundraising campaign to install lights for night games and to equip the team. The Pittsburgh Pirates affiliate moved from Ontario, Canada, and— voila!—baseball was back. Maury Wills played in Hornell during 1951 and 1952.

FMI: Fiesthumel, *"Pent-Ups"*; John Pardon and Jerry Jackson, "New York State Ball Clubs," in Puff, *The Empire State of Base Ball*; "Hornell, NY," *Bullpen.*

NORWICH

UNKNOWN NAME

Location: unknown

Dimensions: unknown

Home Team(s)s: Norwich/Central New York League
Built/In Operation: 1886

Seats/Capacity: unknown

Fun Facts: Norwich took first that year in the Central New York League.

FMI: John Pardon and Jerry Jackson, "New York State Ball Clubs," in Puff, *The Empire State of Base Ball*; "Central New York League," *Bullpen*.

ONEONTA

FAIRGROUNDS

Location: on the east side of Oneonta

Dimensions: unknown

Home Team(s): Oneonta Hustlers/New York State League

Built/In Operation: 1889/1890

Seats/Capacity: unknown

Fun Facts: "Ball" was being "played" in Oneonta in the streets of the village as early as the first year of the Civil War. There weren't any official baseball diamonds or designated "grounds" at that time. These informal games evolved into an "organized" team in 1876. The squad was named "Atnoeno" (Oneonta spelled backwards). Little more is known about those early years. By 1888, the Atnoenos had been joined locally by the Blue Labels.

Nothing more is known about these initial field locations (possibly the fairgrounds) and teams until 1890. A meeting in the spring of 1889 laid down a plan for a professional franchise the following year. The organization would be called the Hustlers, and join a new league for New York State teams. Unfortunately, the Hustlers played so badly in 1890 that the squad was disbanded at the end of the season. While amateur baseball contests were happily staged, attempts to bring back pro ball in the ensuing years were a failure. The next time professionals wore "Oneonta" colors was well into the 20th century.

FMI: Fiesthumel, *"Pent-Ups"*; Whittemore, *Baseball Town*; John Pardon and Jerry Jackson, "New York State Ball Clubs," in Puff, *The Empire State of Base Ball*.

NEAHWA FIELD/MORRIS PARK/ELM PARK/
DUTCH DAMASCHKE STADIUM

One of the many photographs made around 1940 by General Electric to document and promote their newly installed lighting systems at area ballparks. Neahwa "Park," shot during July of the 1940 season, was located in Oneonta. Courtesy miSci/Museum of Innovation and Science, Schenectady, New York.

Location: Neahwa Park, 15 James Georgeson Avenue

Dimensions: left 337', center 403', right 341'

Home Team(s): Oneonta Giants/Eastern League and New York-Penn League; Oneonta Indians and Red Sox/Can-Am League; and Oneonta Red Sox, Yankees, and Tigers/New York-Penn League

Built/In Operation: 1905/1906, 1908, 1919, 1921, 1924, 1940 through 1942, 1946 through 1951, and 1966 through 2009

Seats/Capacity: 3,700 to 4,500

Fun Facts: In its online publicity materials, Oneonta calls itself "the City of the Hills." The vista from the seats of Damaschke Stadium fully illustrate that nickname.

The land for the ballfield and the park surrounding it were donated to the city in the fall of 1908 by Dr. Lewis Rutherford Morris, for whom the area was initially known. The oldest section of seating in Morris Park was the wooden grandstands, added for that season. By 1911, the facility had become Neahwa Park, with the name supposedly from the language of local Native Americans. Some boosters of the area have interpreted "neahwa" to mean "gift," while other scholars purport it to resemble the Mohawk word for "thank you."

With a ballpark over a century old, one would rightly assume that many changes have been made over the years to keep the facility up and functioning. The dugouts were first added in 1920, with running water, fencing, and other improvements made to parking and sidewalks in 1923. Lighting has been upgraded multiple times as well.

The first major renovations came during 1939 and 1940. Funded by a consortium including local businessman William Eggelston, the WPA (Works Progress Administration), and the city, the wooden seating from 1908 was replaced with a concrete and steel structure. WPA workers also redid the playing surface of the diamond. Reporter Bob Whittemore repeats one legend that

> the reason for the excellent [field] drainage was WPA workmen in the thirties dumped as many as 25 old cars into the area [of play] . . . cover[ing] them with . . . dirt. . . . But complete renovation of the playing surface in the fall of 1993 ended Damaschke Field's unique ability to absorb water and the car theory has been questioned in recent months.

Neahwa Field was relabeled in 1968 to honor longtime Oneonta Parks and Recreation Commission chairman and an official with the Can-Am League, Ernest "Dutch" Damaschke. Damaschke's name currently adorns the front gate of Damaschke Stadium in large blue letters.

The latest major modernization for the stadium was executed in the lead up to the 2007 schedule. Wooden bleachers were replaced with metal, and a picnic area was built past the right field bleachers, along with new sidewalks, clubhouses, concession stands, and landscaping.

During the 1906 schedule, imported players were partially compensated with jobs on the local railroad. That season also saw a tie exhibition game between Oneonta and the barnstorming Cuban (Negro Leagues) Giants.

A highlight for 1908 was the visit in August by a traveling team of "Cherokee Indians." During this road trip, the "Indians" also played in Elmira, Waverly, and Lestershire. The Cherokee brought along female pitcher Maud Nelson (who was white; see **Ridgewood Park [II]**) and their own lights. This would have been the first night game played at Elm Park. And, according to David Pietrusza's *Baseball's Canadian-American League*, "collegiate players from Brown, Holy Cross, Syracuse and Williams College played ball there in the summers circa 1910–1912."

Like many other surrounding communities hosting professional baseball, Oneonta had their own set of "blue laws" prohibiting play on Sundays. During a 1919 contest, the ball team's manager and two players were arrested and removed to jail. Strangely, the game was allowed to continue in their absence. It took another five years and the return of professional baseball for the local laws to be repealed to legally allow baseball on the Sabbath.

During most of the 1920s and 1930s, the ballfield was home to semiprofessional teams: that is, squads of mostly local players augmented by paid, imported talent. One of these, the Oneonta Cubs, played an August 1920 exhibition game against the barnstorming Brooklyn Royal Giants (Negro Leagues), losing by a score of 13 to 3. Two months later, the baseball squad from Endicott-Johnson entertained Babe Ruth and his All Stars at Damaschke Stadium.

The Oneonta Red Sox took two Can-Am League championships (in 1948 and 1951), and made the league playoffs during all six years of their Can-Am membership. The Can-Am League folded after 1951 and professional baseball would not return to Oneonta until 1966. That affiliation, with the Boston Red Sox, lasted just one season. A relationship with the New York Yankees followed, one that would last over 30 years!

The Oneonta Yankees won an astonishing 10 New York-Penn League championships with 12 total playoff appearances. Between 1979 and 1981, the prospective major leaguers captured three league pennants in a row. After the 1998 season, the Yankees went elsewhere and Oneonta became a Detroit Tigers affiliate for the last years that professional baseball graced the diamond of Damaschke Stadium. Don Mattingly, Al Leiter, Bernie Williams, Jorge Posada, Curtis Granderson, Mike Pagliarulo, Willie McGee, Bob Tewskbury, Jair Jurrgens, Will Rhymes, Guillermo Moscoso, and Don Kelly: these are just a few of the names of major leaguers that began their professional baseball careers at Oneonta's stadium.

The Oneonta Outlaws collegiate team played their first season at Damaschke in 2010.

FMI: *digitalballparks.com* on Damaschke Field; Whittemore, *Baseball Town*; David Pietrusza, "Upstate New York's Ballparks," in Puff, *The Empire State of Base Ball*; Pietrusza, *Baseball's Canadian-American League*; Perfect Game Collegiate Baseball League, "Ballparks of the PGCBL: Damaschke Field"; Walsh and Murphy, *The Fields of New York*; Benson, *Ballparks of North America*; Bennett, "Dutch Damaschke Field in Oneonta NY"; Simonson, "The Early Years: Local Area Benefactor Morris Honored in 1936"; "Real Novelty for Saturday," *Star-Gazette*, July 20, 1908; *Press and Sun-Bulletin*, July 25, 1908; *Press and Sun-Bulletin*, July 28, 1908; *Press and Sun-Bulletin*, July 28, 1908.

WAVERLY

ELM STREET GROUNDS

Location: a few blocks north of the **Howard Street Grounds**

Dimensions: unknown

Home Team(s): unknown

Built/In Operation: 1887

Seats/Capacity: unknown

Fun Facts: In 1886, the amateur Waverly Spauldings were sponsored by the Spaulding Hose Company, a fire department named for a distant cousin of baseball mogul Al Spaulding. The following year was the only season for games by a semiprofessional, unaffiliated Waverly team. Elm Street was used for amateur and school baseball and football from 1908 until 1929.

FMI: unknown

HOWARD STREET GROUNDS

Location: south of the cemetery, on the south side of Providence Street, east of Spaulding Street, west of Cayuta Avenue, and north of Broad Street, on the site of the old circus grounds

Dimensions: unknown

Home Team(s): Cortland and Waverly Wagonmakers/New York State League

Built/In Operation: 1887/1887, 1896, and 1900 through 1901

Seats/Capacity: 700/1,800

Fun Facts: This semiprofessional/professional facility briefly flourished during a local push for a Waverly team. In May of 1896, in anticipation of the baseball season, members of the Waverly Athletic Club "improved" the Howard Street Grounds by extending the fences and grading the diamond. The playing schedule proceeded before seating could be completed; a grandstand was finished in July.

For 1896, the Waverlys included local African-American "laborer" and infielder John "Bud" Waller. Waller was also good with a bat. A season's-end visit by the Cuban (Negro Leagues) Giants included former Buffalo Bison, Frank Grant.

A new fence greeted the public for 1900, and Waverly welcomed a combination of professional, semipro, and amateur nines from June through September. Among those on the schedule included the Cuban X Giants (Negro Leagues), who beat Waverly by a score of 6–5.

The baseball enthusiasts among Waverly's residents still held out the hope for bringing professional baseball to town. William H. Brewster, a son of the area and the proudest promoter of local ball lore, wrote that, for 1901,

> in preparation for Opening Day on April 29 . . . team officials further enhanced the Howard Street Grounds beyond the improvements made the previous year. They enlarged the grounds, re-graded the field, doubled the size of the grandstand, and erected a new ticket office. They also improved the grandstand's seating arrangements, and even provided several seats

for the press. . . . In addition to improvements to the grounds themselves, the team added a walkway from Broad Street to the grounds' entrance on Howard Street. This would help ensure that Broad Street businesses profited from a successful season as much as the team would.

The Waverlys began 1901's schedule as a semiprofessional squad playing similar organizations as the previous year. For example, the Cuban X Giants again visited, in June of 1901. However, ongoing negotiations with the New York State League finally yielded results. During the second week of July, the league moved the Wagonmakers franchise from Cortland to Waverly, making the town an official professional league affiliate. The Wagonmakers played out their schedule in Waverly. Unfortunately, the State League again moved the franchise at the conclusion of the season, ending Waverly's history of professional baseball.

FMI: Brewster, *The Workingman's Game*; Brewster, *That Lively Railroad Town*; John Pardon and Jerry Jackson, "New York State Ball Clubs," in Puff, *The Empire State of Base Ball*; *Star-Gazette*, June 13, 1900; *Star-Gazette*, November 16, 1903; *Press and Sun-Bulletin*, April 29, 1905; *Star-Gazette*, March 21, 1903; *Star-Gazette*, September 26, 1900; *Star-Gazette*, October 11, 1900; *Star-Gazette*, July 21, 1900; *Star-Gazette*, July 26, 1900.

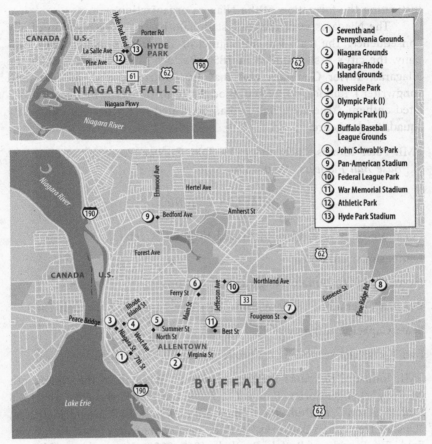

①	Seventh and Pennsylvania Grounds
②	Niagara Grounds
③	Niagara-Rhode Island Grounds
④	Riverside Park
⑤	Olympic Park (I)
⑥	Olympic Park (II)
⑦	Buffalo Baseball League Grounds
⑧	John Schwabl's Park
⑨	Pan-American Stadium
⑩	Federal League Park
⑪	War Memorial Stadium
⑫	Athletic Park
⑬	Hyde Park Stadium

Map 6. Buffalo Ballparks.

SEVENTH AND PENNSYLVANIA GROUNDS

Location: at the intersection of Seventh Street and Pennsylvania Street

Dimensions: unknown

Home Team(s): Buffalo Niagaras; and Eries

Built/In Operation: 1857/1857 through 1858

Seats/Capacity: unknown

Fun Facts: These were the first "grounds" used for baseball by the Buffalo Niagara club, succeeded by the Eries. The "New York rules" had been introduced in the city by two former members of the Brooklyn Excelsiors, instigating the formation of the Niagara organization.

The Niagaras were the earliest Buffalo baseball organization of any consequence. The team was an adjunct of Taylor Hose No. 1 Fire Company, the city's first, founded in 1850. Besides supplying players for the Niagaras, Taylor Company also may have nurtured club member and songwriter J. Randolph Blodgett. Blodgett contributed the first baseball-related anthem, "The Base Ball Polka," dedicated to Rochester's Flour City squad, to the genre.

FMI: Peter Morris, "Niagaras of Buffalo, Prewar+Postwar," in Morris et al., *Base Ball Pioneers, 1850–1870*.

NIAGARA GROUNDS

Location: on a vacant lot, Main and Virginia Streets

Dimensions: unknown

Home Team(s): Buffalo Niagaras and Cliftons

Built/In Operation: 1858/1858 through 1861, and 1867 through 1869

Seats/Capacity: unknown

Fun Facts: The second field utilized by the Buffalo Niagaras.

FMI: Johnson, *Ballparks Database*; Astifan, "Baseball in the Nineteenth Century"; Langendorfer, *Baseball in Buffalo*; Joseph Overfield, "The 1878 Buffalo Bisons," in Puff, *The Empire State of Base Ball*; David Pietrusza, "Upstate New York's Ballparks," in Puff, *The Empire State of Base Ball*; Overfield, *The Seasons of Buffalo Baseball, 1857–2020*; protoball.org, "Niagara Grounds, Buffalo"; Peter Morris, "Niagaras of Buffalo, Prewar+Postwar," in Morris et al., *Base Ball Pioneers, 1850–1870*.

SIXTH AND NORTH/YORK STREETS FIELD

Location: Sixth Street and North/York Streets

Dimensions: unknown

Home Team(s): Buffalo Niagaras and Buffalo (Negro Leagues) Mutuals

Built/In Operation: 1866/1866 through 1870

Seats/Capacity: unknown

Fun Facts: In 1866, the Niagaras moved to what might have been the first enclosed field in Buffalo, which also eventually boasted grandstand seating. In June of 1868, the Niagaras took on the (legendary) touring Brooklyn Atlantics. Somehow, the Niagaras pulled off the unthinkable, defeating Brooklyn by a score of 19–14.

An unknown combination of factors saw the Niagaras play elsewhere during 1869, freeing up the field for use by other local teams. On August 4, 1869, what was described in the *Buffalo Morning Express* as the "colored" championship game was played between the Utica Fearless club and Buffalo's own Invincibles. Unfortunately, Buffalo didn't live up to their name, losing to Utica 88–18 (August 6, 1869).

The Niagaras returned in 1870, although financial problems led to the team's demise after that season. For the remainder of the decade, college and amateur matches continued here, eventually becoming less and less frequent.

FMI: Johnson, *Ballparks Database*; Astifan, "Baseball in the Nineteenth Century"; Langendorfer, *Baseball in Buffalo*; Joseph Overfield, "The 1878 Buffalo Bisons," in Puff, *The Empire State of Base Ball*; David Pietrusza, "Upstate New York's Ballparks," in Puff, *The Empire State of Base Ball*; Overfield, *The Seasons of Buffalo Baseball, 1857–2020*; protoball.org, "Niagara Grounds, Buffalo"; Peter Morris, "Niagaras of Buffalo, Prewar+Postwar," in Morris et al., *Base Ball Pioneers, 1850–1870*.

RACING PARK

Location: East Ferry Street, one mile outside of Buffalo

Dimensions: unknown

Home Team(s): Buffalo Niagaras

Built/In Operation: 1869

Seats/Capacity: unknown

Fun Facts: For some reason, for this one season, the Niagaras were "forced" to play at "an unfavorable site outside of the city." Hoping that this move was only temporary (which it proved to be), portable seating was employed for the fans.

FMI: Peter Morris, "Niagaras of Buffalo, Prewar+Postwar," in Morris et al., *Base Ball Pioneers, 1850–1870*; "Portable Seats to Be Constructed for Niagara's New Grounds," *Buffalo Morning Express*, July 31, 1869.

NIAGARA-RHODE ISLAND GROUNDS/PROSPECT SKATING CLUB

Location: the west side of Niagara Street between Vermont and Rhode Island Streets

Dimensions: unknown

Home Team(s): Buffalo "Buffalos"

Built/In Operation: 1876/1877

Seats/Capacity: 3,000

Fun Facts: The Buffalos are credited in *The Seasons of Buffalo Baseball*, an update of the classic *The 100 Seasons of Buffalo Baseball* by Joseph M. Overfield, as "Buffalo's first professional team." This was a "non-league" organization (i.e., not affiliated with any association) that only played for several months at the end of the 1877 baseball season. The team added a scoreboard to center field and had the players sell score cards to spectators in between at bats.

Although this 1877 squad wasn't league affiliated, it played against teams that were members of the National League and International Association, as well as challenging other autonomous squads. These included the Louisville (Kentucky) Reds, Rochester Rochesters, Syracuse Stars, as well as the Indianapolis Blues.

FMI: "Three to Nothing," *Buffalo Morning Express*, August 15, 1877; Johnson, *Ballparks Database*; Astifan, "Baseball in the 19th Century"; Langendorfer, *Baseball in Buffalo*; Overfield, "The 1878 Buffalo Bisons," in Puff, *The Empire State of Base*; David Pietrusza, "Upstate New York's Ballparks," *The Empire State of Base Ball*; Overfield, *The Seasons of Buffalo Baseball, 1857–2020*.

RIVERSIDE PARK/GROUNDS

The Directors have dubbed the ballgrounds "Riverside Park." The name is not appropriate, but it will do.

—*Buffalo Commercial*, April 29, 1882

Location: Fargo Avenue (southwest), Rhode Island Street (northwest), West Avenue (northeast), Vermont Street (southeast)

Dimensions: left 250', center 410', right 250'

Home Team(s): Buffalo Buffalos and Bisons/International Association and National League

Built/In Operation: 1878/1878 through 1883

Seats/Capacity: under 3,000/3,000 to 5,000

Fun Facts: As you might have gathered from the above quote, Riverside Park's ballfield didn't exactly have a view of the Niagara River. However, the ball diamond *was* brand new for 1878, rising from leased land on Buffalo's west side that winter and spring before the start of the new season.

For a new group on a new field in a new league, the Bisons played exceptionally well. The team won the International Association and New York State championships, and earned an outstanding win/loss record against the clubs of the National League of a bit under .600. Unfortunately, their lease ran out after the 1883 season, forcing the Bisons to find a new home.

FMI: Johnson, *Ballparks Database*; Astifan, "Baseball in the Nineteenth Century"; Langendorfer, *Baseball in Buffalo*; Overfield, "The 1878 Buffalo Bisons," in Puff, *The Empire State of Base Ball*; David Pietrusza, "Upstate New York's Ballparks," in *The Empire State of Base Ball*; Overfield, *The Seasons of Buffalo Baseball, 1857–2020*; Stats Crew, "Niagara-Rhode Island Grounds"; Cichon, "From 1880 to Today."

OLYMPIC PARK (I)/RICHMOND AVENUE GROUNDS

Location: Richmond Avenue (west), Summer Street (south), Norwood Avenue (east)

Dimensions: unknown

Home Team(s): Buffalo Bisons/National League and International League

Built/In Operation: 1884/1884 through 1888. Dismantled and moved after the 1888 season, and the land divided into building lots.

Seats/Capacity: 3,748/9,000

Fun Facts: At the end of the 1883 season, the owner of the land upon which sat the **Riverside Grounds** refused to renew the Bison's lease. Therefore, team president Josiah Jewett was forced to find a new location for his ball club. A site was located on Richmond Avenue and rented for five years at a fee of $5,000 per anum, and a brand-new wooden stadium was fabricated.

Supervised by contractor William F. Burrows at a cost of $6,000 ($163,502 in 2021 dollars), the ballpark was 350 by 608 feet, larger than the previous facility. The curved, covered grandstand seating 1,064 was set back from Summer Street facing north, and topped with a press box. The visitor's clubhouse sat behind the grandstand, as did carriage parking, which was separated from the ballpark proper by a 12-foot-high fence between the rear of grandstand and the street. The home dressing rooms were behind the grandstand's right wing, with uncovered seats holding almost 2,000 running parallel to the side streets. "State of the art" improvements over the old facility included an enclosed grandstand back to protect fans from the rain, built-in ventilation, and wider seats with footrails. Female fans were provided a separate grandstand section on the left wing to insulate them from the often-vulgar behavior of male baseball fans of the day.

To raise more income, the field was flooded during the winter of 1886 for ice skating, and a bicycle track around the diamond was also proposed. Concessions included ginger beer, peanuts, fruit, cigars, and cigarettes, with roaming vendors making sure you were never without an opportunity. When the Bisons were on the road, the facility was busy with amateur contests, and the playing of other sports, including cricket and lacrosse.

Opening day for the new ballpark was May 21, 1884, when the Bisons defeated the Detroit Wolverines by a score of 11–4. Before the end of the 1885 season, the franchise and all its players were sold to Detroit. Somehow, the Bisons finished out their schedule by recruiting a rag-tag bunch of locals and unsigned professionals as replacements for the departing pros.

After the Bisons left the National League, they helped found the International League. From 1886–1888, the club was managed by former Brooklyn player Jack Chapman. As an outcome of signing African-American second baseman and power hitter Frank Grant during his first season, Chapman was ostracized by other squad members. This type of racism permeated all levels of baseball at that time and resulted in an end to the integration of the sport until the second half of the 20th century.

The final complete professional game for Olympic Park (I) occurred at the conclusion of September 1888, when the Buffalo Bisons met the barnstorming Cuban Giants, called by some historians the first professional team of Black players. Rather than, as one might assume, being based in Cuba (they had nothing to do with the Island nation), at that time, the Giants played their home contests in Trenton, New Jersey.

FMI: Johnson, *Ballparks Database*; Gilbert, *How Baseball Happened*; David Pietrusza, "Upstate New York's Ballparks," in Puff, *The Empire State of Base Ball*; Overfield, *The Seasons of Buffalo Baseball, 1857–2020*.

OLYMPIC PARK (II)/BUFFALO BASE BALL PARK/ QUEEN CITY BASEBALL AND AMUSEMENT COMPANY

Location: East Ferry Street and Michigan Avenue

Dimensions: unknown

First run for Buffalo professional baseball at Olympic Park (II), also known as Buffalo Base Ball Park. Unknown date. Joseph Overfield Collection, Buffalo History Museum.

Home Team(s): Buffalo Bisons/International League, Brotherhood-Players League, Eastern Association-League, and Western-American League

Built/In Operation: 1888 through 1889/1889 through 1923. Demolished between the 1923 and 1924 seasons and replaced in this location by **Offermann Stadium**.

Seats/Capacity: 10,000/30,000

Fun Facts: With the land under the first **Olympic Park (I)** slated to be divided into residential building lots, Bison franchise directors chose a location for their new ballpark near the grounds of the International Fair. At the conclusion of the 1888 season, the old wooden Olympic Park (I) was dismantled and the materials recycled for this recently acquired real estate at Michigan Avenue and East Ferry Street.

The latest grandstand was designed by the firm of Bethune, Bethune, and Fuchs, the husband-and-wife team based in Buffalo. Louise Blanchard Bethune was America's first female architect. The firm also advised on the **Federal League Park**. Local lore has it that, on the first opening day, one of contractors who still had not been paid stood with a shotgun blocking the entrance to the field until his accounts had been settled.

In 1897, the current grandstand was razed and seating expanded. Unfortunate timing, as the new grandstand burned to the ground in March of 1898. Again in 1903, the grandstand and bleachers were expanded, and barely avoided similar destruction by fire through the quick actions of local police and firemen.

For the 1890 schedule, the Bisons became affiliated with the Players' League, an organization founded and run by the competitors themselves. The league collapsed at season's end, sending the Buffalo Bisons to the Eastern Association. The year 1891 proved to be a good one, as the reorganized team, in their dark-blue uniforms, won the league championship. In 1893, a change to Kelly-green inspired the unofficial fan nickname of the Hibernians.

An opinion piece in the *Buffalo Morning Express* (August 1, 1893) states that a Sunday baseball game at Olympic Park (II) instigated a ban by the police commissioners of future Sabbath contests therein. This "first" (and last for the moment) Sunday game at Olympic (II) evidently was played on July 30, 1893. Protestations by neighbors led to the prohibition, and forced the Bisons' management to find other, less obvious facilities for these games (see **East Side Baseball Grounds** et al.).

During their residency at Olympic Park (II), the Bisons' roster included Connie Mack (for the 1890 season), most famously later the skipper of the Philadelphia Athletics, and Joe McCarthy (during the mid-1910s), who went on to manage the New York Yankees. Early in his professional baseball career, Babe Ruth came with the Baltimore Orioles to pitch against the Buffalo Bisons. Evangelist Billy Sunday held a revival at Olympic Park (II) for two months during the winter of 1917. Finally, the Bisons won four league championships here—1904, 1906, 1915, and 1916.

FMI: *digitalballparks.com* on Offerman Stadium; Langendorfer, *Baseball in Buffalo*; Overfield, "Offermann Stadium in Buffalo," in Puff, *The Empire State of Base Ball*; David Pietrusza, "Upstate New York's Ballparks," in Puff, *The Empire State of Base*; Overfield, *The Seasons of Buffalo Baseball, 1857–2020*; Fox, "Louise Blanchard Bethune"; Bennett, "Buffalo Base Ball Park and Offermann Stadium"; "Olympic Park Also a Hoodoo on Sunday," *Buffalo Morning Express*, July 31, 1893.

BUFFALO BASEBALL LEAGUE GROUNDS/CITY BASEBALL PARK/ FRANKLIN PARK/EAST SIDE BASE BALL GROUNDS

Location: the North side of Genesee and Barthel Streets: Urban Street (north), Belt Line Railroad (east), Fougeron Street (south, about a block away from the Belt Line and Genesee Street crossing).

Dimensions: unknown

Home Team(s): (the other) Buffalo Bisons/International Association; and (the original) Buffalo Bisons/Eastern League and Western League

Built/In Operation: 1878/1890, and 1893 through 1899. The stands and fences were dismantled in 1900.

Seats/Capacity: 1,000 to 3,000/3,500

Fun Facts: Referred to in *The Seasons of Buffalo Baseball* as a "jerrybuilt ballpark," the original East Side Grounds were first enclosed and rented out for amateur play in 1878. The following year, improvements included raising the fence by five feet and adding additional seating, including a lady's section, to the grandstand and bleachers.

During 1879 and 1880, the local amateur nines formed an association, and planned a full schedule of Sunday contests. Unfortunately, a change of the city's administration precipitated the arrests of players, effectively ending the games.

Amateur ball on Sundays was back for at least 1883–1887. For 1886, a new semicircular grandstand seating 1,000 fans was built, with 2,000 additional seats replacing the old bleachers. At the beginning of 1890, high winds badly damaged the fencing and stands.

During 1890, there were actually two different Buffalo baseball teams named the Bisons. The original Bisons played most of their home games at **Olympic Park (II)** and are the direct ancestor for all professional ball in Buffalo that came afterwards. Those Bisons occasionally used the Buffalo Baseball League Grounds for Sunday games. The *other* Bisons, who played all of their home contests at Buffalo Baseball League Grounds, were referred to in the local newspapers as the "little Bisons." That team only lasted a month before first moving to Montreal, Canada, and then, a bit more than a week later, to Grand Rapids, Michigan. As Sunday games were either limited by the city or prohibited by the Bisons' management, it appears that, after Bisons number two left Buffalo, no professional baseball was played by the original Bison team in this facility for two years.

In 1893, baseball on the Sabbath was once again attempted at **Olympic Park (II)**, provoking a ban on Sunday games therein by the commissioner of police. Therefore, from 1893–1899, East Side/Franklin Park (named I believe for team owner and local politician James Franklin) again became the Bisons "other" venue.

One of the area drivers for the Sunday playing ban was the Christian Endeavorers organization. Led by the Reverend O. P. Gifford, the group led a concerted campaign throughout the area to stop baseball on the Sabbath. Gifford actively interfered with games by both local amateurs and the professional Bisons throughout 1897, 1898, and into 1899. By then, because of the disruptions the arrests caused, it just wasn't worth the trouble to stage contests at Franklin Park. In May of 1900, the seats and fences were removed and brought to **John Schwabl's Park**.

FMI: Overfield, *The Seasons of Buffalo Baseball, 1857–2020.*

ELDORADO PARK/IDLEWILD PARK

Location: the Eldorado resort, East River Road on Grand Island

Dimensions: unknown

Home Team(s): Buffalo Bisons/Eastern League

Built/In Operation: 1892, and one game in 1893

Seats/Capacity: 1,200

Fun Facts: Eldorado Park/Idlewild Park was an amateur baseball facility that existed from around 1892 until 1906. The Buffalo Bisons played one Sunday game here in August of 1893, beating the Binghamton Bingos by a wide margin. Ultimately, it was decided that the size of the playing field was not conducive to professional baseball, and the Bisons went elsewhere for contests on the Sabbath.

FMI: Overfield, *The Seasons of Buffalo Baseball, 1857–2020*.

JOHN SCHWABL'S PARK/FOREST GROVE PARK

Location: Pine Ridge Road south of Genesee Street, Cheektowaga

Dimensions: unknown

Home Team(s): Buffalo Bisons/Eastern League

Built/In Operation: 1900/1900 through 1903, and 1918

Seats/Capacity: 1,000/4,000

Fun Facts: After leaving **Franklin Park**, the Buffalo Bisons reconstructed their stands at John Schwabl's Park. Because the Park was outside of the Buffalo city limits, the Bisons management believed that, finally, they would be able here to circumvent local "blue laws." Also known locally as "Little Germany," the site included a restaurant, rides, a zoo, a bowling alley, a pool hall, and shooting galleries.

However, sporadic interference from law enforcement continued unabated. Somehow, despite the harassment, baseball persisted here through 1911. The local semiprofessional Pullmans used Schwabl's as their home field from 1909 to 1911, playing touring teams such as the Cuban Giants (Negro Leagues). By March 1912, the baseball facility had been razed, with John Schwabl planting the former diamond with onions.

FMI: Langendorfer, *Baseball in Buffalo*; Overfield, *The Seasons of Buffalo Baseball, 1857–2020*.

PAN-AMERICAN STADIUM

Pan-American Stadium in an illustration from the *Buffalo Sunday Morning News*, January 20, 1901.

Location: between Delaware Avenue, Elmwood Avenue and Great Arrow Avenue, on the western edge of current day Delaware Park

Dimensions: unknown

Home Team(s): Buffalo Bisons and Pan-Ams/Eastern League

Built/In Operation: 1901. Demolished in March of 1902.

Seats/Capacity: 12,500

Fun Facts: On June 28 and 29, 1901, the Buffalo professional baseball franchise played two games here in conjunction with the Pan-American Exposition. The facility cost $55,000 (around $1.8 million today), and was typical of other "over the top" structures built in tandem with large fairs. Designed by the firm of Babb, Cook, and Willard, this multipurpose stadium referenced the architecture of the Spanish renaissance, as well as ancient Athens. This World's Fair is best known as the site, later that year, where President William McKinley was assassinated.

FMI: Overfield, *The Seasons of Buffalo Baseball, 1857–2020*.

TONAWANDA DRIVING PARK

Location: south of Park Avenue, Tonawanda

Dimensions: unknown

Home Team(s): Buffalo Bisons/Eastern League

Built/In Operation: 1869, and one game in 1904. Demolished beginning in 1911, and housing built on this area.

Seats/Capacity: 5,000

Fun Facts: Originally constructed for harness racing, at least two parks with a similar name and function have graced this site. Tonawanda Driving Park was utilized for baseball as early as August of 1869, when the Niagaras played the Central Citys. Amateur athletes added a diamond and stands in 1892, and the Bisons attempted a Sunday contest here in 1904. But you can already guess the outcome. The game began, local clergy called the sheriff, who arrived and promptly arrested three players. Even though charges were later dropped, the "win" went to the men of God, as, once again, the Buffalo boys looked elsewhere for a Sabbath field.

FMI: Overfield, *The Seasons of Buffalo Baseball, 1857–2020*; Growing Up in Tonawanda, "Tonawanda Driving Park."

FEDERAL LEAGUE PARK/
INTERNATIONAL FAIR ASSOCIATION GROUNDS

> Know every blade of grass in your park, is my motto for taking care of a baseball field. I never fail to go over the field myself, every day. . . . The home plate and the pitchers' box, like an impatient baby, always need attention.
>
> —Frank Hart

Location: Northland Avenue and Jefferson Street-Lonsdale Road

Dimensions: left 290', center 400', right 300'

Home Team(s): Buffalo Buffeds, Blues, and Electrics/Federal League

Built/In Operation: 1914/1914 through 1915. Demolished early in 1917.

Seats/Capacity: 11,800 to 16,300/20,000

Fun Facts: This location originally housed a succession of fair grounds and horse racing tracks. Horter and Lockwood had built the original park behind the Cold Spring Hotel. Opening in 1858, it was sold off in the immediate aftermath of the Civil War. By the time of the spring races in 1868, Cicero Jabez Hamlin and company had rehabbed and renamed the track the Buffalo Driving Park. It eventually became known as "The Kentucky Derby of the North." For the rest of the 19th century, various organizations and events controlled the property.

The year 1914 saw the formation of the Federal League as a major competitor to the National and American League organizations. In cities like Buffalo, the Feds also competed for fans with other professional teams such as the Bisons.

The owners of the native Federal League franchise leased this property for $20,000. The locally based architects Bethune, Bethune, and Fuchs, founded by the husband-and-wife team of Louise Blanchard Bethune and Robert A. Bethune, had previous experience working on the designs for **Olympic Park (II)**. They teamed up with builder Charles Mosier of Mosier and Summers to produce Federal League Park.

Ground was broken during a not unexpected late March upstate New York snowstorm. The builders optimistically aimed for completion by the end of April, but construction dragged on into early May. After 30 days playing on the road, the Feds opened their first homestand on May 11 with a parade and other appropriate pomp and ceremony. This modern ballpark of steel and concrete featured a covered "V" shaped grandstand extending east and south along Northland Avenue and Lonsdale Road. Under the grandstand were the team locker rooms. Other stands were located along the base lines, and parking for automobiles was included. Improvements continued into the season with the addition of an "electric" scoreboard and a "no smoking" section created for female fans. The total cost of construction ran around $75,000 (a bit over $2 million in today's money).

At the end of the 1914 season, when Federal League president James A. Gilmore toured Buffalo's latest baseball facility, he commended the architects, builders, and groundskeeper Frank Hart:

> This is the prettiest park that I have seen in the league. . . . It
> is the cleanest park that I have ever been in and it certainly
> looks as though the stands, ground, and the entire equipment
> was given a thorough scrubbing with all the sapolio [soap] in
> Buffalo.

Coming from the Cleveland Naps, Hart had constructed a miniature garden around the center field flagpole.

First baseman Hal Chase played for Buffalo during these two seasons despite being signed to the Chicago White Stockings of the American League and taken to court by Sox owner Charles Comiskey. In fact, the

Buffeds management rubbed Chicago's face in the signing by actively promoting Chase with featured newspaper articles. Ultimately, it was all about the money—Buffalo offered Hal Chase more than Comiskey, causing Hal to opt out of his agreement with Chicago.

After the second Federal League season for Buffalo, intense negotiations began between the management and owners of the Feds and the major and minor league commissioners. By the end of 1915, the Federal League proprietors got what they wanted from major league baseball—ownership stakes in American and National League teams.

With the end of the Federals, the stadium was offered to the city for $125,000, but Buffalo passed on the purchase. Instead, the structures were sold for salvage and homes were built on the site. Today, the location is part of the Hamlin Park Historic area, named for the early developer of the racetrack, with some of the plantings and features designed by Frederick Law Olmsted, the famous landscape architect.

FMI: Cichon, "Torn-Down Tuesday"; "Federal League Park (Buffalo)," *curveinthedirt.com*; Langendorfer, *Baseball in Buffalo*; David Pietrusza, "Upstate New York's Ballparks," in Puff, *The Empire State of Base Ball*; Overfield, *The Seasons of Buffalo Baseball, 1857–2020*; Healey, "Federal League Park"; "The Federal League Ballparks"; Goldman, "Buffalo's Historic Neighborhoods: Hamlin Park"; Cichon, "From 1880 to Today: Hamlin Driving Park, Buffalo's famed Horse Track"; Puma, "The History of Hamlin Park"; "Work on Federal League Park Progressing," *Buffalo Evening News*, March 28, 1914; "Hart Praised by Gilmore," *Buffalo Enquirer*, September 19, 1914.

OFFERMANN STADIUM/BISON STADIUM/BUFFALO BASEBALL PARK

Location: East Ferry Street and Michigan Avenue

Dimensions: left 321', left-center 346', right 297'

Home Team(s): Buffalo Bisons/International League

Built/In Operation: 1923 through 1924/1924 through 1960. Demolished in 1961 and 1962, and Woodlawn Junior High School (now Buffalo Academy for Visual and Performing Arts) built on this site. In 2012, a plaque commemorating the stadium was placed here.

Seats/Capacity: 14,000/23,000

Fun Facts: Bison Stadium was built at a cost of $265,000–$400,000 (around $4–$6 million in 2021). The first "modern" ballpark of the International

Offermann Stadium field, showing Joe Brown, ground superintendent, and Joe Ziegler, general manager, standing at home plate. Unknown date. Collection of the Buffalo History Museum.

League, this steel and concrete stadium is locally credited as inspiring other sporting grounds throughout the association. Utilizing the same field as **Olympic Park (II)**, new structures were built for Bison Stadium during the 1923 season and completed just in time for opening day of 1924 (of course, weather delayed that game six times!). With great sight lines, the park's short distance to left-center field joined with winds blowing out from the plate to carry many well-hit balls over the fence.

The stadium was renamed for team owner (from 1920 until his death in January of 1935) Frank J. Offermann after his passing. Offermann had presided over the introduction to the Bisons and the International League of lights for night games (July 3, 1930), as well as, starting with the 1931 season, the broadcast of contests over the radio. According to the owners, lights were necessary so that fans who worked a regular job could attend weekday games. The original system, costing a modest $10,000, included 44 lamps on four 56-foot poles or mounted on the roof of the grandstand. These were the first permanent illumination for professional baseball in New York State and the eastern United States. In the long run, the system proved inadequate, and updated lights were installed for the 1939 season.

Radio broadcasts of games was another matter. Frank Offermann was going against the prevailing opinion of the other league owners, who felt that, rather than pay to attend games, fans would choose to stay home and listen to the free transmissions. These programs were the first such attempts at regular broadcasts of professional baseball.

For at least some of its history, the stadium's wooden scoreboard was hand-operated. Additionally, in the early days predating public address systems, announcements at Offermann Stadium were made through a large megaphone.

Typical for most fields of the period, Offermann was in a densely settled section of Buffalo. Therefore, no space was available for automobile parking. Additionally, the close proximity to area homes meant that residents had a free, unencumbered view of games. Some even erected illegal bleachers on their garages and charged other fans bargain prices for seats. The downside of living near the ballpark was that solidly hit baseballs often came crashing through the front windows of dwellings alongside of the stadium. The Presbyterian house of worship behind home plate showed the scars from the many foul balls that had careened off its walls over the years. Eventually, the original 12-foot-high concrete fences were supplemented in the 1930s with another tier. This, plus an eventual third addition effectively ended "bootleg" seating.

From 1932 to 1937, the double A–level Bisons were managed by Ray Schalk, who, while a member of the Chicago White Sox, was one of the whistleblowers during the 1919 "Black Sox" betting scandal. Player Lou Boudreau went from the Bisons to the Cleveland Indians and then into the Baseball Hall of Fame. Jim Bunning spent 1955 pitching in Buffalo before careers in the major leagues and the United States Senate.

Affiliations for the Buffalo Bisons included the Cleveland Indians (1939), Detroit Tigers (a working agreement for 1940–1949, with ownership by the Tigers during 1951–1955), the Kansas City Athletics (1957–1958) and the Philadelphia Phillies (during 1950 and 1959–1962). After Detroit discontinued their support in the mid-1950s, the Bisons team was threatened with extinction. However, local investors took over expenses and the Bisons became community owned for about the next 10 years.

Two traveling Negro Leagues teams based themselves at Offermann Stadium: in the 1940s, the New York Black Yankees of the Negro National League and, during the first half of the 1950s, the Negro American League Indianapolis Clowns.

FMI: *digitalballparks.com* on Offerman Stadium; Langendorfer, *Baseball in Buffalo*; Violanti, *Miracle in Buffalo*; Joseph Overfield, "Offermann Stadium in Buffalo," in Puff, *The Empire State of Base Ball*; Mandelaro and Pitoniak, *Seasons*; Overfield, *The Seasons of Buffalo Baseball, 1857–2020*; Bennett, "Buffalo Base Ball Park and Offermann Stadium."

WAR MEMORIAL STADIUM/"THE ROCKPILE"/CIVIC STADIUM/ GROVER CLEVELAND STADIUM/ROESCH STADIUM

> The Old Rockpile was a mess. Thousands of gray wooden seats were peeling and cracking. . . . On the outside, it was cracking and rusting. Grass grew wild. The terribly scarred infield was a sea of mud. The lights didn't work, and neither did most of the toilets, sinks and urinals.
>
> —Anthony Violanti, *Miracle in Buffalo*

Location: Jefferson Avenue (east, left field), Best Street (south, right field), Dodge Street (north, third base), Masten Avenue (west, first base), in the Masten Park neighborhood

An aerial view of War Memorial Stadium. Date unknown. Collection of the Buffalo History Museum.

Dimensions: unknown

Home Team(s): Buffalo Bisons/International League, Eastern League, and American Association

Built/In Operation: 1935 through 1937/1961 through 1970, and 1979 through 1987. Demolished in 1988.

Seats/Capacity: 33,000 to 46,500

Fun Facts: Originally the site of a reservoir, between 1935 and 1937, the WPA (Works Progress Administration) built this concrete and steel football stadium for $3 million (almost $57 million today!). The original monikers affixed to the stadium were in honor of Buffalo mayors Charles Roesch and Grover Cleveland.

When the Bisons made the move to War Memorial Stadium in 1961, a lot of sweat and money was required to bring the facility up to snuff. Unfortunately, even with all the investments by the team and their owners, the facility remained problematic. Fans complained about poor sight lines from the first base box seats, bad parking, and traffic. As the neighborhood deteriorated following the 1967 race riots, all but Sunday daytime games were moved to **Hyde Park Stadium** in Niagara Falls. Finally, with the loss of a workable local facility and major league affiliation, the franchise was moved to Canada. No professional baseball was played in Buffalo between the end of the 1970 season and 1978.

After the return of baseball, the Rockpile had one last comeback. When director Barry Levinson and producer Mark Johnson were looking for a ballpark to use in their movie *The Natural* (1983), they fell in love with War Memorial Stadium. Anthony Violanti relates Johnson's reaction:

> The first time I walked in that place, I said, "What a great stadium! This is perfect." It was a combination of things. I loved the size of the stadium; it was clearly big enough to be a major-league park. I loved the place; it had an old-fashioned feel that was just right for the film.

Barry Levinson concurred, remarking that "it was the only park we could find that was big enough to resemble a major-league stadium from the 1930s. There was nothing like it anywhere else." Additionally, in 1984, the Beach Boys performed the first of four yearly concerts in conjunction with Bisons' games at (appropriately) the Rockpile.

While playing at the War Memorial, the Bisons were affiliated with the Philadelphia Phillies (1961–1962), New York Mets (1963–1965), Cincinnati Reds (1966–1967), Washington Senators (1968–1969), Montreal Expos (1970), Pittsburgh Pirates (1979–1982), Cleveland Indians (1983–1984, 1987), and the Chicago White Sox (1985–1986).

The sports pavilion that replaced War Memorial Stadium preserves the original entrance at Dodge Street and Jefferson Avenue, as well as some other features of the stadium's exterior.

FMI: *digitalballparks.com* on Offerman Stadium; Langendorfer, *Baseball in Buffalo*; Violanti, *Miracle in Buffalo*; Overfield, "Offermann Stadium in Buffalo," in Puff, *The Empire State of Base Ball*; Mandelaro and Pitoniak, *Silver Seasons*; Overfield, *The Seasons of Buffalo Baseball, 1857–2020*; Bennett, "The Rockpile—Buffalo's War Memorial Stadium."

CELORON

CELORON (ORIGINALLY SPELLED CELERON) PARK

Location: "Prendergast Point" on Lake Chautauqua

Dimensions: left 325', center 362', right 287'

Home Team(s): Acme (Negro Leagues) Giants/Iron and Oil League; Jamestown Hill Climbers and Dubois Miners/Interstate League; Jamestown Oseejays/Interstate League; Jamestown Lohrels, Rabbits, and Giants/Interstate League; and Jamestown Jaguars and Pirates/PONY League

Built/In Operation: 1893/1895, 1898, 1905 through 1906, 1914 through 1915, and 1939. Demolished (remnants remain).

Seats/Capacity: 3,240

Fun Facts: This lavish amusement park on the southern shore of Lake Chautauqua was named for the French explorer Pierre Joseph Céloron de Blainville, who led an expedition through the area in the mid-1700s. Known as "the Coney Island of Western New York," Celoron Park was built by the Broadhead family atop of what had formerly been a swamp. In operation by 1893, besides the ballfield, there were rides, a zoo, a bandshell, a penny arcade, and an indoor theater that was later refurbished as a dance hall. At one point in its existence, the baseball facility contained a covered grandstand as well as bleacher seating.

There was a veritable procession of teams that used the diamond at Celoron. The 1895 Iron and Oil League squad moved from Sharon, Pennsylvania on July 18. The 1898 Celoron team was unusual, as the Acme Giants were a Black organization playing in an otherwise white minor league. Unfortunately, their win/lose record was so poor that the team quit the Iron and Oil League two months into the season. The owners replaced the African-American players with whites, supposedly the members of a lineup from Kentucky.

Three Jamestown organizations appear to have used Celoron Park. In 1905, the Hill Climbers-Dubois Miners were loosely affiliated with the New York Hilltoppers-Highlanders-Yankees. During the next season, the Oseejays of the Interstate League split their home games between Celoron and Oil City, Pennsylvania. That team beat the Cuban (Negro Leagues) Giants in May of 1906. By the way, that team name is the phonetic pronunciation of the initials for Oil City (OC) and Jamestown (J).

For the two seasons between 1914 and 1915, the Lohrels-Rabbits-Giants were in residence. Their nicknames came partially from speedy base running (Rabbits) and an affiliation with a major league New York squad (the Giants). Although Jamestown took the pennant in 1914, after the park had the grandstand painted, with permanent seating and a protective screen added between seasons, the Rabbits hopped away in mid-August of 1915.

The final gasp for professional baseball at Celoron came in 1939. Unfortunately, by then lacking basic amenities such as restrooms and concessions, the PONY squad decamped at season's end for London, Ontario.

Over the years, Celoron Park hosted exhibition games by most of the major league baseball franchises of the day, as well as "barnstorming" athletes like Jim Thorpe and Babe Ruth. The Babe hit a 500-foot homerun into the lake during practice. These days, what remains of the facility is named for the locally raised actress, Lucille Ball.

FMI: *digitalballparks.com* on the New York-Penn League; Village of Celoron, "Park History"; Burk, "The Babe"; Riggs, "Jamestown Played a Role in Black Baseball History"; John Pardon and Jerry Jackson, "New York State Ball Clubs," in Puff, *The Empire State of Base Ball*; Langendorfer, *Baseball in Buffalo*; Violanti, *Miracle in Buffalo*; David Pietrusza, "Upstate New York's Ballparks," in Puff, *The Empire State of Base Ball*; Overfield, *The Seasons of Buffalo Baseball, 1857–2020*; Yankeebiscuitfan, "Minor League History: Iron and Oil League"; *Stats Crew*, "Celeron Park"; "The Chautauqua Community"; "70 Years of Jamestown Pro Baseball to Be Celebrated"; John Pardon and Jerry Jackson, "New York State Ball Clubs," in Puff, *The*

Empire State of Base Ball; *Stats Crew*, "Sports in Jamestown, New York"; *Stats Crew*, "1890 Jamestown Roster"; "Jamestown, New York," in Worth, *Baseball Team Names*; "Roots of Local Baseball"; *Olean Democrat*, July 9, 1895; "Iron and Oil League," *Bullpen*.

DUNKIRK

TURNERS' NEW GROUNDS

Location: West Fourth Street

Dimensions: unknown

Home Team(s): Dunkirk Dandies/New York-Penn League and Western New York League

Built/In Operation: 1890

Seats/Capacity: unknown

Fun Facts: When the Dandies moved in, fences and a grandstand were lacking at the New Grounds. Maybe that's why the team also played home games at Dunkirk's **Driving Park Grounds**.

FMI: "The Western New York League," *Dunkirk Evening Observer*, June 2, 1890.

DRIVING PARK GROUNDS

Location: Dunkirk

Dimensions: unknown

Home Team(s): Dunkirk Dandies/New York-Penn League; and Dunkirk and Fredonia Stars/Iron and Oil League

Built/In Operation: 1883/1890 and 1898

Seats/Capacity: unknown

Fun Facts: Another in a succession of racetracks converted for use as ballfields.

FMI: John Pardon and Jerry Jackson, "New York State Ball Clubs," in Puff, *The Empire State of Base Ball*; "New York-Penn League, 1890–1891," *Bullpen*.

JAMESTOWN

MARVIN PARK

Location: located in the southwestern portion of the park near the boat landing and the Chautauqua Lake railway passenger station

Dimensions: unknown

Home Team(s): Jamestown/Western New York-Penn League

Built/In Operation: 1890/1890 through 1891

Seats/Capacity: 1,000

Fun Facts: In 1884, the county fairgrounds relocated to this land owned by local lawyer, businessman, and politician, R. P. Marvin. The Jamestown team's home games were delayed during the 1890 season because wet weather prolonged the construction of the grandstand and fences. Because the grounds were located on land that had formerly been a swamp, the field flooded easily. Local historian Greg Peterson tells the story about how the owner of the Warner Dam held the team hostage, choosing inopportune times just before games to flood the baseball field. Evidently, some type of remuneration was adjudicated, and the flooding ceased. In 1890, Jamestown came in first in the Western New York-Penn League.

One notable member of Jamestown's squad was Black baseballer R. A. Kelly. Kelly played first base here, and later joined the Celoron Acme Giants (Negro Leagues).

A horse track was added during the 1891 baseball season. Cricket was also played at Marvin Park.

FMI: John Pardon and Jerry Jackson, "New York State Ball Clubs," in Puff, *The Empire State of Base Ball*; *Stats Crew*, "Sports in Jamestown, New York"; *Stats Crew*, "1890 Jamestown Roster"; Riggs, "Jamestown Played a Role in Black Baseball History"; "Jamestown, New York," in Worth, *Baseball Team Names*; "The Marvin House"; Chautauqua Sports Hall of Fame, "Old Baseball Ticket Discovered"; "Roots of Local Baseball."

ALLEN PARK

Location: West Virginia Boulevard and Elizabeth Avenue

Dimensions: unknown

Home Team(s): Niagara Falls Rainbows and Jamestown Falcons/PONY League

Built/In Operation: 1940

Seats/Capacity: unknown

Fun Facts: Allen Park, as are the surrounding streets, is named for Virginia Allen, who donated this land to the city. It's been a public park since 1906.

Problems with the lack of adequate "professional-grade" facilities carried over from the end of the 1939 season (see **Celoron**). At that time, the Pittsburgh Pirates had discontinued their affiliation with Jamestown, moving their team to Canada because the city could not provide an acceptable ballpark. On July 19, 1940, Jamestown replaced the Pirates with a franchise from Niagara Falls.

Although the 1940 team survived without a major league agreement, the field at Allen Park was deemed inadequate to sustain a professional squad. Many battles with the Jamestown common council followed, before an agreement was reached, and a proper facility approved (see **Jamestown Municipal Stadium**).

FMI: Anderson, "JCB Journal: 1940"; Robinson, "The Magic of Allen Park."

JAMESTOWN MUNICIPAL STADIUM/COLLEGE STADIUM/ RUSSELL E. DIETHRICK, JR., PARK

Location: 485 Falconer Street

Dimensions: left 356', center 404', right 346'

Home Team(s): Jamestown Falcons/PONY League and New York-Penn League; and Jamestown Tigers, Dodgers, Braves, Falcons, Expos, and Jammers/New York-Penn League

Built/In Operation: 1941/1941 through 1957, 1961 through 1973, and 1977 through 2014. Now part of the campus for Jamestown Community College.

Seats/Capacity: 3,000 to 5,077

Fun Facts: At the end of the 1940 schedule, it looked as though the history of PONY League baseball in Jamestown was at an end. Throughout the season, discussions had been underway to build a modern sports facility, necessary for maintaining the PONY League in Jamestown. Initially, the mayor and city council refused to subsidize the initiative, suggesting that a fundraising effort among the public be attempted. In mid-September, it was announced in the local newspapers that the ruling council had again rejected approving the $28,000 needed toward building a new baseball stadium when privately raised funds could not reach that goal. Finally, later that fall, the city agreed to issue bonds for the $23,000 necessary to build the grandstand. In January of 1941, the common council raised an additional $27,000 through an increase in the local tax rate to finish construction. When building was completed, $60,000 was the total projected cost (that's a little over $1 million today). The first game at Municipal Stadium was on May 7, 1941.

Falconer is an area municipality, and the team's name came (obviously) from the ballpark's location (half way between Jamestown and Falconer). The Falcons won pennants during 1941 and 1942, their first two years of play. The Jammers name, according to one source, came from a name-the-team contest. A fan suggested the moniker because of Jamestown's association with the jelly-making industry.

Recent photographs depict the original brick-covered grandstand structure housing bleacher-style seating, a press box atop the grandstand, unroofed more recent bleachers down the left and right field lines, and lights, with the visitor's bullpen off left field.

Renamed Russell E. Diethrick, Jr., Park in 1997 for that ardent supporter of local baseball, the field is now home to a summer collegiate league team.

FMI: O'Reilly, *Charlie's Big Baseball Parks Page*; Benson, *Ballparks of North America*; Anderson, "JCB Journal: 1940"; Hyde, "A Look Back at the Jamestown Falcons"; "Russell Diethrick Park," *In the Ballparks*; "Jamestown, New York," in Worth, *Baseball Team Names*; "Jamestown Rejects Stadium," *Times Herald*, September 17, 1940; "1941 Tax Rate for Jamestown Raised," *Dunkirk Evening Observer*, January 21, 1941.

LOCKPORT

OUTWATER STADIUM

Location: Outwater Drive near Charlotte Street

Dimensions: unknown

Home Team(s): Lockport White Sox, Cubs, Socks, and Reds/PONY League; and Lockport Locks/Mid-Atlantic League

Built/In Operation: 1942/1942 through 1951

Seats/Capacity: 3,500 to 4,500

Fun Facts: The stadium was built in Outwater Park; the original/core parcel of land had been donated by Dr. Samuel Outwater in 1920. The effort to bring baseball to Lockport was spearheaded by a group of eleven baseball enthusiasts who called themselves "the Screwball Club." The group worked with a locally formed booster organization to gain a PONY League franchise.

FMI: John Pardon, and Jerry Jackson, "New York State Ball Clubs," in Puff, *The Empire State of Base Ball*; "Lockport, NY," *Bullpen*; Linnabery, "Niagara Discoveries: The Screwball Club"; *Stats Crew*, "Outwater Park"; Linnabery and Boles, "Over the Hill: A Brief History of Outwater Park."

NIAGARA FALLS

ATHLETIC PARK/NU-CRUME PARK

Location: Sugar Street (now Hyde Park Blvd.), just west of current-day **Hyde Park Stadium**

Dimensions: unknown

Home Team(s): Niagara Falls/International League

Built/In Operation: 1905/1908

Seats/Capacity: unknown

Fun Facts: The International League (as in the United States and Canada) was an association of four teams based at Athletic Park. The locals were dubbed "Yankees" by the Buffalo newspapers, although this could have been a function of the Niagara Falls players being the only non-Canadian squad in the league. The Internationals played the Cuban Giants and the Cuban Stars (both of the Negro Leagues) in the preseason.
The ballfield was still extant in 1918.

This area appears to have had another ballpark close by, located about a five-minute walk from Hyde Park, Athletic Park, and the future location of **Hyde Park Stadium**. With the address of Woodlawn Avenue and 27th Street, this other facility of 2,000 seats played host to local semiprofessional teams approximately between 1914 and 1916.

FMI: John Pardon and Jerry Jackson, "New York State Ball Clubs," in Puff, *The Empire State of Base Ball*; Higgs, "What's in a Name?"; *Stats Crew*, "Nu-Crume Park."

HYDE PARK STADIUM/SAL MAGLIE STADIUM

Location: Hyde Park Boulevard

Dimensions: left 327', center 410', right 327'

Home Team(s): Niagara Falls Rainbows/PONY League; Niagara Falls Frontiers and Citizens/Middle Atlantic League; Buffalo Bisons/International League; Niagara Falls Pirates, White Sox, Tigers, and Rapids/New York-Penn League; and Niagara Falls Mallards/North Atlantic League

Built/In Operation: 1933 through 1936/1939 through 1940, 1946 through 1947, 1950 through 1951, 1967 through 1979, 1982 through 1985, 1989 through 1993, and 1995. Demolished.

Seats/Capacity: 2,500 to 4,000/7,000

Fun Facts: Hyde Park Stadium was located within Hyde Park on land donated by Charles B. Hyde before his death in 1921. Hyde is the largest city park in New York State outside of Manhattan. One of the myriads of "New Deal" projects funded in the 1930s by the Federal government through the WPA (Works Progress Administration), the stadium was originally designed for football. Built and initially used over a four-year period, the icing on the cake was the WPA-installed lights costing $26,000 (almost $500,000 today) that were in operation by June of 1937.

As noted in the section on **the Rockpile**, Hyde Park Stadium was used by the Buffalo Bisons for nighttime home games between 1967 and 1969. During that period, Niagara Falls refurbished the stadium to the tune of $200,000, adding new sod, fences, lights, and paint. Hyde Park Stadium, renamed Sal Maglie Stadium, was redone again between 1982 and 1983. Maglie was a local product who was a Bison before going to the majors. Sal pitched for all three of the New York City major league teams in the late 1940s and early 1950s. Because Sal Maglie was known for giving batters a "close shave" (throwing near them), a barber chair was placed outside this facility in his memory.

Sal Maglie Stadium was utilized as a practice space for the actors to hone their baseball skills during the filming in Buffalo for *The Natural*. Other uses included motor cycle races, political events, and collegiate and semiprofessional athletics, including the Niagara Falls' Honeymooners baseball squad.

FMI: O'Reilly, *Charlie's Big Baseball Parks Page*; Violanti, *Miracle in Buffalo*; Walsh and Murphy, *The Fields of New York*; Benson, *Ballparks of North America*; John Pardon and Jerry Jackson, "New York State Ball Clubs," in Puff, *The Empire State of Base Ball*; "Niagara Falls, NY," *Bullpen*; "Light Huge Outdoor Field, Niagara Falls," *Daily Messenger*, September 2, 1936; "Wings Start with Win on Falls Lot," *Democrat and Chronicle*, September 25, 1933.

OLEAN

ATHLETIC ASSOCIATION GROUNDS

> In the afternoon a great part of the populace . . . hied themselves [went quickly] to the Athletic association grounds to see the Olean base ball team give an exhibition of its inability to play ball.
>
> —*Olean Democrat*, July 9, 1891

Location: Higgins Avenue and Main Street. The grounds borders Olean Creek on the modern map.

Dimensions: unknown

Home Team(s): The Olean/Western New York-Penn League and Iron and Oil League

Built/In Operation: 1887/1890 through 1891, and 1898. Demolished. The site is now behind a Pizza Hut.

Seats/Capacity: 2,300

Fun Facts: John McGraw began his professional career as a teenager on the 1890 squad. The Iron and Oil League disbanded mid-July of 1898.

FMI: John Pardon and Jerry Jackson, "New York State Ball Clubs," in Puff, *The Empire State of Base Ball*; *Stats Crew*, "Sports in Olean, New York"; *Stats Crew*, "Athletic Grounds"; Brewster, *The Workingman's Game*; "New York-Penn League," *Bullpen*.

INTERSTATE LEAGUE PARK

Location: Union Street, possibly in or adjoining Boardman Park

Dimensions: unknown

Home Team(s): Olean Oleaners, Candidates, Refiners, and White Sox/ Interstate League

Built/In Operation: 1905/1905 through 1916

Seats/Capacity: 900 to 1200/3000

Fun Facts: In April of 1905, the *Star-Gazette* announced that "A new baseball park is being built." The very next season, the local nine tied Hornell for the pennant. In 1915, playing in a recently remodeled ballpark, Olean took first in the Interstate League. The grandstand was again enlarged for the 1916 season. Although a visit by the New York Yankees was predicted, the locals appear to have quit the league by early August.

FMI: John Pardon and Jerry Jackson, "New York State Ball Clubs," in Puff, *The Empire State of Base Ball*; *Stats Crew*, "Sports in Olean, New York"; *Stats Crew*, "Athletic Grounds"; Eberth, "History of Bradner Stadium"; "Saturday Will Be Pennant Day at Interstate Park," *Times Herald*, August 4, 1915; "Southern Tier Baseball Plans," *Star-Gazette*, April 5, 1905; "Echoes of the Past," *Times Herald*, May 26, 1936; *Times Herald*, May 20, 1915; "Additional Seats to Be Built at Interstate Park," *Times Herald*, April 22, 1916; "New Schedule Arranged for Six Remaining Interstate Teams," *Times Herald*, August 5, 1916.

BRADNER STADIUM

Location: East State Street and Front Street

Dimensions: unknown

Home Team(s): Olean Oilers, Yankees, Giants, Athletics, and Red Sox/ PONY League and New York-Penn League

Built/In Operation: 1926 through 1927/1939 through 1959, and 1961 through 1962

Seats/Capacity: 4,000 to 6,000/10,000

Fun Facts: During the second decade of the 20th century, a local group was formed in Olean with the purpose of building a city sporting facility. By 1924, enough money had been raised to purchase property near the intersection of the Olean Creek and the Allegheny River by the Genesee Valley Canal basin. However, it took a $50,000 donation on top of a loan approaching another $20,000 from John Howe and Marcia Boardman Bradner for the project to move forward (combined, that's about a million in today's dollars). The Bradners owned a local department store in Olean.

A. G. Spaulding and Brothers, the sporting goods manufacturer founded by former baseballer Albert Spaulding, designed the facility. Their plan called for a baseball diamond, football field, running track, and tennis courts. One feature was a fence on the east side of the stadium. It included a canvas curtain that was raised during games to block the view of spectators outside of the park.

Contractor Havens Construction Company of Olean carried out Spaulding's blueprint. The resulting stadium of reinforced concrete was projected to open in the spring of 1927 with a contest between the Boston Braves and the Detroit Tigers. However, a flooded field effected the game's cancellation, closing the facility for two weeks. Another "official" opening was scheduled for June of the following year. However, that exhibition by Pittsburgh Pirates/Boston Red Sox was also rained out.

Over the years, flooding continued to be an issue, as the stadium's pumping system occasionally failed. Ironically, to use Bradner for winter ice skating, if the field wasn't already naturally flooded, the city had to shut down the pumps, effectively filling the field with water.

Lighting for night games was installed during July of 1935. Since that time, several travel squads have visited Bradner, including the Homestead Grays (twice in 1935 and 1936, and again in 1937, 1938, 1941 and 1942), the Philadelphia Stars, the New York Cubans (all Negro Leagues), and one from the House of David.

The year 1939 featured the first full season of professional baseball, with the Oilers taking the pennant. Between that time and the final loss of the pros in 1962, Olean was affiliated with the Brooklyn Dodgers, the St. Louis Browns, and the Philadelphia Phillies. Jackie Robinson played here as a Dodger in an exhibition game during his first year in the major leagues.

After the conclusion of professional baseball, Bradner Stadium was renovated in 1969–1970, with the addition of a new entrance, drainage system, and lights. This facilitated the stadium's use as a concert venue. By the early 2000s, the old grandstand with locker rooms was demolished. At some point, the diamond was converted to a football oval and, beginning in 2009, dedicated exclusively for that sport. From 2012 to 2019, baseball returned with a collegiate summer "wooden bat" team, and further improvements were made between 2012 and 2017. Those makeovers included a complete rebuild to the tunnel entrance under East State Street, as well as the reinstallation of a baseball diamond with permanent dugouts.

FMI: O'Reilly, *Charlie's Big Baseball Parks Page*; *Stats Crew*, "Sports in Olean, New York"; "Bradner Stadium, Olean, New York," *RochesterAreaBallparks. com*; "Sox-Pirates Game Plans to Be Aired," *Times Herald*, May 14, 1928; "Official Opening of Stadium Will Be on June 18th," *Times Herald*, May 1, 1928; *Times Herald*, June 16, 1927; "Pirates and Red Sox Play Here June 18," *Times Herald*, March 8, 1928; *Times Herald*, July 18, 1935.

WELLSVILLE

ISLAND PARK

Location: on the property known as "Farnum's Island"

Dimensions: unknown

Home Team(s): Wellsville/Western New York League; Wellsville Oil Drillers/ Southern Tier League; and Addison and Wellsville Strippers/Southern Tier League

Built/In Operation: 1890/1890 and 1903 through 1905

Seats/Capacity: unknown

Fun Facts: Purchased by the town of Wellsville a few years before professional baseball was played here, Island Park hosted the initial Western New York League season. Unfortunately, the league lasted less than a month in September of 1890. The Oil Drillers played on the Island for two seasons, although the second in 1904 was terminated partway through the schedule. From the end of June or early July until the third week of August 1905, the Addison-Wellsville Strippers could have played here, or possibly just in Addison.

FMI: *Star-Gazette*, August 25, 1903; Boyce, photo of Island Park sign.

TULLAR('S) FIELD

Location: between what is now Route 19 and South Main Street, on Piper Place, surrounded on two sides by Dyke Creek

Dimensions: left 335', center 357', right 300'

Home Team(s): Wellsville Rainmakers/Interstate League; Wellsville Yankees, Nitros, Senators, Rockets, and Braves/PONY League; and Wellsville Braves and Red Sox/New York-Penn League

Built/In Operation: 1911/1914 through 1915, 1942 through 1956, 1957 through 1961, and 1963 through 1965. Structures removed in 1967, and the size of the field reduced in 1969.

Seats/Capacity: 2,000 to 2,500/2,600

Fun Facts: Tullar('s) Field was built on a former pasture purchased in April of 1911 by local philanthropist Angeline "Angie" Cobb Tullar for use by the city. Flooding was a problem during the early years for this stadium. In 1936, lights costing $7,000 were installed, and, three years later, a new entrance dedicated to Mr. Tullar was constructed. The entry included two 18-foot columns of concrete topped with globes and bronze letters spelling "Tullar Field."

In anticipation of the Yankee's PONY League club playing at Tullar('s), locker rooms with showers and new fencing were erected. In 1952, Wellsville was affiliated with the St. Louis Browns and the 1955 Milwaukee Braves associates were rewarded with a new replacement scoreboard. The following season, the Wellsville nine took the PONY League pennant, a feat they repeated when the league was renamed the New York-Penn League in 1957, again in 1958 and 1959.

In 1957, the fences were rebuilt and new third base line stands were added. For 1960, the grandstands and restrooms were improved. After a year off, the 1963 Boston Red Sox–affiliated team received a newly repaired and painted Tullar('s) Field, with a 12 by 20 foot addition to their clubhouse. Unfortunately, this did not prevent the ballpark from showing its age in various ways throughout the Red Sox tenure. After the 1965 schedule, the Sox moved their franchise to Oneonta.

For all intents and purposes, that was the end of the original Tullar('s) Field. In the next year, the grandstands and dugouts were demolished and the field integrated into a similarly titled new city recreational facility. In 1969, parts of the outfield were taken for the construction of the Route 17 and Route 19 arterial.

FMI: John Pardon and Jerry Jackson, "New York State Ball Clubs," in Puff, *The Empire State of Base Ball*; "Wellsville, NY," *Bullpen*; Stats Crew, "Tullar Field"; "Decorative Columns Projected for Entrance to Tullar Field," *Democrat and Chronicle*, July 2, 1939; *Times Herald*, March 3, 1942; "Braves in Town after Trip from Waycross," *Wellsville Daily Reporter*, April 24, 1957; "Braves Minor to Return for 1960 NY-P Season," *Wellsville Daily Reporter*, January 27, 1960; "Baseball Park, Stands Improved for Opener," *Wellsville Daily Reporter*, April 10, 1963; "Bill Contractor for Water Line Repairs," *Wellsville Daily Reporter*, June 24, 1969.

The Northern Tier

AUBURN

DRIVING PARK

Location: unknown

Dimensions: unknown

Home Team(s): Syracuse Arctics; Union Springs Frontenacs; Rochester Atlantics; Rochester Excelsiors; Macedon Macedons; Utica Hiawathas; Auburn; and Geneva Hobarts

Built/In Operation: 1866

Seats/Capacity: 20,000

Fun Facts: A week of baseball occurred here in early October 1866, and was supposed to settle the championship between 12 upstate New York nines.

FMI: Kissel, "The Pumpkin and Cabbage Tournament of 1866."

WALNUT STREET BALLPARK

Location: Walnut Street

Dimensions: unknown

Home Team(s): Auburn Auburnians/League Alliance

Built/In Operation: 1877

Seats/Capacity: unknown

Fun Facts: The League Alliance was an association of minor league professional clubs affiliated with the National League that followed their rules and regulations.

FMI: Roe, "Meet Some of Auburn's Earliest Baseball Players"; Helander, "The League Alliance."

SEWARD AVENUE PARK

Location: Seward Avenue

Dimensions: unknown

Home Team(s): Auburn Auburnians/League Alliance and National Association; Auburn Yankees/Central New York League; Auburn Yankees, Maroons, and Pioneers/New York State League; and Utica Harps/Empire State League

Built/In Operation: 1877 through 1878, 1888 through 1889, 1897 through 1899, 1906 through 1907, and 1910

Seats/Capacity: unknown

Fun Facts: Auburn won the Central New York League pennant in 1888. The League then disbanded, and Auburn moved to the New York State League, where the team again came out on top in 1889. The *Stats Crew* website reports that, on August 24, Auburn played Utica at Seward for (possibly) the first minor league New York game under lights.

Part way through the 1899 season, the Auburn Pioneers moved to Troy, New York. The Central New York League of 1910 was typical of the other lower-level, small town organizations. Poor finances drove the league out of business in early June, attempting to continue by replacing the worse performing franchises, and finally closing up shop a week or two later.

Seward Avenue Park was named for the street, which was labeled to honor Secretary of State William H. Seward. The secretary, who maintained a local residence, is best known today by his acquisition of Alaska (aka "Seward's Folly") for the United States.

FMI: John Pardon and Jerry Jackson, "New York State Ball Clubs," in Puff, *The Empire State of Base Ball*; Helander, "The League Alliance"; *Evening Sun*, June 1, 1910; *Post-Standard*, June 3, 1910; *Democrat and Chronicle*, August 25, 1889; *Stats Crew*, "Seward Avenue Park."

FALCON PARK (I)

Location: 108 North Division Street

Dimensions: left 326', center 382', right 325'

Home Team(s): Auburn Bouleys and Colts/Can-Am League; Auburn Cayugas and Falcons/Can-Am League and Border League; Auburn Yankees, Mets, Twins, Phillies, Sunsets, Red Stars, Americans, and Astros/New York-Penn League; and Syracuse Chiefs/International League

Built/In Operation: 1926 through 1927/1938, 1940, 1946 through 1950, 1958 through 1980, and 1982 through 1994. Demolished after the 1994 season, and replaced with a new ballpark.

Seats/Capacity: 3,000 to 3,600/4,037

Fun Facts: The original wooden grandstand was built by and named for the Polish Falcons organization, who initially fielded a semipro team here. The first professional team playing their home games at Falcon Park (I) was the Smith Falls Beavers of the Can-Am League. The Smith Falls franchise was purchased between the 1937 and 1938 seasons by local businessman William Bouley, for whom the team was renamed. After a last place finish, Bouley resold the team, which then moved to Utica.

Can-Am baseball returned to Auburn in 1940, when the stadium gained permanent lighting. However, again finishing in last place, the franchise left town.

After World War II, baseball resumed in Auburn. A "new" grandstand was moved to Falcon (I) from another location in 1946. With a much better squad, the newly named Cayugas ascended that year to the top of the Border League. In 1948, the Cayugas became a Boston Red Sox affiliate. The league and the team disbanded mid-season in 1951.

For 1958, their first year as both a Yankee affiliate and a member club of the New York-Penn League, the squad featured a young rookie named Joe Pepitone. Later future stars included pitchers Jim Bouton and Mel Stottlemyre. When the Mets took over the Auburn team, players included Ed Kranepool and Tug McGraw.

Falcon Park (I) briefly became the home for the Syracuse Chiefs after the team lost their stadium to fire. For a month in the spring of 1969, Auburn welcomed the Chiefs when the local nine was on the road.

With major league baseball becoming more demanding of their minor league affiliates, and Falcon Park (I) continuing its deterioration, the baseball club invested $60,000 in 1988, building a new press box and upgrading drainage on the diamond. Unfortunately, by the early 1990s, the amount needed to bring the facility up to the standards required by the pros had increased to closer to $500,000–$1,000,000 (almost double in today's dollars). It made more sense to build a new facility, dooming the original Falcon Park (I) to demolition.

FMI: *digitalballparks.com* on Falcon Park (I); David Pietrusza, "Upstate New York's Ballparks," in Puff, *The Empire State of Base Ball*; Pietrusza, *Baseball's Canadian-American League*; Benson, *Ballparks of North America*;

Ithaca Journal, June 26, 1991; Croyle, "Throwback Thursday: Syracuse Chiefs Left Homeless after Big Mac Burns"; "New York-Penn League, 1957–2019," *Bullpen.*

BATAVIA

(FAIR) ASSOCIATION GROUNDS

Location: Swan Street

Dimensions: unknown

Home Team(s): Batavia/Western New York League

Built/In Operation: 1887

Seats/Capacity: unknown

Fun Facts: The first game to be played at this new facility was on June 22, 1887, between Batavia and Le Roy. Unfortunately, the league descended into disarray, with Batavia the last team standing. Attempts at reorganizing occurred in 1888 and 1889, but, except for scattered games by amateur and touring teams, were unsuccessful. By 1890, the locals had abandoned plans for professional baseball, and the lease for the Association Grounds was assigned to the local YMCA.

FMI: *Buffalo Morning Express,* June 23, 1887; *Democrat and Chronicle,* August 13, 1887; *Buffalo Courier,* March 9, 1889; *Buffalo Courier,* June 5, 1889; *Buffalo Morning Express,* June 9, 1889; *Democrat and Chronicle,* May 20, 1890.

DWYER STADIUM (I)/STATE STREET PARK/MACARTHUR STADIUM

Location: Denio Street

Dimensions: left 326', center 382', right 325'

Home Team(s): Batavia Clippers, Trojans, Indians, and Pirates/PONY League and New York-Penn League

Built/In Operation: 1939/1939 through 1953, 1957 through 1959, and 1961 through 1995. Demolished in 1995, and replaced with new stadium structures while maintaining the original diamond.

Seats/Capacity: 3,000/4,000

Fun Facts: State Street Park was funded through the WPA (Works Progress Administration). Unfinished at the start of its inaugural season, State Street was probably the only ballpark in history to have temporary seating supplied by the local mortuary. By year's end, work on the wooden structures such as the covered grandstand, outfield fencing, and lights costing $7,500 was completed. Years later, when Auburn and Batavia were concurrently reworking their baseball facilities, the old seating at the park was upgraded to aluminum stands. State Street Park was twice renamed, during World War II (as with Syracuse's park) after General Douglas MacArthur and, finally, for local director of baseball Edward D. Dwyer.

FMI: *digitalballparks.com* on Dwyer Stadium (I); David Pietrusza, "Upstate New York's Ballparks," in Puff, *The Empire State of Base Ball*; Walsh and Murphy, *The Fields of New York*; Benson, *Ballparks of North America*; " 'Clippers' Tag for Batavia," *Democrat and Chronicle*, April 26, 1939.

CANANDAIGUA

FAIRGROUNDS

Location: unknown

Dimensions: unknown

Home Team(s): Canandaigua/Central New York League; Canandaigua Rustlers/New York State League; and Penn Yan Grape Pickers/Southern Tier League

Built/In Operation: 1888/1888 through 1889, 1896 through 1898, and 1902 through 1903

Seats/Capacity: unknown

Fun Facts: The Rustlers won the New York State League pennant in 1897 and 1898.

FMI: "Iroquois Trail League," *Fandom*; "Empire State League (NY)," *Bullpen*; *Stats Crew*, "New York State League Team Rosters and Statistics"[a]; *Democrat and Chronicle*, March 8, 1889; *Democrat and Chronicle*, July 12, 1888; *Star-Gazette*, August 25, 1903; "Grape Pickers Beat Locals," *Star-Gazette*, June 25, 1904; advertisement, *Democrat and Chronicle*, July 24, 1905.

CANTON

UNKNOWN NAME

Location: unknown

Dimensions: unknown

Home Team(s): Canton/Northern New York League

Built/In Operation: 1901

Seats/Capacity: unknown

Fun Facts: unknown

FMI: John Pardon and Jerry Jackson, "New York State Ball Clubs," in Puff, *The Empire State of Base Ball*; "Northern New York League," *Fandom*; *Stats Crew*, "Canton Franchise History (1901)."

CORTLAND

COUNTY FAIRGROUNDS

Location: Fisher Avenue

Dimensions: unknown

Home Team(s): Cortland Hirelings and Wagonmakers/New York State League

Built/In Operation: 1897 through 1898

Seats/Capacity: unknown

Fun Facts: The team was nicknamed "Wagonmakers" because Cortland was home to multiple wagon manufacturers.

FMI: unknown

ATHLETIC FIELD

Location: Main Street

Dimensions: unknown

Home Team(s): Cortland Hirelings and Wagonmakers/New York State League; Cortland Wagonmakers/Empire State League; and Cortland/Central New York League

Built/In Operation: 1899 through 1901, 1905, and 1910

Seats/Capacity: 2,000

Fun Facts: Cortland didn't have much luck maintaining a professional team. Part way through the 1901 season, the team moved to Waverly, New York. In 1905, the franchise folded in July, and, for 1910, the Central New York League disbanded due to its financial collapse on June 1.

FMI: John Pardon and Jerry Jackson, "New York State Ball Clubs," in Puff, *The Empire State of Base Ball*; Lang, "Mountain Athletic Club at Fleischmanns Park Gains Historic Designation"; "Mountain Athletic Club, 1895–1914"; *Evening Sun*, June 1, 1910; "Central League Will Continue," *Post-Standard*, June 3, 1910.

FULTON

EMPIRE LEAGUE GROUNDS

> Work on the grand stand, fence and grading of the local field is going merrily on, the setting of posts being expected to be finished this week.
>
> —"Fulton Granted Franchise,"
> *Democrat and Chronicle*, May 3, 1906

Location: unknown

Dimensions: unknown

Home Team(s): Fulton/Empire State League; and Fulton/Central New York League

Built/In Operation: 1905 through 1906/1905 through 1908, and 1910

Seats/Capacity: unknown

Fun Facts: In July of 1905, the Ilion team was moved to Fulton. The Central New York League disbanded on June 1, 1910, due to a lack of finances.

FMI: John Pardon and Jerry Jackson, "New York State Ball Clubs," in Puff, *The Empire State of Base Ball*; Stats Crew, "Ilion/Fulton Franchise History (1905–1907)"; "Fulton Leaguers Win over Auburn," *Post-Standard*, May 21, 1910; *Evening Sun*, June 1, 1910; "Central League Will Continue," *Post-Standard*, June 3, 1910.

GENESEO

UNKNOWN NAME

Location: unknown

Dimensions: unknown

Home Team(s): Geneseo Livingstons/League Alliance

Built/In Operation: 1877

Seats/Capacity: unknown

Fun Facts: Geneseo is in Livingston County, hence the team name.

FMI: John Pardon and Jerry Jackson, "New York State Ball Clubs," in Puff, *The Empire State of Base Ball*; Helander, "The League Alliance."

GENEVA

PRE EMPTION PARK/FAIRGROUNDS

Location: Pre Emption Road

Dimensions: unknown

Home Team(s): Batavia and Geneva Alhambras/New York State League; and Geneva Opticians/Empire State League

Built/In Operation: 1884/1897, and 1905 through 1908

Seats/Capacity: unknown

Fun Facts: As early as 1879, Pre Emption Park featured a horse and bicycle racing track. The facility was in use for local baseball by August of 1884, when the Syracuse Revolts played the Utica Fearless at the fairgrounds. Amateur baseball continued in 1896. In 1897, the first year for professional baseball in Geneva, the park was utilized by Batavia of the New York State League for games after the franchise moved to Geneva at the end of July.

The mayor put the kibosh on local Sunday baseball in 1900, which didn't prevent the Geneva Opticians from replacing Palmyra's Empire State team at the end of June 1905. Of course, it didn't exclude players from being arrested that season either for playing on the Sabbath. By 1906, fencing and grandstand improvements were needed.

The Pre Emption Park moniker disappeared from local newspapers between 1914 and 1954, when the last notice appeared. It's not certain when the ballfield met its demise.

FMI: *Democrat and Chronicle*, August 7, 1884; "Good Pitching Won," *Democrat and Chronicle*, July 5, 1896; "An Exhibition Game," *Democrat and Chronicle*, June 23, 1897; "Geneva Won Again," *Democrat and Chronicle*, July 31, 1897; "May Be Admitted To-Day," *Democrat and Chronicle*, June 27, 1905; "Baseball Boom in Geneva," *Democrat and Chronicle*, April 14, 1906.

PULTENEY STREET GROUNDS

Location: Pulteney Street

Dimensions: unknown

Home Team(s): Geneva/Central New York League

Built/In Operation: 1910

Seats/Capacity: unknown

Fun Facts: The Central New York League disbanded June 1, 1910, due to a lack of financial support.

FMI: John Pardon and Jerry Jackson, "New York State Ball Clubs," in Puff, *The Empire State of Base Ball*; *Stats Crew*, "New York State League Team Rosters and Statistics"[a]; *Stats Crew*, "Geneva Franchise History (1906–1907)"; "Geneva, NY," *Bullpen*; "Border League," *Bullpen*; *Evening Sun*, June 1, 1910.

STOCO PARK/SHURON PARK/MCDONOUGH PARK

Location: Lyceum Street at Nursery Avenue

Dimensions: left 315', center 370', right 305'

Home Team(s): Geneva Red Wings, Red Birds, and Robins/Border League; and Geneva Redlegs, Senators, Pirates, Rangers, Twins, and Cubs/New York-Penn League

Built/In Operation: 1919 through 1920/1947 through 1951, 1958 through 1973, and 1977 through 1993

Seats/Capacity: 2,300 to 3,500

Fun Facts: During the winter of 1918–1919, Geneva's Standard Optical Company (STOCO) fielded an indoor baseball team and took the city

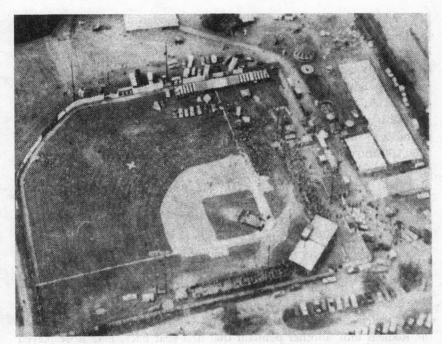

Aerial photograph of Shuron Park. From the *Democrat and Chronicle*, May 31, 1965.

title. This inspired Standard's semiprofessional squad to move outside for their 1919 schedule, when they won the pennant in the local industrial league. For the following three outdoor seasons, Standard Optical joined forces with their neighbor United States Lens to field a team under the moniker of STOCO Lens. This amalgamation played at the ballpark built by Standard Optical named STOCO Park. The original facility featured a covered grandstand seating 800, with another 800 accommodated in bleachers along the first and third baselines. Parking was available beside each stand. In 1923, the ballpark hosted an independent Geneva team, and the following year, the semipros played the Brooklyn (Colored) Giants.

In 1925, Standard Optical became Shur-On Standard Optical Company, and the name of the ballpark was altered to Shuron Park to reflect that change. At end of July 1925, the wooden bleachers collapsed, prompting a fundraising campaign to build new ones out of concrete.

From 1925 until 1928, amateur and industrial baseball was played at the park. That last season, Geneva played the Rochester Cuban Giants (Negro Leagues).

After the 1928 season, with Shur-On Standard loaning the field for local high school football, the company proposed that the city rent (for one dollar) as well as maintain the facility. This proved amenable, and Geneva added lights for night games in 1930. Amateur sports called Shuron Park home through World War II.

In 1947, professional baseball returned when the Red Sox franchise in Granby, Quebec, was moved to Geneva. The Red Wings requested upgrades to Shuron from the city, including $16,000 worth of lights (almost $200,000 today), a wooden fence costing $3,000 ($36,000), as well as a covered steel grandstand and baseline bleachers for $13,000 (currently $156,000). Rain delayed construction, so, even at the end of May, much of the outfield enclosure was constructed out of temporary snow fencing and the clubhouse was also unfinished.

In 1948, Geneva became an affiliate of the Brooklyn Dodgers. The Robins took the Border League championship that year. After the Dodgers left, the city was without a professional team until 1958, when the Cincinnati Reds' Hornell franchise was moved to Geneva. The municipality gave Cincinnati free use of Shuron Park, reconditioning the facility in time for the start of the season. Geneva and the Reds were rewarded when the Redlegs took another pennant that first year back. Pete Rose played for Geneva during 1960, but, even so, the squad slipped into last place. For 1961, a new fence was installed at the park, along with an enlarged clubhouse and new front entrance. The last year Geneva hosted Cincinnati, 1962, the Redlegs were once again in the cellar at the end of the season.

From 1963 to 1968, the Washington Senators controlled the Geneva association. Drainage problems caused by misguided field alterations haunted the diamond during these years, impeding play and leading to other issues. The Senators were succeeded by the Pirates, and, when Pittsburgh arrived, the current corporate owners of Shuron Park gifted it to the city. Then came (briefly) the Texas Rangers, and, in 1973, the Minnesota Twins, prompting new paint and lights for the stadium, along with an enlarged clubhouse. Similar upgrades occurred in 1977, the first year for the Geneva (Chicago) Cubs, at a cost to the city of $50,000–60,000 (the equivalent to $220,000–$265,000 today). At that time, Geneva rebranded the stadium McDonough Park in honor of the late Joseph McDonough, former chief of police and the team director since 1958.

Fifteen years passed before the next stadium refurbishment by Geneva. However, in 1991 and 1992, major league baseball began to require significant upgrades and improvements for all affiliated minor league ballparks. After investing $250,000 (about twice as much in today's dollars) for a new clubhouse and other repairs, the majors expected another $100,000–$200,000 expenditure the following year for new lights, bathrooms, and visitors' clubhouse. Since attendance had been poor, Geneva was unable to oblige. At the end of the 1993 season, professional baseball left Geneva for the last time.

FMI: John Pardon and Jerry Jackson, "New York State Ball Clubs," in Puff, *The Empire State of Base Ball*; *Stats Crew*, "New York State League Team Rosters and Statistics"[a]; *Stats Crew*, "Geneva Franchise History (1906–1907)"; "Genevan, NY," *Bullpen*; "Border League," *Bullpen*; Walsh and Murphy, *The Fields of New York*; Benson, *Ballparks of North America*; "New State League to Open Tomorrow," *Press and Sun-Bulletin*, May 13, 1921; "Baseball and Geneva," *Democrat and Chronicle*, October 7, 1993; "Geneva Ballpark Shows Off Recent Facelift," *Democrat and Chronicle*, June 24, 1992; "Red Wings Ask Park Equipment," *Post-Standard*, April 5, 1947; "Geneva Waits May 16 Debut," *Democrat and Chronicle*, May 3, 1947; "Baseball and Geneva," *Democrat and Chronicle*, October 7, 1993; *Ithaca Journal*, June 26, 1991.

GOUVERNEUR

UNKNOWN NAME

Location: unknown

Dimensions: unknown

Home Team(s): Gouverneur/Northern New York League

Built/In Operation: 1900

Seats/Capacity: unknown

Fun Facts: unknown

FMI: "1900 Northern New York League," *Baseball Reference*.

ILION

CHISMORE DRIVING PARK

Location: the west side of Central Avenue (then named Railroad Street)

Dimensions: unknown

This historic image from 1890 shows the racetrack and grandstand used for harness racing at Chismore Driving Park. Courtesy the Ilion Free Public Library.

Home Team(s): Ilion Independents; and Ilion Riflemen and Ilionites/ Empire State League

Built/In Operation: 1889/1898 and 1905. Sometime between 1906 and 1909, Chismore was converted to an industrial site and homesteads.

Seats/Capacity: unknown

Fun Facts: Ilion baseball dates to the Clippers. Organized in 1869, this first uniformed club competed against touring major league teams. Sporting goods mogul Al Spaulding, when still a player, pitched against Ilion. In 1905, the Riflemen played at Chismore.

FMI: John Pardon and Jerry Jackson, "New York State Ball Clubs," in Puff, *The Empire State of Base Ball*; Keetz, *"Doff Your Caps to the Champions!"*; Messenger, "Ilion Is Remington and Remington Is Ilion"; "Ilion Recreation and Sports"; Ilion Free Public Library, "Chismore Pk. View from N. Ilion"; "New Trotting Circuit," *Democrat and Chronicle*, July 14, 1895.

TYPEWRITER FIELD

Ilion Is Remington and Remington Is Ilion.

—local saying

The park was laid out about 1900 with a screened, covered grandstand, [and] bleachers along the first and third base lines.

—Ernest Sitts, "Ilion Park 'Comeback,'"

Location: Between East River Road and the railroad tracks

Dimensions: unknown

Home Team(s): Ilion Typewriters/New York State League; and Ilion Riflemen and Ilionites/Empire State League

Built/In Operation: 1900/1901 through 1905.

Seats/Capacity: unknown

Fun Facts: This short-lived New York State League franchise was named for the Remington company, who, along with firearms, sewing machines, and bicycles, produced the first commercial typewriters in Ilion.

In 1901, Ilion had a difficult time procuring players for their State League organization. After 13 different managers, the team stabilized, finishing the 1902–1904 schedules second in the standings. After the 1904 season, their New York State League franchise transferred to Wilkes-Barre, Pennsylvania, and Ilion joined the Empire State League. Unfortunately, that league also moved Ilion's team, this time, in July of 1905, to Fulton.

Typewriter Field in about 1916. Courtesy the Ilion Free Public Library.

Following the exit of professional ball, Remington was used for travel squads such as the Bloomer Girls and the House of David. From 1921 to 1930, the locals played in the Sunset League. With the decline in baseball interest during the 1930s, the grandstands were torn down, and the field was utilized as a landfill by the factory. The ballpark came back into use in 1953, with the facility being restored for youth baseball, with new bleachers, back stop, scoreboard, dugouts, and fencing.

FMI: John Pardon and Jerry Jackson, "New York State Ball Clubs," in Puff, *The Empire State of Base Ball*; Keetz, *"Doff Your Caps to The Champions!"*; Messenger, "Ilion Is Remington and Remington Is Ilion"; "Ilion Recreation and Sports"; "Search for Ilion Parks Underway in 1880," *Evening Telegram*, January 11, 1966; Ernest Sitts, "Ilion Park 'Comeback,'" unknown newspaper, June 13, 1954, from Ilion Public Library; *New Century Atlas of Herkimer County, New York.*

ITHACA

DRIVING PARK

Location: unknown

Dimensions: unknown

Home Team(s): Ithaca Ithacas

Built/In Operation: 1876

Seats/Capacity: unknown

Fun Facts: Driving Park was utilized for a variety of sports, including horse racing and college baseball. The park was still in use during 1901.

FMI: W. Lloyd Johnson, "John Clapp and Club Base Ball in Ithaca," in Puff, *The Empire State of Base Ball.*

LITTLE FALLS

RIVERSIDE PARK

Location: Carden's Flats, bordered by the Mohawk River to the south, the railroad tracks and Herkimer Road to the north

Dimensions: unknown

Home Team(s): Little Falls/Central New York League

Built/In Operation: 1886

Seats/Capacity: 1,000

Fun Facts: Amateur baseball in Little Falls flourished from 1867 until the 1880s, with teams such as Rough & Readys, the Pastimes, the Excelsiors, the Alerts, and the Rocktons utilizing for grounds the Petrie farm on the Eatonville Road (todays Route 169), Casler's Flats (Southern Avenue), the hill behind Furnace Street (Skinner's Flats), and Eastern Park.

In 1886, three local businessmen—Frank Burgor, Horace Tozer, and Stuart Devendorf—formed a "base ball association" in order to (finally) bring professional ball to Little Falls. Amateur players themselves, the trio sold shares in the franchise to raise the necessary funds to build a field and assemble personnel. An invitation from the Central New York League cemented the deal and plans moved forward. On a six-acre plot, Riverside Park, with a diamond, grandstand, and 1,700 feet of board fencing, was quickly erected.

Unfortunately, the Little Falls team only lasted for this one season. Although Riverside Park continued to be used for amateur ball, professional baseball wouldn't return for another 90 years.

FMI: Krutz, "Early Baseball in Little Falls and the Little Falls Baseball Association."

VETERANS MEMORIAL PARK

If I ever saw a jewel, it's Little Falls.

—"the president of the New York-Penn League," quoted on City of Little Falls website

This playing surface is superior to Yankee Stadium and Shea Stadium. It is the best in New York State.

—"a former National League batting champion," quoted on City of Little Falls website

Location: Burwell and Ray Streets

Dimensions: left 373'

Home Team(s): Little Falls Mets/New York-Penn League; and Mohawk Valley Landsharks/Northeast League

Built/In Operation: 1949/1977 through 1988 and 1995

Seats/Capacity: 2,000

Fun Facts: Veterans Memorial Park is typical of the small "bare bones" ballparks doting rural New York State, where a flat space large enough for a ballfield can be hard to find. The first and third baseline bleachers afford scenic mountain views, and the right field scoreboard sits in a grove of trees.

The longest-lived professional squad in Little Falls was affiliated with the New York Mets. Not a particularly strong franchise, they had their moment of glory in 1984, when they won the New York-Penn League championship. That group of players included future major leaguers Rick Aguilera, Wally Backman, Billy Beane, Kevin Elster, Dwight Gooden, and Todd Hundley. In 1988, the Mets moved the team to Pittsfield, Massachusetts. First, they were replaced in 1995 by the Landsharks, and then a collegiate summer wooden bat association team, the Mohawk Valley Diamond Dawgs.

FMI: O'Reilly, *Charlie's Big Baseball Parks Page*; *digitalballparks.com* on Veterans Park; Perfect Game Collegiate Baseball League, "Ballparks of the PGCBL: Shuttleworth Park"; City of Little Falls, "Veterans Memorial Park."

LYONS

UNKNOWN NAME

Location: unknown

Dimensions: unknown

Home Team(s): Lyons/New York State League; and Faatz's Fancies/Empire State League

Built/In Operation: 1897 through 1898, 1905, and 1907

Seats/Capacity: unknown

Fun Facts: In 1898, the Lyons franchise disbanded before the end of the season. Faatz's Fancies (named for former pro first baseman Jayson S.

"Jay" Faatz, who managed Lyons in 1905) lost at home to the Cuban Stars (Negro Leagues) in May of 1907.

FMI: John Pardon, and Jerry Jackson, "New York State Ball Clubs," in Puff, *The Empire State of Base Ball*; "New York State League," *Bullpen*; *Stats Crew*, "Lyons Franchise History (1897–1907)"; Nemec, "Jay Faatz."

MALONE

UNKNOWN NAME

Location: unknown

Dimensions: unknown

Home Team(s): Malone/Northeastern League; and Malone/Eastern International League

Built/In Operation: 1887 and 1896

Seats/Capacity: unknown

Fun Facts: unknown

FMI: unknown

FRANKLIN COUNTY FAIR GROUNDS

Location: unknown

Dimensions: unknown

Home Team(s): Malone Hop Pickers/Northern New York League

Built/In Operation: 1900 through 1902

Seats/Capacity: 2,500

Fun Facts: The earliest newspaper reference to the Franklin County Fair Grounds was in 1883. Initially, the Fair Grounds hosted horse racing on a track viewed from a grandstand. Before professional baseball arrived in 1900, a supplement to the south end of the stand added 52 feet. At the same time, the roof from 1883 was covered with tin.

In 1900, the Malone Hop Pickers joined the Northern New York League, a localized confederation that included, along with Malone, teams from Potsdam, Ogdensburg, and Gouverneur. In July, the Malone nine beat the touring Cuban Giants (Negro Leagues) in eleven innings, going on to take the league championship for that season.

After a new, double-decker grandstand was erected in July of 1901, Malone played their 23 game league schedule against Ogdensburg, Potsdam, Canton, and Plattsburgh. For their final season in 1902, the Hop Pickers contested with Plattsburgh, St. Albans, and Potsdam. It was a miserable year, with poor attendance leading to disintegrating finances. Luckily, the team survived reorganization at the end of August and won a second Northern League pennant.

FMI: John Pardon and Jerry Jackson, "New York State Ball Clubs," in Puff, *The Empire State of Base Ball*; *Stats Crew*, "Malone Franchise History (1887–1902)"; "Malone Winner," *Burlington Free Press*, July 24, 1901; "Northern New York League," *Buffalo Commercial*, February 16, 1900; *Star-Gazette*, September 26, 1902; *Burlington Free Press*, July 26, 1900; *Malone Farmer*, July 25, 1900; *Chateaugay Journal*, April 11, 1901; *Malone Farmer*, July 16, 1902; *Malone Palladium*, August 21, 1902; *Malone Farmer*, September 12, 1900; *Chateaugay Journal*, July 25, 1901; *Franklin Gazette*, April 2, 1886.

MASSENA

ALCOA FIELD

Location: Bishop Avenue

Dimensions: unknown

Home Team(s): Massena Grays/Can-Am League; and Massena Alcoas/ Northern League

Built/In Operation: 1916/1936, and 1940 through 1941

Seats/Capacity: unknown

Fun Facts: This facility was built by the local branch of Alcoa (the Aluminum Company of America). It boasted a covered grandstand and (no surprise here) a set of bleachers made from aluminum.

In the 1920s, the local nine played barnstorming major leaguers here. The later Alcoas franchise was moved to Massena from Watertown. In 1961, Alcoa Field was gifted by the Aluminum Company to the town.

FMI: Pietrusza, *Baseball's Canadian-American League*; "Canadian-American League (1936–1951)," *Fun While It Lasted*; *Post-Standard*, January 18 and March 15, 1961.

NEWARK

COLBURN PARK

Location: 1160 East Union Street

Dimensions: left 310–30', center 375–90', right 293–360'

Home Team(s): Newark Co-Pilots and Orioles/New York-Penn League; and Newark Barge Bandits/North Atlantic League

Built/In Operation: 1938/1968 through 1979, 1983 through 1987, and 1995 through 1996

Seats/Capacity: 1,200 to 3,000

Fun Facts: According to mayor Arthur Christy, this area close to the Erie Canal was dubbed Colburn Park in 1913 after another local politician, E. Douglass Colburn. The baseball facility was built by the WPA (Works Progress Administration of the New Deal) in the spring of 1938. The resulting ballpark, which scholar David Pietrusza labels as "tiny," boasted wooden bleacher seats along both baselines, with a picturesque view over the green outfield fence of traffic on the canal. The press box was located to the right of home plate.

Even though Colburn Park was built in the 1930s, it did not house professional baseball until the late 1960s. By that time, to draw an affiliation with a major league franchise, the park needed a concrete block clubhouse with locker rooms for the players (added in left field), dugouts, additional lights, and a larger diamond. In 1966 and 1967, to raise money for improvements and to attract an alliance with the majors, the locals sponsored professional contests for the paying public. The resulting upgrades brought the Seattle Pilots to Newark, an affiliation that remained even after the Pilots left Seattle and became the Milwaukee Brewers in 1970.

In 1971, Colburn Park was painted and a manager's office added along the third base line, along with a new box office and concession stand. For 1978, better visibility for the fielders was encouraged by rotating the field. The foul lines were extended, but, strangely, contracted again five years later.

The 1975 season was the Co-Pilots best, with a pennant and a league championship. Three years later, Milwaukee pulled out, and the Co-Pilots attempted one unaffiliated schedule before folding at the end of 1979. Professional baseball returned to Coburn in 1983 with the Baltimore Orioles, lasting through 1987, when the O's moved the franchise to Erie,

Pennsylvania. At that time, the field was just too old and funky for even minor league ball.

Again, money seemed to be the issue. Luckily, the city ponied up around $80,000 ($140,000 today) to repair the fencing and bleachers, add seating, enlarge the clubhouse, concessions, and office, and improve the public address system. Fences were again moved back; I guess someone thought all this adjusting would help the players!

Newark's new affiliation was with the independent North Atlantic League. All the team needed was a nickname. So, when a fan suggested "Barge Bandits" for the nearby Erie Canal, the moniker stuck. After two years, professional ball made its final exit from Newark. Today, Coburn Park hosts the summer collegiate wooden bat team, the Newark Pilots.

FMI: O'Reilly, *Charlie's Big Baseball Parks Page*; David Pietrusza, "Upstate New York's Ballparks," in Puff, *The Empire State of Base Ball*; Perfect Game Collegiate Baseball League, "Ballparks of the PGCBL: Colburn Park"; Benson, *Ballparks of North America*; "4 at Newark Honored For Village Service," *Democrat and Chronicle*, May 2, 1959; "WPA Project Begins Today," *Democrat and Chronicle*, April 2, 1937; "WPA to Build New Roadway, Ball Diamond," *Democrat and Chronicle*, January 29, 1938; Charley Ross, "Newark Eyes June 22 Start for New Entry in Class A," "Realignment Plans Shelved at Newark Baseball Park," and "Colburn Park Refurbished for Co-Pilots Home Opener," *Democrat and Chronicle*, May 7 and 20, and June 2, 1968.

OGDENSBURG

RIVERSIDE PARK/MORISSETTE PARK

Location: Riverside Avenue

Dimensions: unknown

Home Team(s): Ogdensburg/Northern New York League; and Ogdensburg/ Empire State League

Built/In Operation: 1895/1900 through 1901, and 1908

Seats/Capacity: unknown

Fun Facts: unknown

FMI: John Pardon and Jerry Jackson, "New York State Ball Clubs," in Puff, *The Empire State of Base Ball*; Baxter and Boyesen, *Historic Ogdensburg*.

WINTER PARK/FATHER MARTIN FIELD

Location: Hasbrouck and Patterson Streets

Dimensions: left 260', center 450', right 386'

Home Team(s): Ogdensburg Colts/Can-Am League; Ottawa and Ogdensburg Senators/Can-Am League; and Ogdensburg Maples/Border League

Built/In Operation: 1936/1936 through 1940, and 1946 through 1951. Lights and grandstands have been removed; the diamond remains.

Seats/Capacity: 1,800 to 3,000

Fun Facts: When one discusses Ogdensburg's sporting history, the name Father Harold J. Martin is unavoidable. Without Father Martin, professional baseball in New York's northern tier wouldn't have been as widespread, nor as important, as it was in the 1930s and 1940s.

Harold Martin, like many of his ilk, played ball as a youth, pitching for Fordham University between 1915 and 1920. A few years later, Father Martin helped organize the semiprofessional Ogdensburg nine of the Northern New York League for whom Martin participated between 1923 and 1935. Lastly, Martin had a short minor league career that helped finance his way through the seminary.

In 1936, assigned by the parish to Ogdensburg, Father Martin developed the Winter Recreation Center, adding a low-fenced baseball diamond, minimally covered grandstand, and clubhouse on the site of a former skating rink. Martin ran the Colts franchise of the Canadian-American League, ascending to head the league in 1937. In 1939, the parish granted the city and the Ogdensburg Colts-Senators a free lease on the park. An affiliation with the Philadelphia Phillies followed in 1940.

After the suspension of Ogdensburg baseball during World War II, Father Martin helped to form the Border League. An attachment by Ogdensburg to the New York Giants brought the Maples three league championships between 1948 and 1950. Lights had been installed in 1946 by the Syracuse firm of Bradley and Williams at a cost of $17,500. Unfortunately, six years later, the league went under, and the lights were sold. Seven years after the loss of pro ball, the hero of the local minor leagues, Father Harold Martin, passed away at the age of sixty-two.

FMI: *Stats Crew*, "Winter Park"; David Pietrusza, "Upstate New York's Ballparks," in Puff, *The Empire State of Base Ball*; Pietrusza, *Baseball's Cana-*

dian-American League; "Border League," Bullpen; "Teaching Baseball Priest's Hobby," Ithaca Journal, December 22, 1936; "Priest Repays Debt to Game Guiding League," Brooklyn Daily Eagle, November 7, 1937; "Ogdensburg to Continue Franchise in Can-Am," Post-Star, January 31, 1939; "Border Loop Prepares to Quit," Post-Standard, July 16, 1951; Daily News, May 9, 1958.

ONEIDA

UNKNOWN NAME

Location: unknown

Dimensions: unknown

Home Team(s): Oneida Oneidas and Indians/Central New York League; and Oneida/New York State League

Built/In Operation: 1886, 1889, and 1894

Seats/Capacity: unknown

Fun Facts: Oneida was leading the Central League at the end of August 1886. For both State League seasons, the league pulled the plug in July. There would be no professional baseball in Oneida again until 1889. That year, with attendance dwindling, the team played some of the time at **Sylvan Beach**.

FMI: "1894 New York State League," Baseball Reference; Buffalo Times, August 25, 1886.

CITIZENS PARK

Location: unknown

Dimensions: unknown

Home Team(s): Oneida/Empire State League

Built/In Operation: 1904/1905, 1908, and 1910. The grandstand burned in September of 1912.

Seats/Capacity: 1,200

Fun Facts: Citizens Park was a privately held facility built for horse racing and previously used for football. In discussing the park, the Post-Standard commented that it "is about the only place in this city where the game [of baseball] could be played and an admission charged, as the grounds are fenced in and contain a good grandstand."

FMI: John Pardon and Jerry Jackson, "New York State Ball Clubs," in Puff, *The Empire State of Base Ball*; "Oneida Meets Norwich To-Day in First Game," *Post-Standard*, May 14, 1910; "Would Enter Empire League," *Post-Standard*, January 29, 1907; "Citizen Park Grand Stands Fired by Tramps," *Press and Sun-Bulletin*.

OSWEGO

EAST PARK (FREE ADMISSION)/
ORPHAN ASYLUM HILL (PAID ADMISSION)

Location: unknown

Dimensions: unknown

Home Team(s): Oswego Ontarios

Built/In Operation: 1859, 1864 through 1867, and 1869 through 1870

Seats/Capacity: unknown

Fun Facts: Baseball in Oswego dates to 1859's Frontier Club. The Ontarios, who succeeded the Frontiers, utilized East Park for free-to-the-public contests. Orphan Asylum Hill, because it was fenced and facilitated collecting admission fees, was utilized for games against visiting professional squads that required payment to play. Those in the latter category included the Brooklyn Eckfords (1869), Washington Olympics, Chicago White Stockings, and Cincinnati Red Stockings (all in 1870).

FMI: Peter Morris, "Ontarios of Oswego," in Morris et al., *Base Ball Pioneers, 1850–1870*.

RICHARDSON FIELD/PARK

Location: unknown

Dimensions: unknown

Home Team(s): Oswego Sweegs/New York State League; Oswego Starchboxes/International League and Eastern International League and Association; Oswego Oswegos, Grays, and Starchmakers/New York State League;

and Oswego Starchmakers/Empire State League and Central New York League

Built/In Operation: 1885 through 1888, 1898 through 1900, 1905 through 1907, and 1910. Demolished and replaced with a county garage.

Seats/Capacity: 650

Fun Facts: Richardson Field was possibly named for attorney, real estate developer and Oswego mayor Maxwell Richardson. As Oswego was known for their local laundry and corn starch industry, it's no surprise that the city's baseball nicknames often include references to those products.

As with many smaller municipalities and leagues, Oswego's seasons were often truncated when finances evaporated. In 1887, the team disbanded on May 31 and, for 1899, they went bust by mid-July, although (somehow) the nine finished the season. Oswego's franchise was transferred to Elmira at the end of July 1900. In 1910, it was the Central New York League that went kaput, on June 1.

FMI: John Pardon and Jerry Jackson, "New York State Ball Clubs," in Puff, *The Empire State of Base Ball*; David Pietrusza, "Upstate New York's Ballparks," in Puff, *The Empire State of Base Ball*; Pietrusza, *Baseball's Canadian-American League*; *Stats Crew*, "Richardson Park"; "History" [Richardson-Bates House]; William G. Pomeroy Foundation, Richardson background; McCarthy, *Rochester Diamond Echoes*; Perfect Game Collegiate Baseball League, "Ballparks of the PGCBL: Damaschke Field"; *Stats Crew*, "New York State League Team Rosters and Statistics"[a]; *Stats Crew*, "1888 Eastern International League"; *Stats Crew*, "New York State League Team Rosters and Statistics"[b]; *Dunkirk Evening Observer*, September 15, 1885; *Democrat and Chronicle*, May 14, 1887; *New York Times*, June 1, 1887; *Star-Gazette*, July 17, 1899, January 23, 1900; "Richardson Park Goes to Billy Patterson," *Post-Standard*, May 10, 1910; *Evening Sun*, June 1, 1910; *Post-Standard*, June 3, 1910.

OTIS FIELD

Location: the end of West Oneida Street

Dimensions: left 550–354', center 585–491', right 428–347'

Home Team(s): Oswego Netherlands/Can-Am League

Built/In Operation: 1931 through 1932/1936 through 1940. Demolished after the 1955 amateur season and replaced with Frederick Leighton Elementary School.

Seats/Capacity: 2,000 to 3,000

Fun Facts: Otis Field was named for mayor John Otis and erected on the former site of the Oswego city dump, which would inadvertently lead to sinkage issues. The team's name was derived from the local Netherlands Milk and Ice Cream Company.

With the arrival of professional baseball, stands and fences were added. However, the diamond stayed with a grass covering. Lights, installed in 1936, were ruled inadequate, and sold in 1939.

The Netherlands had agreements in place during their prewar run in the Can-Am League with the Cleveland Indians as well as the Washington Senators. After the 1940 season, the team was sold and moved to Massachusetts. As the ballpark stood empty, local stories tell of the illegal dismantlement of the outfield fences for firewood by Oswego residents.

FMI: David Pietrusza, "Upstate New York's Ballparks," in Puff, *The Empire State of Base Ball*; John Pardon and Jerry Jackson, "New York State Ball Clubs," in Puff, *The Empire State of Base Ball*; Pietrusza, *Baseball's Canadian-American League*; Benson, *Ballparks of North America*; Stats Crew, "Otis Field."

PALMYRA

PAL-MAC AQUEDUCT COUNTY PARK

Location: 555 West Main Street

Dimensions: unknown

Home Team(s): Palmyra Mormons/New York State League and Empire State League

Built/In Operation: 1897 through 1898, and 1905

Seats/Capacity: unknown

Fun Facts: Palmyra's New York State team won the pennant in 1897, but disbanded in late July the following year and moved to Johnstown. For 1905, the Mormons relocated to Geneva.

FMI: John Pardon and Jerry Jackson, "New York State Ball Clubs," in Puff, *The Empire State of Base Ball*; "Palmyra Clinches Pennant," *Buffalo Courier*, September 11, 1897; "Johnstown Is in State League Circuit," *Democrat and Chronicle*, August 4, 1898.

PENN YAN

YATES COUNTY FAIRGROUNDS

Location: Monell and Lake Streets

Dimensions: unknown

Home Team(s): Penn Yan/Central New York State League; Penn Yan Grape Pickers/Southern Tier Association; Penn Yan/Empire State League; Penn Yan Cuban Giants (Negro Leagues, semiprofessional); and Penn Yan Colored Giants (semiprofessional)

Built/In Operation: 1871/1888, 1904, 1906, and 1924 through 1925. The grandstand was sold in August of 1952, and the site eventually became the Lake Street Plaza Shopping Center.

Seats/Capacity: unknown

Fun Facts: In 1871, the County Agricultural Society acquired what became the fairgrounds, grading a horse racing course enclosed with a fence. Several abortive attempts at professional baseball followed, including with the Southern Tier Association of 1904 and, two years later, in the Empire State League.

The proudest years for Penn Yan occurred in 1924 and 1925, the two seasons for local semiprofessional Black baseball. Because of the fierce competition for fans in the New York Metropolitan area, the Cuban Giants of Brooklyn relocated to town in June of 1924. It needs to be mentioned that the Giants took the "Cubans" name because associating players with the Caribbean seemed to reduce the number of racist tropes directed at the team. Earlier versions of the Giants had barnstormed New York State, previously playing Penn Yan teams at this facility. Home games occurred on Thursday and Saturday afternoons on a diamond relocated in front of the grandstand. Unfortunately, the local public refused to support the squad, the only crowds occurring during the county fair and a visit by the International League's Toronto Maple Leafs in September.

Nevertheless, the Cuban Giants were planning to return for the 1925 season. However, a rival squad, the Penn Yan Colored Giants, formed that winter. After a defection of their core players, the Cuban Giants decided to move their home base to Cumberland, Maryland. The Penn Yan Giants played one season and then disbanded.

FMI: John Pardon and Jerry Jackson, "New York State Ball Clubs," in Puff, *The Empire State of Base Ball*; *Stats Crew*, "1898 New York State League"; *Stats Crew*, "No Known Name"; *Stats Crew*, "Penn Yan Franchise History (1888–1906)"; MacAlpine, "The Penn Yan Cuban Giants (1924)"; MacAlpine, "The Penn Yan Colored Giants (the 1925 Season)"; "Yates County Fair—Once Attracted Carrie Nation and Billy Sunday"; "Yates County Fair"; "Sale of Familiar Site Ends Cycle in Yates Fair History," *Chronicle-Express*, July 17, 1952; "Grape Pickers Beat Locals," *Star-Gazette*, June 25, 1904.

POTSDAM

UNKNOWN NAME

Location: unknown

Dimensions: unknown

Home Team(s): Zouave Baseball Club; and Potsdam/Northern New York League

Built/In Operation: ca. 1865, and 1900 through 1902

Seats/Capacity: unknown

Fun Facts: unknown

FMI: John Pardon and Jerry Jackson, "New York State Ball Clubs," in Puff, *The Empire State of Base Ball*.

ROCHESTER

BROWN'S SQUARE, UNIVERSITY GROUNDS, FRANKLIN SQUARE

Location: unknown

Dimensions: unknown

Home Team(s)s: Flour City Club and Live Oak Club

Built/In Operation: 1858

Seats/Capacity: unknown

Fun Facts: Author Scott Pitoniak quotes *Big Leagues* by Stephen Fox as dating Rochester baseball to 1825. The sport continued as an amateur pursuit, with teams organizing around locale, vocation, religion, and race.

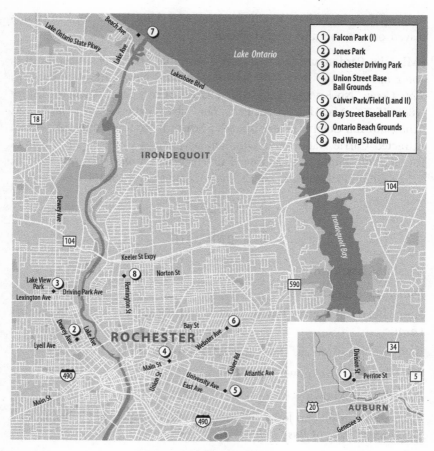

Map 7. Rochester Ballparks.

Early African-American players from Rochester included the namesake son of Abolitionist Frederick Douglass, Jr. According to Mandelaro and Pitoniak, a local newspaper estimated in 1858 that there could be as many as 1,000 baseball aggregations in the greater metropolitan area.

Among those was the Flour City Club, playing the first game reported in the local press in June of 1858, in a meadow later chosen for the new university campus. Along with Brown's Square, which was designated by the city during August for baseball play, the University Grounds continued to be utilized during the remainder of 1858.

Another union founded within the wave toward the professional game was the Live Oak Club, whose games were governed by the "New

York rules." Their first match against another team was with Flour City at the University Grounds. Live Oak was honored with the second piece of music inspired by baseball, "The Live Oak Polka," the first having been dedicated to Flour City.

Other "playing grounds" located within Rochester City were Franklin Square and the **Babbitt Tract**, the later located at the corner of High and Troup Streets. By the way, none of these public spaces had officially marked fields, nor, it goes without saying, any special amenities such as clubhouses with dressing rooms, seating for viewers, nor concessions of any kind.

As far back as the founding of the Live Oaks, local pundits took a dim view of sporting events being held on Sundays. In a May 1858 edition of the *Union and Advertiser*, an unknown journalist reported large numbers of community males playing baseball on the day of rest, which they justified by staging these contests just outside of the city limits. "What a narrow view some people take of infinity," remarked this author.

Whether using open spaces within a cityscape or claiming an unused field for play, early baseball required at least a minimum of facility development. The grounds needed leveling and any foreign objects hazardous to players had to be removed. A set of bases—canvas sacks painted white and initially filled with sand and, later, sawdust or horse hair—were required. Eventually, a set of foul line markers in the form of posts, were introduced locally.

One of the strangest grounds used for baseball was the surface of Irondequoit Bay. Frozen solid in the coldest part of the winter, at least two contests on its ice are documented in the run-up to the Civil War.

FMI: Bielewicz, *Hallowed Grounds: The Baseball Grounds of Rochester*; Pitoniak, *Baseball in Rochester*; Brancato, "Researching Rochester's Live Oak Baseball Club of the 19th Century"; Rochester Baseball Historical Society, "Research Projects"; Astifan, "The Dawn of Acknowledged Professionalism and Its Impact on Rochester Baseball"; Astifan, "Rochester's Last Two Seasons of Amateur Baseball"; Mandelaro and Pitoniak, Scott. *Silver Seasons*; Priscilla Astifan, "Clubs of Rochester," in Morris et al., *Base Ball Pioneers, 1860–1870*.

BABBITT TRACT

Location: the corner of High and Troup Streets
Dimensions: unknown
Home Team(s): Live Oak and Flour City

Built/In Operation: 1857/1859 and 1860

Seats/Capacity: unknown

Fun Facts: Other "playing grounds" located within Rochester City included the Babbitt Tract, located at the corner of High and Troup Streets. This 10-acre lot became the "field of choice" for local baseball during 1859.

One of the first road trips by a squad of players took the Brooklyn Excelsiors across New York State in the summer of 1860. First visiting Buffalo, the Excelsiors then journeyed to Rochester and defeated both the Flour City and Live Oak squads.

FMI: Bielewicz, *Hallowed Grounds: The Baseball Grounds of Rochester*; Pitoniak, *Baseball in Rochester*; Brancato, "Researching Rochester's Live Oak Baseball Club of the 19th Century"; Rochester Baseball Historical Society, "Research Projects"; Astifan, "The Dawn of Acknowledged Professionalism and Its Impact on Rochester Baseball"; Astifan, "Rochester's Last Two Seasons of Amateur Baseball"; Mandelaro and Pitoniak, *Silver Seasons*; Priscilla Astifan, "Clubs of Rochester," in Morris et al., *Base Ball Pioneers, 1860–1870*.

JONES SQUARE (JONES SQUARE PARK)

Location: Jones Avenue (southeast), Saratoga Avenue (southwest), Lorimer Street (northwest), Plymouth Avenue North (northeast)

Dimensions: unknown

Home Team(s)s: Alerts Baseball Club and Lone Star Baseball Club
Built/In Operation: 1869, 1877, and 1890

Seats/Capacity: unknown

Fun Facts: During the State Fair, held in Rochester during September of 1864, a baseball contest was held at Jones Square. In this United States versus Canada game, the Atlantics of Brooklyn, not a squad of Rochester locals, represented the United States. By the way, the Atlantics beat the Canadian team handily.

After the Civil War, both Rochester and Niagara Falls could boast African-American organizations populated by local men. Frank Stewart organized the Unexpected in Rochester for the 1866 season, while Niagara Falls hosted the Lincoln. Eventually, Rochester would add other squads of African-American players, including the Hartfords, Summer Base Ball

Rochester's Jones Square, as shown on the sheet music for J. H. Kalbfleisch's "Live Oak Polka." 1860. From the Music Division, Library of Congress. https://www.loc.gov/item/2009541120/.

Club, Flyers, and the Slow Goers. There were also a few all-female squads playing around the state.

The Alerts had been using Jones Square and, for their season-opening game of 1869, the Rochester nine took on the Cincinnati Red Stockings. Cincinnati was the first team to openly embrace professionalism, acknowledging to the public that all their talent was paid to play. Also at this time, local squads such as the Alerts were touring throughout New York State, determined to improve their game by taking on similar teams from other locales. This arrangement was soon formalized with the establishment of leagues.

FMI: Bielewicz, *Hallowed Grounds: The Baseball Grounds of Rochester*; Pitoniak, *Baseball in Rochester*; Brancato, "Researching Rochester's Live Oak Baseball Club of the 19th Century"; Rochester Baseball Historical Society, "Research Projects"; Astifan, "The Dawn of Acknowledged Professionalism and Its Impact on Rochester Baseball"; Astifan, "Rochester's Last Two Seasons of Amateur Baseball"; Mandelaro and Pitoniak, *Silver*

Seasons; Priscilla Astifan, "Clubs of Rochester," in Morris et al., *Base Ball Pioneers, 1860–1870*.

MONROE COUNTY FAIRGROUNDS

Location: Brighton

Dimensions: unknown

Home Team(s): Live Oak; Flower City; and Rochesters

Built/In Operation: 1858, and 1870

Seats/Capacity: unknown

Fun Facts: In 1870, the Rochester City Council responded to calls from property owners and began limiting and, eventually, removing baseball from the various squares and public spaces around the municipality. Thereafter, the president of the Flower City club leased a field at the Fairgrounds, which the Live Oak Club had begun using for games as early as 1858. Starting that same year, the Agricultural Society started sponsoring an all-city baseball championship. Unfortunately, this site proved inconvenient for fans journeying from downtown Rochester, prompting the search for other venues.

During the post–Civil War period, a vacant lot known as the Commons at the back of City School Number 14 also served as a ballfield. Among the contests witnessed there included a game with a squad of locals taking on the Mutuals, a club of Black players from Washington, DC.

FMI: Astifan, "The Dawn of Acknowledged Professionalism and Its Impact on Rochester Baseball"; Priscilla Astifan, "Clubs of Rochester," in Morris et al., *Base Ball Pioneers, 1860–1870*.

ROCHESTER DRIVING PARK

Location: a race track "about one mile and three-quarters from the Court House, between Rochester and Lake Ontario." McCracken Street (now Driving Park Avenue), Dewey Avenue, Birr Street. and the Pennsylvania Central Railroad tracks.

Dimensions: unknown

Home Team(s): Rochester Rochesters

Built/In Operation: 1874/1875, and 1876. The last race was in 1895, and the grandstands burned in November 1899. The property was foreclosed on in the fall of 1902, and divided into building lots in February 1903.

Seats/Capacity: 6,000 to 10,000/20,000

Fun Facts: The structures for Rochester Driving Park were designed by commercial architect Charles Coots in collaboration with civil engineer Oscar H. Peacock (who supervised the new Poughkeepsie course as well). Coots, born in England, came to Rochester as a boy, where he was in business from 1869 to 1880. Oscar Henry Peacock, who was from Wayne County, New York, served as a "musician" during the Civil War. Peacock came to Rochester after the conflict, working for the city in a variety of positions, including "surveyor," today known as "city engineer."

Opened in 1874, the race track boasted all the amenities of a modern stadium. This included tiered grandstand seating, luxury boxes, press section, clubhouse, fencing, restaurants, wine rooms, and a hotel. "They are to be built in the ornamental Swiss style," wrote the *Democrat and Chronicle*. Baseball games were played on the "infield" within the actual racing track.

While the majority of the Rochesters' games in 1875 and 1876 were played at the Driving Park, conflicts inevitably occurred with race days. When baseball could not be scheduled, a limited number of contests were held on the field of the Western House of Refuge reformatory located south of the race track. Opened August 11, 1849, the Western House property fronted on Backus Street near the intersection with Phelps Avenue, now in Edgerton Park.

Notable professional teams faced by the Rochesters at home included the Philadelphia Athletics, the Chicago White Stockings, and St. Louis Brown Stockings of the National Association. Of course, the local squad also took on other teams from New York State and the surrounding region.

FMI: Astifan, "Rochester's Last Two Seasons of Amateur Baseball"; "Western House of Refuge," *Lost Rochester*; "Western House of Refuge," *RocWiki*; Morry, "Tonight There's Gonna Be a Jailbreak"; "The State Fair," *Democrat and Chronicle*, May 23, 1874; advertisement, *Democrat and Chronicle*, November 15, 1873, and October 26, 1874; "Horse Notes," *New York Daily Herald*, February 27, 1874; "Revival," *Democrat and Chronicle*, November 7, 2010.

UNION STREET BASE BALL GROUNDS/ HOP BITTERS BASE BALL GROUNDS

Location: Union Street North at Weld Street

Dimensions: unknown

Home Team(s): Rochester Rochesters/International Association; and Rochester Hop Bitters/National Association, International Association, and New York State League

Built/In Operation: 1877/1877 through 1880, and 1885. Demolished.

Seats/Capacity: unknown

Fun Facts: In 1868, Rochester baseball was allowed to charge admission for the first time, adopting a practice already used by teams in New York City. Events such as the formation of the National Association of Professional Base Ball Players in 1871 (which became the National League five years later) furthered the cause for paying players. These two events led to the first purpose-built enclosed area ballpark at Union and Weld.

The park served the new Rochesters, a group of pros recruited from around the United States to play the 1877 season in the equally new International League. The franchise only lasted for two years.

Replacing the Rochesters was the Hop Bitters. They were sponsored by Asa Soule, whose company marketed the namesake tonic claiming to cure a multitude of ailments. Soule supposedly required his ballplayers to use his preparation before games, one assumes in a (misguided?) effort to improve their play. According to the Philadelphia, Pennsylvania, *Times*, the Hop Bitters were directly descended from the Capital City Club of Albany, who moved to Rochester in May of 1879.

In the fall after the 1879 season, the Hop Bitters played their way out to San Francisco, and then, by boat, on to Cuba and New Orleans. The team finally returned by steamboat up the Mississippi River to Rochester. After a second season, this time as a member of the National Association, the club disbanded.

FMI: Bielewicz, *Hallowed Grounds: The Baseball Grounds of Rochester*; Astifan, "1877—Rochester's First Year of Professional Baseball"; McCarthy, *Rochester Diamond Echoes*; John Pardon and Jerry Jackson, "New York State Ball Clubs," in Puff, *The Empire State of Base Ball*; Mandelaro and Pitoniak, *Silver Seasons*; Benson, *Ballparks of North America*; *Buffalo Commercial*, November 26, 1878; *Times*, May 10, 1879.

CULVER PARK/FIELD (I + II)

Location: the northwest corner of University Avenue and Culver Road

Dimensions: unknown

Home Team(s): Hop Bitters/International League, International Association, American Association, and Eastern Association; and Rochester Bronchos and Beau Brummels/Eastern League

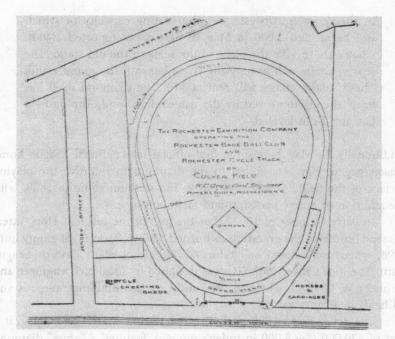

The plan for Culver Field (II), as shown in the Rochester *Democrat and Chronicle*, March 20, 1898.

Built/In Operation: 1886/1886 through 1892, and 1898 through 1907. Demolished. Culver is currently the industrial site for the Gleason Works, which was built at 1000 University Avenue in 1911.

Seats/Capacity: (I): 4,000/7,000; (II): 6,000/10,000

Fun Facts: Both Culver Park/Field (I+II) and Culver Road bear the name of this prominent local family. Scholar Paul J. Bielewicz describes the original Culver Park (I) as a rectangle oriented in a north/south manner. The primary Culver (I) contained grandstands with a press box below, accommodating two thousand spectators along the park's southern end on Culver Road. Each baseline featured bleachers holding 1,000 fans. Culver (I) was completed in the spring of 1886 between exhibition contests and the first league game on May 8.

The following year, the stadium was upgraded by architect Otto Block. Block, the son of an area contractor, mostly conceived local residences and commercial buildings. As described in the *Democrat and Chronicle* newspaper, the improvements included a grandstand extension:

to the fence northwest . . . , the seating capacity of which will be at least 1,000 [a May 10 newspaper reported 1,400]. Chairs are to take the place of the seats in the old stand. The season chairs will occupy the space beneath the grand stand. These season chairs will rent at $10. The diamond itself has been already improved by the use of dark sand. The outfield has also been leveled.

Additionally, in May, before the first official International League home season began, clay was added to the diamond to improve the playing surface of the field. Another refresh to the stadium came in 1888, with the addition of a new backstop and team entrance.

In early October of 1893, after the loss of the resident Hop Bitters baseball franchise, the grandstands burned. Culver Park (I) sat empty until 1898, when professional ball returned with Rochester's Eastern League team. The new Culver Park (II) was designed by local civil engineer and architect W. C. Gray, who had previously worked building railroads and oil fields in Pennsylvania.

The reimagined 1898 park, erected during March and April at a cost of $20,000 ($665,000 in today's money), featured a "grass" diamond and grandstands behind home plate, as well as bleachers along the first base side and a "cycling stand" along the third base line. Like **Riverside Park**, Culver (II) included a bicycle track, probably due to one of the new owners helming the American Bike Racing Association. A drawing of the new facility appeared in the *Democrat and Chronicle* on March 20, 1898.

On May 19, 1906, during the fifth inning of a home stand, the north end of the first base bleachers collapsed. A quarter of the seats gradually sank to the ground in somewhat of a chain reaction, resulting in 300 traumatized fans and 50 injuries. Even though the old bleachers were immediately removed, rebuilt, and enlarged, the ensuing lawsuits bankrupted the franchise, affectively ending their use of the Culver (II). At the end of 1906, Culver (II) was sold at auction. The final season of professional baseball at Culver (II) saw the 1907 Rochester Bronchos reduce the size of the outfield and add both a new scoreboard and two ticket offices.

The period that Rochester pro baseball called Culver Field (I+II) home was a rough and ready time for the game. Gambling was an everyday sight, and some franchises were even funded by monies from that pursuit. Brewery owners were also likely to invest in ballclubs. Of course, spectators and players alike could avail themselves of the beer sold at the ballpark that added appeal and profitability to local baseball. Therefore, it's not surprising that the 1887 Rochester squad earned the dubious distinction as the most intemperate drinkers in the league. Strangely enough, considering the laisse faire acceptance of drinking and wagering at games, players were forever getting suspended when caught gambling or drunk (or both).

Considering the commonality of player inebriation, overt on-the-field intimidation outweighed verbal taunts. The Bronchos specifically were infamous for spitting tobacco juice at umpires and players alike, and fistfights at their contests were a common occurrence.

FMI: *digitalballparks.com* on Bay Street Ball Grounds; Bielewicz, *Hallowed Grounds: The Baseball Grounds of Rochester*; Johnson, *Ballparks Database*; Pitoniak, *Baseball in Rochester*; McCarthy, *Rochester Diamond Echoes*; "New Name for Rochester Club," *Democrat and Chronicle*, February 16, 1909; Mandelaro and Pitoniak, *Silver Seasons*; "House for V. F. Whitmore"; "William C. Gray," *Biographies of Monroe County People*; Gleason Works, "This Is Our Story"; "Was Well Known Here as Architect," *Democrat and Chronicle*, October 20, 1921; "Grand Stand Gone," *Democrat and Chronicle*, October 9, 1893; "Section of Stand Falls at Baseball Park; Many Injured," *Democrat and Chronicle*, May 20, 1906; *Democrat and Chronicle*, March 28, 1888; "Changes at Culver Park," *Democrat and Chronicle*, March 4 and May 1, 1887.

WINDSOR BEACH BASE BALL GROUNDS

[Even] if the grounds there are put in proper condition and the grand stand moved to its proper place, no more fatal mistake could be made than playing a majority of the games so far away from the Four Corners [I believe meaning in town]. Every club in the association is opposed to playing its Rochester games there.

—"The Beach or Culver Park,"
Democrat and Chronicle, March 21, 1888

Location: near Lake Ontario; on the Rome, Watertown, and Ogdensburg Railroad (RW&O). Windsor Beach, Summerville neighborhood, Irondequoit.

Dimensions: unknown

Home Team(s): Rochesters; and Rochester Hop Bitters/International Association, American Association, and Eastern Association

Built/In Operation: 1885/1888 through 1892. Demolished.

Seats/Capacity: 3,000

Fun Facts: Windsor Beach was used for Sunday games to circumvent Rochester's "blue laws," which banned Sabbath play on public lands. Since Windsor Beach was privately held, the Sunday prohibition did not apply. Access from the city was guaranteed by streetcar lines linking downtown Rochester to the Beach, which had allowed amateur baseball to thrive there since as early as 1885. This raised the hopes of professional teams requiring a stress-free location for games on the only day that their fans were off work.

However, in June of 1890, an Irondequoit farmer claimed that baseball organizations had violated the *state* ordinance against "all fishing, playing public sport, exercise and shows" on Sundays. Even after players were arrested, charged, and released on bail, local residents continued to press their case. Later in the season, the Law and Order League of Irondequoit took over the field to prevent a game from proceeding. When spectators surrounded the protestors, violence seemed unavoidable. Manager Pat Powers brokered a compromise: the game would continue and the players would turn themselves in the following day. Unfortunately, a state judge supported the "Law and Order" side, and Sunday games were eventually suspended. This caused the team to be sold mid-season, and professional baseball temporarily exited Rochester.

FMI: Bielewicz, *Hallowed Grounds: The Baseball Grounds of Rochester*; Johnson, *Ballparks Database*; Bielewicz, *Hallowed Grounds: A Look at Rochester's Ballparks*; Astifan, "Baseball in the Nineteenth Century"; Astifan, "Baseball in the Nineteenth Century, Part Two"; John Pardon and Jerry Jackson, "New York State Ball Clubs," in Puff, *The Empire State of Base Ball*; Mandelaro and Pitoniak, *Silver Seasons*.

RIVERSIDE PARK

Location: North St. Paul Street near Norton Street, just outside the Rochester city limits in Irondequoit, about a half mile west of the eventual **Red Wing Stadium** site

Dimensions: unknown

Home Team(s): Rochester Brownies and Patriots/Eastern League

Built/In Operation: 1895/1895 through 1897. Demolished.

Seats/Capacity: 4,000/10,000

Fun Facts: In the lead-up to the 1895 season, William C. Gray (see **Culver Park [I+II]**) had been contracted to "lay out the grounds and erect the grand stand." Either his work was substandard or the workmen hired did not follow his directions, because a section of the stands collapsed before March of 1896. The replacement grandstand at the east end of the ballpark was designed by (Otto) Block and Barnes (see **Culver Park [I+II]**). At 265-feet long and 30-feet wide, Block and Barnes's structure seated 1,500, increasing Riverside's total capacity to around 4,000 fans. The new designers additionally reoriented the diamond, adding a press box behind home plate and making improvements to the fences.

The Rochester Brownies was probably named for Palmer Cox's popular books and comics. On April 18, 1896, the Brownies welcomed the Cuban Giants (Negro Leagues) in preseason play. Rochester took the two contests, winning 5–1 the first day, following with a 9–2 victory on the second. The Giants also played them the following season.

Games scheduled on Sundays continued to be an issue, ironically, because the ballfield had purposely been built in Irondequoit just outside the Rochester city limits to avoid such issues. The Law and Order League of Irondequoit, who had opposed Sabbath baseball at **Windsor Beach**, continued to champion the enforcement of "blue laws" at Riverside.

Tragically, on July 16, 1897, a fire at Riverside Park destroyed its fences and seating. The only remnants were a part of the fence. The *Democrat and Chronicle* reported a loss of $10,000 (around $330,000 in 2021), only partially covered by insurance.

This was the final nail in the coffin for the Rochester baseball franchise. With their ballpark burned to the ground, and six players found guilty of Sunday play, the owners moved the organization to Canada mid-season, ending professional baseball at Riverside.

Somehow, amateur ball continued at Riverside Park after the Brownies moved to Montreal. In the summer of 1902, the YWCA leased and improved the park for use by amateur female athletes. In April 1906, the semiprofessional Rochester Blue Labels took over Riverside Park. Bleachers seating 1,000 were built. The Blue Labels (or a team using that name) also played here for a few games in May of 1908 while their own ballpark was being readied. The *Democrat and Chronicle* described Riverside at that time as "resemble[ing] a cow pasture."

FMI: Bielewicz, *Hallowed Grounds: The Baseball Grounds of Rochester*; McCarthy, *Rochester Diamond Echoes*; newspapers.com; "The New Grand Stand," *Democrat and Chronicle*, March 11 and 31, April 1, and December 17, 1896, and March 14, 1897; "Baseball Stands Destroyed by Fire," *Democrat and Chronicle*, July 17, 1897; "City League Games Off," May 24, 1908.

ONTARIO BEACH GROUNDS

Location: Ontario/Charlotte Beach on the west side of the Genesee River outlet

Dimensions: unknown

Home Team(s): Rochester Bronchos and Beau Brummels/Eastern League

Built/In Operation: 1894/1898 through 1902

Seats/Capacity: unknown

Fun Facts: Yet *another* site for Sunday baseball. The field at Ontario Beach included a three-sided grandstand behind home plate and bleacher seating along the first base line. Semipro and amateur matches featuring professional players in their ranks date back here to at least 1894.

FMI: Bielewicz, *Hallowed Grounds: The Baseball Grounds of Rochester*; Bielewicz, *Hallowed Grounds: A Look at Rochester's*; John Pardon and Jerry Jackson, "New York State Ball Clubs," in Puff, *The Empire State of Base Ball*.

BAY STREET BASEBALL PARK

Location: Bay Street near Webster Avenue

Dimensions: unknown

Home Team(s): Rochester Bronchos, Hustlers, Colts, Tribe, Beau Brummels, and Red Wings/Eastern League and International League

Built/In Operation: 1908/1908 through 1928. Dismantled in 1928.

Seats/Capacity: 8,000/11,000

Fun Facts: In 1909, new manager John Ganzel requested that local fans rename the Bronchos. "Hustlers" was the winning choice, although it seems not to have taken, as the original moniker continued in use for the world in and outside of Rochester. The Hustlers won three pennants in a row—in 1909, 1910, and 1911.

New York Giants' great Fred Merkle, remembered only for his one "boneheaded" baseball moment (neglecting to touch the base by a runner has been known since his time as a "Merkle" play), finished out his professional career as a regular player for the Rochester Tribe.

Over the 26-year period Bay Street was in use, changes included the addition of a press box on the grandstand roof and the expansion of the first baseline bleachers. After using benches for the teams, proper dugouts were built in 1922.

However, these improvements could not save the facility from decay. By the time the St. Louis Cardinals transferred their affiliation from Syracuse to Rochester, rotting wooden bleachers and fencing spelled the end of the Bay Street field. At the end of the 1928 season, the ballpark was dismantled and the parts sold off, to be replaced by the new **Red Wing Stadium**.

FMI: *digitalballparks.com* on Bay Street Ball Grounds; Bielewicz, *Hallowed Grounds: The Baseball Grounds of Rochester*; McCarthy, *Rochester Diamond Echoes*; "New Name for Rochester Club," *Democrat and Chronicle*, February 16, 1909; *Buffalo Enquirer*, March 1, 1909; Mandelaro and Pitoniak, *Silver Seasons*; Benson, *Ballparks of North America*.

RED WING STADIUM/SILVER STADIUM

It was like going from a barn to a palace.

—Jack Lustik, Red Wings' fan,
quoted in Mandelaro and Pitoniak, *Silver Seasons*

Drawing by architect Gustavus William Thompson of the proposed Red Wing Stadium. From the *Democrat and Chronicle*, November 17, 1926.

Location: 500 Norton Street

Dimensions: left 320', center 415', right 315'

Home Team(s): Rochester Red Wings/International League; and New York Black Yankees/Negro National League

Built/In Operation: 1928 through 1929/1929 through 1996. Demolished in 1997.

Seats/Capacity: 11,500 to 15,000/19,000

Fun Facts: In 1926, the local organization that ran the International League's franchise decided that a new ballpark was needed to replace the rapidly decaying **Bay Street Baseball Park**. Toward that end, a site on Norton Street previously used, among other amusements, by the touring Barnum and Bailey Circus, was purchased, and civil engineer Gustavus William Thompson brought in to draw up the plans.

Thompson, a native of Baltimore, Maryland, is best known in baseball circles through his association with Branch Rickey when the later man ran the St. Louis Cardinals. Besides the Rochester facility, Gustavus Thompson designed ballparks for the Houston Buffs (upon which Red Wing Stadium was based) and the Columbus Red Birds, both St. Louis affiliates. During the same time, Thompson also conceived Albany's **Hawkins Stadium**.

Initially aiming to open in the summer of 1927, Rochester baseball proposed funding the construction of the stadium through a public offering to the tune of $300,000 (around $4.6 million today). It's unclear why this plan wasn't put into action. Instead, when the Cardinals assumed control of the franchise in 1928, they also undertook the stadium project. A consortium of locals joined with St. Louis to fund G. W. Thompson's vision.

With the new facility already almost three years in the making, construction was hurriedly begun at the end of 1928. By early 1929, one could begin to see Thompson's concept approaching reality. Shrewdly, Gustavus Thompson curved the steel-framed stadium structures in a horseshoe shape, giving the cream and maroon painted Red Wing a unique appearance. The covered, single-decker grandstand, topped with a press box and including dressing rooms underneath, contained 8 rows of box seats and 32 rows of regular seats. Uncovered bleachers traced both foul lines and a green wooden fence enclosed the outfield.

By the spring of 1929, 600 tons of steel had been utilized and the Cardinals had spent $415,000 (a bit over $6 million today). So many fans were projected to attend opening day that many thousand temporary bleacher seats were added, boosting capacity to 19,000, although inclement weather kept the crowd to just under 15,000 fans. This steel and concrete wonder was thereafter nicknamed "the Taj Mahal of the Minor Leagues."

During the summer of 1933, lights were installed at a cost of $23,000 to facilitate night games. The New York Black Yankees relocated from the Bronx to Red Wing Stadium in 1948, a "last-gasp" move to save the team. Unfortunately, the integration of major league baseball had caused the death for Negro League baseball. Both the Negro National League and the Black Yankees collapsed after the season. In 1960, the Cardinals terminated their working agreement with the Red Wings and were replaced by the Baltimore Orioles.

Red Wing alumni include future Cardinals Stan Musial and Bob Gibson, as well as Orioles John "Boog" Powell, Curt Schilling, and Mike Mussina. The O's also sent Ron Shelton to Rochester, who, after a stint in the minors, used that experience to craft a script for the movie *Bull Durham*. Probably the most famous alum of the Red Wings is Cal Ripken, Jr. Ripken spend his final minor league season (1981) in the International League, where he won Rookie of the Year.

In 1968, Red Wing Stadium was renamed Silver Stadium. Local music store owner Morrie Silver, who had worked tirelessly to promote and "save" professional baseball in Rochester, was honored through the revamped moniker. Stadium improvements in 1980 included a new public address system, added advertising signs on the roofs of the dugouts, and a scoreboard sign promoting the locally based Kodak corporation. Three years later, an additional $300,000 funded reinforcing and replacing parts of the grandstands and roof, as well as improvements to the press box. At that time, new stadium lights were installed, a new screen fitted behind home plate, and new water lines laid. Finally, aluminum bleachers were built along the left-field line and the scoreboard was updated. Alas, the scoreboard only lasted a year, when, in 1984, it caught fire and burned up!

Stopgap stadium renovations during 1986–1987 included a complete gut and rebuild of the facility (baseball historian David Pietrusza writes of costs approaching $4.5 million). Wooden seats were replaced with wider, brightly colored (by section) aluminum, new supports built, and three restrooms added. A rebuilt box office and concession stands, expanded home clubhouse, and a beer and wine garden completed the redo. Writing in the *Times-Union*, and quoted in *Silver Seasons*, Bob Matthews told how "Silver Stadium has gone from worst to first. From the pits to the Ritz. . . . Rochester's 'new' old baseball stadium is a wonder to behold."

Unfortunately, this only delayed the inevitable. With parking still an issue, long lines at the concessions, and fans unenthusiastic about the beer garden, professional baseball moved to the brand-new Frontier Field in 1997.

Today, the former ticket/administration building is still extant, utilized by the city as a community center. The history of the site is memorialized through plaques on the structure.

FMI: Pitoniak, "Gem of Local Baseball History Found"; *digitalballparks.com* on Silver Stadium; Bielewicz, *Hallowed Grounds: The Baseball Grounds of Rochester*; Pitoniak, *Baseball in Rochester*; Evershed, *A Farewell to Silver*; David Pietrusza, "Upstate New York's Ballparks," in Puff, *The Empire State of Base Ball*; Mandelaro and Pitoniak, *Silver Seasons*; "Silver Stadium," Emporis; Cody, "500 Norton Street: A Rochester Destination"; Benson, *Ballparks of North America*; Bennett, "There Once Was a Ballpark"; "John P. Ryan Will Admitted by Surrogate" and "G. W. Thompson, 80, Builder of Baseball Parks, Dies," *Times Record*, January 12 and 6, 1965; "Redwing Stadium Ready for Opening Contest May 20; Engineer Pleased with Park," *Democrat and Chronicle*, April 21, 1929; "To Finish Plant for Opening of Spring Play," *Democrat and Chronicle*, November 17, 1926.

ROME

RIVERSIDE PARK

Location: Parkway and Floyd Avenue, on the Mohawk River

Dimensions: unknown

Home Team(s): Rome Romans/New York State League, Empire State League, and Central New York League

Built/In Operation: 1898 through 1901, 1905, and 1909 through 1910. Still standing, now part of a city facility.

Seats/Capacity: 500/2,500

Fun Facts: Eight New York State municipalities featured a Riverside Park, including Rome. Located next to the fairgrounds, fans and players alike could smell the abutted cattle shed, and foul territory off of left field led onto a race course and, eventually, a steep cliff. Initially utilized by amateur teams, the grandstand at Riverside was enlarged for professional play.

In 1899, the Romans took the pennant for the New York State League. Unfortunately, this didn't prohibit their players from getting arrested (and later acquitted) for playing baseball on a Sunday. On June 1, 1910, the Central League disbanded, ending professional ball at this Riverside Park.

FMI: Pietrusza, *Minor Miracles*; Stats Crew, "Riverside Park"; *Evening Sun*, June 1, 1910; "Central League Will Continue," *Post-Standard*, June 3, 1910; *Buffalo Courier*, June 26, 1899.

MURRAY'S PARK/LEAGUE PARK

Location: Parkway and Floyd Avenue

Dimensions: unknown

Home Team(s): Rome Colonels/Can-Am League

Built/In Operation: 1937

Seats/Capacity: 1,000

Fun Facts: The team that played here and at **Colonels Park** was owned by Dr. Don Mellon, who "operated" the franchise through the 1949 season. When not utilized for pro ball, Murray's Park was home to local industrial league organizations. Professional baseball brought with it improvements to the grandstand, scoreboard, and concession stands, as well as the addition of bleachers. The Colonels had the fence expanded and painted, and a sign was added to the facility proclaiming it "League Park, Fort of the Rome Colonels."

FMI: David Pietrusza, "Upstate New York's Ballparks," in Puff, *The Empire State of Base Ball*.

COLONELS PARK

Location: Black River Boulevard and Pine Streets

Dimensions: left 360', center 380', right 320'

Home Team(s): Rome Colonels/Can-Am League

Built/In Operation: 1938/1938 through 1942, and 1946 through 1951. Demolished in 1952. This location is now a public park, Franklyn's Field.

Seats/Capacity: 2,250 to 3,500

Fun Facts: Colonels Park was built specifically for the team at a cost of $15,000 (around $285,000 today). The Colonels new home boasted 80 box seats, a press box, dressing rooms, showers, and public restrooms, none of which you would have found at **Murray's Park**, where the Rome Colonels spent the 1937 season. The dirt diamond boasted short foul lines, making Colonels Park ideal for power hitters. A 1941 experiment with night baseball utilizing portable illumination for five contests proved a success and led to the installation of permanent lighting the following season.

Before World War II, Rome's parent Philadelphia Phillies visited and beat the Colonels by a score of 6–4. After the war, the Rome club was associated with the Detroit Tigers and, for the last year at Colonels Park, the Philadelphia Athletics.

FMI: John Pardon and Jerry Jackson, "New York State Ball Clubs," in Puff, *The Empire State of Base Ball*; David Pietrusza, "Upstate New York's Ballparks," in Puff, *The Empire State of Base Ball*; Pietrusza, *Baseball's Canadian-American League*.

SENECA FALLS

CAYUGA LAKE PARK

Location: 2678 Lower Lake Road, possibly in what is now a state park

Dimensions: unknown

Home Team(s): Seneca Falls Maroons/New York State League and Central New York League; and Seneca Falls Pump Makers/Empire State League

Built/In Operation: 1886/1887 through 1889, and 1905 through 1907

Seats/Capacity: unknown

Fun Facts: Cayuga Lake Park was typical of the amusement resorts popular in the 19th and early 20th centuries. The park featured an opera house, electric lights, a dance pavilion, and, according to the *Post-Star* newspaper, a "professional baseball" grounds. The Haines Brothers provided rail service from town.

The two short runs of pro ball at Cayuga included two to three years for the Maroons, as well as the three seasons where the Pump Makers took first in the Empire State League.

Of course, Seneca Falls was the birthplace for the suffragette movement. Which doesn't seem to have had any effect on promoting local women's baseball.

FMI: John Pardon and Jerry Jackson, "New York State Ball Clubs," in Puff, *The Empire State of Base Ball*; *Stats Crew*, "1905 Empire State League Standings"; *Stats Crew*, "1906 Empire State League Standings"; *Buffalo Commercial*, April 6, 1905; newspapers.com; *Post-Star*, August 19, 1886; *Post-Star*, April 14, 1887; *Post-Star*, June 17, 1887; *Catholic Union and Times*, June 14, 1888; *Democrat and Chronicle*, July 12, 1888.

SYRACUSE

UNKNOWN NAMES

Location: Otisco and Catherine Streets, West Fayette and Geddes Streets, Lodi Street

Dimensions: unknown

Home Team(s): Syracuse Base Ball Club

Built/In Operation: 1858 through 1860

Seats/Capacity: unknown

Fun Facts: unknown

FMI: Benson, *Ballparks of North America*; Peter Morris, "Syracuse Base Ball Club," in Morris et al., *Base Ball Pioneers, 1850–1870*.

ARMORY PARK

Location: unknown

Dimensions: unknown

Home Team(s): Syracuse Central Citys

Built/In Operation: 1865 through 1867

Seats/Capacity: unknown

Fun Facts: This team was the successor to the Syracuse Base Ball Club, which existed as early as 1862.

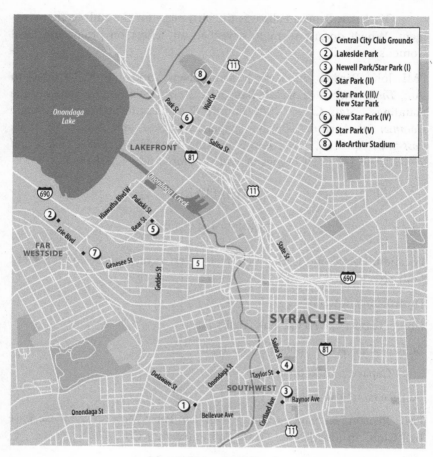

Map 8. Syracuse Ballparks.

FMI: Benson, *Ballparks of North America*; Peter Morris, "Syracuse Base Ball Club," in Morris et al., *Base Ball Pioneers, 1850–1870*.

CENTRAL CITY CLUB GROUNDS

Location: the south side of West Onondaga Street where it currently intersects Delaware Street

Dimensions: unknown

Team(s): Syracuse Central Citys

Built/In Operation: 1868/1868 through 1870

Seats/Capacity: 3,000/10,000

Fun Facts: These grounds were 900 by 300 feet, and enclosed by an 11-foot fence. Historian Peter Morris writes that, to pay for the building of the ballpark, the club began charging a substantial admission fee. This, in turn, necessitated the scheduling of contests against the best national clubs to convince spectators to buy tickets.

One of those crack squads was the Brooklyn Atlantics. In June of 1868, having the Troy part of their tour rained out, the Atlantics took on the Central Citys at their Club Grounds, which the visitors took by a score of 20–14.

FMI: Benson, *Ballparks of North America*; Richard Hershberger, "Upstate New York" introduction," in Morris et al., *Base Ball Pioneers, 1850–1870*; *Brooklyn Union*, June 15, 1868.

LAKESIDE PARK

A park where you didn't have to worry about the ball rolling very far. The outfield was a soggy marsh of weeds. The soil in the all-skin [dirt] infield had a salty texture, and the damp grass was allowed to grow so long in the outfield that balls could get lost in it.

—Michael Benson, *Ballparks of North America*

Location: Hiawatha Boulevard, State Fair Boulevard, New York Central Railroad tracks, Onondaga Lake, Geddes

Dimensions: unknown

Home Team(s): Syracuse Stars/International Association and National League

Built/In Operation: 1869/1869 through 1870, and 1875 through 1879

Seats/Capacity: unknown

Fun Facts: The Syracuse Stars played in 1878 at Lakeside Park, moving to **Newell Park** in early August. Michael Benson adds that the Stars of 1879 only played Sunday games here.

FMI: David Pietrusza, "Upstate New York's Ballparks," in Puff, *The Empire State of Base Ball*; Benson, *Ballparks of North America*; *Buffalo Commercial*,

April 5, 1878; *Buffalo Morning Express*, August 3, 1878; "Buffalo Courier," February 22, 1879.

NEWELL PARK/STAR PARK (I)

Location: East Raynor Avenue and South Salina Street

Dimensions: unknown

Home Team(s): Syracuse Stars/International Association and National League

Built/In Operation: 1869/1878 through 1879, and 1883 through 1884

Seats/Capacity: over 1,000/3,000

Fun Facts: unknown

FMI: *Stats Crew*, "Syracuse Stars Franchise History (1877–1941)"; W. Lloyd Johnson, " 'We Wuz Robbed!' Syracuse in 1878," in Puff, *The Empire State of Base Ball*; David Pietrusza, "Upstate New York's Ballparks," in Puff, *The Empire State of Base Ball*; Benson, *Ballparks of North America*.

STAR PARK (II)

Location: Salina Street and Taylor Street

Dimensions: unknown

Home Team(s): Syracuse Stars/New York State League, International League, International Association, Eastern League, Eastern Association, and American Association

Built/In Operation: 1885/1885 through 1900, and 1902 through 1904. Demolished. South Clinton Street now runs through the former stadium site.

Seats/Capacity: unknown

Fun Facts: In 1885 and 1888, the Stars won the pennant, first in the New York State League and then for the International Association. Black baseball pioneer Moses Walker caught for Syracuse in 1888 and 1889. The Chicago Cubs visited in September of 1904, after which the Lackawanna Railroad, who owned the property, passed the lot along to the city, facilitating the team's move to **Star Park (III)**.

FMI: *Stats Crew*, "Syracuse Stars Franchise History (1877–1941)"; L. Robert Davids, "Bud Fowler: Black Baseball Star," in Puff, *The Empire State of*

Base Ball; John Pardon and Jerry Jackson, "New York State Ball Clubs," in Puff, *The Empire State of Base Ball*; Benson, *Ballparks of North America*.

CRESCENT PARK

Location: unknown

Dimensions: unknown

Home Team(s): Syracuse Stars/Eastern Association

Built/In Operation: 1891

Seats/Capacity: unknown

Fun Facts: unknown

FMI: David Pietrusza, "Upstate New York's Ballparks," in Puff, *The Empire State of Base Ball*.

STAR PARK (III)/NEW STAR PARK

Location: between Marsh, Pulaski and Liberty Streets

Dimensions: unknown

Home Team(s): Syracuse Stars/New York State League and Empire State League

Built/In Operation: 1900 through 1901, and 1905 through 1906

Seats/Capacity: unknown

Fun Facts: During the fall of 1906, the grandstand collapsed during a football game, causing the death of at least one individual.

FMI: *Stats Crew*, "Syracuse Stars Franchise History (1877–1941)"; John Pardon and Jerry Jackson, "New York State Ball Clubs," in Puff, *The Empire State of Base Ball*.

NEW STAR PARK (IV)/HALLOCK PARK/
FIRST WARD PARK/LEMOYNE SPRING GROUNDS

Men were set at work yesterday by Contractor St. Pierre taking down the old bleachers and the present grandstand. The plan now is to thoroughly reconstruct both of them, and a bleacher will also be built at the other end of the stand. . . . A new ten-foot fence will be built on one side of the inclosure . . . and the old fence will be thoroughly overhauled and put in condition. The diamond . . . will be put into good shape and its position somewhat changed. As for the creek that crossed one corner of the park it will probably be filled up.

—"Contract Has Been Signed," *Post-Standard*, April 3, 1907

Location: the end of North Salina Street

Dimensions: unknown

Home Team(s): Syracuse Stars/New York State League and International League

Built/In Operation: 1907/1907 through 1918. Demolished. The property is now under the entrance and exit ramps for I-81.

Seats/Capacity: 2,500

Fun Facts: After the Cuban Stars visited in 1907, the Brooklyn Royal Giants helped initiate a new fence in the spring of 1910 (both teams Negro Leagues).

FMI: Benson, *Ballparks of North America*; "Work Will Start To-Day on Stars' New Playing Ground" and "Contract Has Been Signed," *Post-Standard*, April 2 and 3, 1907.

STAR PARK (V)/SYRACUSE ATHLETIC FIELD/
INTERNATIONAL LEAGUE PARK

Location: 1420 West Genesee Street, along the New York Central Railroad tracks

Dimensions: unknown

Home Team(s): Syracuse Stars/International League and New York-Penn League

Built/In Operation: 1919 through 1920/1920 through 1929. Acquired by the City in 1939, and then sold in 1947 to Sacred Heart Church for use as a playground.

Seats/Capacity: unknown

Fun Facts: unknown

FMI: Benson, *Ballparks of North America*.

MACARTHUR STADIUM (AKA "BIG MAC")/MUNICIPAL STADIUM

Location: East Hiawatha Boulevard, Second Street North, LeMoyne Park, off Court Street

Dimensions: left 320–35', center 434–64', right 320–42'

Home Team(s): Syracuse Chiefs/International League and Eastern League

Built/In Operation: 1934/1934 through 1957, and 1961 through 1996. Demolished. The current (as of this writing) ballpark parking lot occupies this site.

Seats/Capacity: 8,416 to 10,000/13,000

Fun Facts: Built at a cost of $300,000 ($6 million in today's money), Municipal Stadium was renamed during World War II for General Douglas MacArthur (although a song describing it never followed).

During the fall of 1945, the stadium's lighting towers were damaged in a windstorm, necessitating an upgraded system. The new lights were installed the following year by the Crouse-Hinds Company at a cost of $13,000. Other damaged items included the wooden fence, replaced with an aluminum one for $10,000.

During 1946 and 1947, Big Mac was visited by Negro League squads the Boston Blues, Pittsburgh Crawfords, Cleveland Buckeyes, Birmingham Black Barons, Indianapolis Clowns, and the Black Yankees. Improvements at a cost of over $40,000 in 1949 and 1952 upgraded concessions, restrooms, the broadcast and press booths, fencing, roofs, and scoreboard.

In 1955, Syracuse's International League Phillies franchise moved to Miami, to be replaced for a season and a half by a Detroit Tigers Eastern League team that itself was relocated mid-season in 1957 to Allentown, PA. After three and a half years, a new Syracuse club affiliated with the Minnesota Twins entered the International League at MacArthur. Eventually, associates included the New York Mets, Washington Senators, the Tigers (again), the New York Yankees, and the Toronto Blue Jays.

In May of 1969, Big Mac sustained up to $500,000 in damages after a massive fire was accidently set by teenagers attempting to burn their way into a safe in the team's office. The resulting blaze took out the center portion of the grandstand, the main entrance, press box, offices and concessions area, including the PA and broadcast equipment. Also lost was a collection of baseball paraphernalia and concessions supplies.

After a month of games at **Falcon Park (I)** in Auburn, the Chiefs returned to play at the damaged ballpark. Because the city lacked the financial resources to maintain the facility after the fire, the county took over the stadium at the end of 1974. Between 1975 and 1977, and again in 1987 and 1988, Onondaga County's government funded extensive renovations that cost over $1.4 million.

FMI: O'Reilly, *Charlie's Big Baseball Parks Page*; *digitalballparks.com* on MacArthur Stadium; Whittemore, *Baseball Town*; David Pietrusza, "Upstate New York's Ballparks," in Puff, *The Empire State of Base Ball*; Keetz, *They, Too, Were "Boys Of Summer"*; Croyle, "Throwback Thursday: Syracuse Chiefs Left Homeless after Big Mac Burns"; "Syracuse Chiefs," *Fun While It Lasted*.

UTICA

UNKNOWN NAME

Location: unknown

Dimensions: unknown

Home Team(s): Utica Base Ball Club

Built/In Operation: 1860 through 1865

Seats/Capacity: unknown

Fun Facts: In 1864, the Utica Base Ball Club faced the Mutuals of New York City, as well as the Brooklyn Atlantics, losing both contests.

FMI: Scott Fiesthumel, "Utica Base Ball Club," in Morris et al., *Base Ball Pioneers, 1850–1870*.

RIVERSIDE PARK

Location: north of the Mohawk River off Genesee Street

Dimensions: left 450', center 450', right 320'

Home Team(s): Utica Pent-Ups/International Association, National Association, International League, and New York State League; and Utica Stars/Eastern League and New York State League

Built/In Operation: 1878/1878 through 1880, 1885 through 1887, 1888 or 1889 through 1890, 1892, and 1894 through 1897

Seats/Capacity: 1,200/7,000

Fun Facts: For the revived team of 1885, new grandstand seating was built at Riverside Park. The 200-foot stands held 1,000 seats, as stated by Pent-Ups historian Scott Fiesthumel, arranged in seven tiers beginning four feet off the diamond.

One interesting feature of an 1886 game against the Detroit Wolverines (which Utica lost 7–3) was the unusual method of communicating the results. At various points in the game, homing pigeons were utilized to carry the outcomes around the region.

Extreme spring rains would often cause the nearby Mohawk River to overflow its banks and flood. On good days, water would only overtake the area around the grandstands. On bad days, the river would completely inundate the diamond. As a result, fans often had to stand around the field or watch from surrounding trees, housetops, and fences.

By 1887, Riverside Park's repeated spring flooding had left it in unplayable condition. This ultimately moved the preseason to other locations and delayed the start of regular games. No matter. Mid-season, the Utica team was sold to Wilkes-Barre. There would be no professional baseball again in town until 1889. That year, with attendance dwindling, the team played some of the time at **Sylvan Beach**, as did the Oneida squad.

In 1892, the Syracuse team moved to Utica, retaining the Stars name from its former home city. During the 1894 season, games ended in July, when the New York State League disbanded.

FMI: Fiesthumel, *"Pent-Ups"*; John Pardon and Jerry Jackson, "New York State Ball Clubs," in Puff, *The Empire State of Base Ball*; *Stats Crew*, "Sports in Utica, New York."

SYLVAN BEACH

Location: Sylvan Beach
Dimensions: unknown

Home Team(s): Utica Pent-Ups/New York State League; and Oneida/New York State League

Built/In Operation: 1889

Seats/Capacity: unknown

Fun Facts: Sylvan Beach was a summer resort on Oneida Lake used by both Utica and Oneida of the State League for some games during the 1889 season.

FMI: *Democrat and Chronicle*, April 7, 1889; *Stats Crew*, "Sports in Utica, New York."

UTICA ATHLETIC FIELD/GENESEE PARK/UTICA PARK/ UTICA DRIVING PARK

> With the commencement of the baseball season next year [1904], the [New York State] league games will be played in Utica at Utica Park, a portion of which will be fitted up as one of the finest baseball grounds in the entire State.
>
> —*Buffalo Evening News*, October 15, 1903

> Utica Athletic Field . . . is regarded as one of the most complete to be found anywhere.
>
> —*Utica Press*, quoted in the *Wilkes-Barre Record*, March 23, 1910

Location: the fairgrounds, Bleecker Street

Dimensions: unknown

Home Team(s): Utica Harps, Asylums, Reds, Pent-Ups, and Utes/New York State League and Western New York-Penn League

Built/In Operation: 1898 through 1917, and 1924

Seats/Capacity: 3,500

Fun Facts: Utica Park contained a racetrack for the second half of the 19th century. In 1889, the park was purchased by the local Masons to house a hall and asylum. In 1890, a new track was built close by. Races continued into the 20th century.

The covered grandstand at Utica Park was built by M. E. Fournier of Syracuse, who also constructed one of Syracuse's **Star Park**s. The center was around 30 feet across, and held 11 rows of attached seating. Accommodations for the press and game officials dominated the front rows. The two wings of the "V" shape were each twice as long as the center, and outfitted with 11 rows of benches. After the 1909 season, extensive renovations to the facility included a grandstand extension of 80 feet, adding 800 seats. The field was also improved at that time.

The Utica Reds brought home the New York State League pennant in 1900. In 1924, the Utes were moved midseason to Oneonta, where they changed their name to the Oneonta Indians.

FMI: John Pardon and Jerry Jackson, "New York State Ball Clubs," in Puff, *The Empire State of Base Ball*; David Pietrusza, "Upstate New York's Ballparks," in Puff, *The Empire State of Base Ball*; *Stats Crew*, "1907 Utica Pent-Ups Roster"; *Stats Crew*, "Sports in Utica, New York"; "Look Back: Photo Gallery of Bleecker St. in Utica"; "State League Gossip," *Wilkes-Barre Record*, January 8 and February 22, 1910.

BRAVES FIELD/AMBROSE MCCONNELL FIELD

One of the many photographs made around 1940 by General Electric to document and promote their newly installed lighting systems at area ballparks. Braves Field was shot during January of 1940 and located in Utica. Courtesy miSci/Museum of Innovation and Science, Schenectady, New York.

Location: Mohawk River/Barge Canal, on the west side of North Genesee Street

Dimensions: left 389', center 503', right 400'

Home Team(s): Utica Braves and Blue Sox/Can-Am League and Eastern League

Built/In Operation: 1939/1939 through 1950. Demolished mid-1950s and replaced by an on-ramp to the New York State Thruway.

Seats/Capacity: 5,000 to 5,500

Fun Facts: Braves Field was often plagued by fog because of its location near the Mohawk River. Lighting for night games was added in 1939 at a cost of $10,000. The facility was renamed Ambrose McConnell Field for the team's owner in 1942. Although most of minor league baseball suspended play during World War II, Utica's attendance was so strong as to allow the team to continue their games. In 1944, the Philadelphia Phillies bought the team and changed its name to the Blue Sox. The Sox were league champions in 1947 and 1948. In 1950, the Phillies moved the franchise to Schenectady.

FMI: *digitalballparks.com* on McConnell Field; *Stats Crew*, "Ambrose McConnell Field"; Dick Beverage, "Good Enough to Dream in Upstate New York," in Puff, *The Empire State of Base Ball*; Pietrusza, *Baseball's Canadian-American League*; Benson, *Ballparks of North America*.

DONOVAN STADIUM/MURNANE FIELD

Location: 1700 Sunset Avenue at Memorial Parkway

Dimensions: left 330', center 400', right 330'

Home Team(s): Utica Blue Jays and Sox/New York-Penn League

Built/In Operation: pre-1939, and 1976 or 1977 through 2001

Seats/Capacity: 2,000 to 4,000/4,500

Fun Facts: Originally utilized for amateur sports, Murnane Field was named in honor of the high school coach Charles F. Murnane. State funding provided the dollars for stadium improvements, dictating a rebranding for Senator James Donovan, who spearheaded the allocation of capitol.

Over their time at Murnane, Utica had agreements with the major league Phillies, Blue Jays, White Sox, Red Sox, and Marlins.

FMI: O'Reilly, *Charlie's Big Baseball Parks Page*; Stats Crew, "Donovan Stadium"; Fiesthumel, *"Pent-Ups"*; Dick Beverage, "Good Enough to Dream in Upstate New York," in Puff, *The Empire State of Base Ball*; Benson, *Ballparks of North America*.

WATERTOWN

ALEX T. DUFFY FAIRGROUNDS

Location: Arsenal Street, 970 Coffeen Street

Dimensions: left 320', center 380', right 320'

Home Team(s): Watertown/Central New York League; Watertown/Empire State League; Watertown-Massena Bucks-Grays/North Country Baseball League and Can-Am League; Watertown Athletics/Border League; Watertown Pirates and Indians/New York-Penn League; Havana (Negro Leagues) and Watertown Red Sox (semiprofessional)

Built/In Operation: 1851/1886, 1910, 1913 through 1923, 1936, 1946 through 1951, and 1983 through 1998

Seats/Capacity: 2,500 to 4,000

Fun Facts: The Alex T. Duffy Fairgrounds are named for the former president of the Jefferson County Agricultural Society and the New York State Association of Fairs. Besides his many other accomplishments, Duffy had even played baseball himself on these grounds.

The Watertown Fairgrounds date to 1817 and still hosts the oldest county fair in the United States. The grandstand was built in 1851, and baseball has been played here since the early 1870s.

Interestingly, the ballfield was unfenced until 1936, which was also the first season the park added a public address system. In September of 1947, the original grandstand burned and was rebuilt.

Today's stadium boasts a large, covered, straight (instead of "U" or "V" shaped) metal grandstand that houses both metal bleacher seats and the more upscale box seats. Interestingly, bleacher seats top the dugouts on both baselines, with the press box behind third base. The scoreboard sits behind the green right-center field wall.

The Watertown Athletics were Border League champs during their first year of existence (1946). Watertown took a trip to the New York-Penn League playoffs in 1987, losing out in the finals to the Geneva Cubs. A decade later, the Watertown Indians took the league title, defeating the Vermont Expos (1995). After the 1998 season, the franchise was moved to Staten Island and became a Yankees associate. Players who have come through Watertown on their way to major league careers include Tim Wakefield, Sean Casey, Brian Giles, Moises Alou, Jay Buhner, Randy Tomlin, Steve Kline, Kelly Stinnett, and former Chicago Cubs manager Mike Quade.

The fairgrounds now host a team in the Perfect Game Collegiate Baseball League, a summer association aimed at developing college age players for professional baseball. Interestingly, these leagues have filled the need for local baseball in locales abandoned by the minor leagues.

FMI: O'Reilly, *Charlie's Big Baseball Parks Page*; digitalballparks.com on Duffy Fairgrounds; "Watertown Indians," *Bullpen*; Botero, "It Took Almost 20 Years, but Pro Baseball Is Finally Back in Watertown"; John Pardon and Jerry Jackson, "New York State Ball Clubs," in Puff, *The Empire State of Base Ball*; David Pietrusza, "Upstate New York's Ballparks," in Puff, *The Empire State of Base Ball*; Pietrusza, *Baseball's Canadian-American League*; Perfect Game Collegiate Baseball League, "Ballparks of the PGCBL: Duffy Fairgrounds"; Benson, *Ballparks of North America*; "Border League (1946–1951)," *Fun While It Lasted*; Karpinski, "Havana Red Sox at Parkhurst"; Keenan, "September 7, 1929: Havana's Luis E. Tiant Knocked Out in Baltimore Exhibition Game"; "1918 Havana Red Sox."

ALBANY

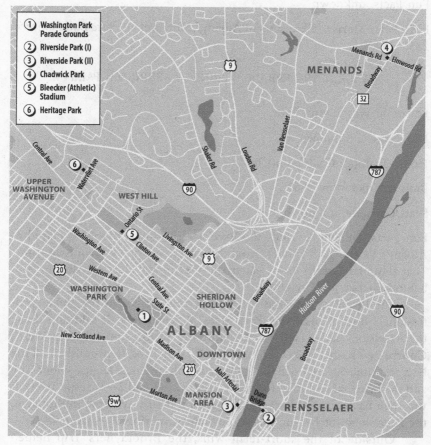

Map 9. Albany Ballparks.

ALBANY CRICKET GROUNDS

Location: unknown

Dimensions: unknown

Home Team(s): Excelsior Club of Albany

Built/In Operation: 1856

Seats/Capacity: unknown

Fun Facts: unknown

FMI: Peter Morris, "Excelsiors of Albany," Morris et al., *Base Ball Pioneers, 1850–1870*.

WASHINGTON PARADE GROUNDS/WASHINGTON PARK

Location: Washington Park

Dimensions: unknown

Home Team(s): Champion Club

Built/In Operation: 1860

Seats/Capacity: unknown

Fun Facts: On July 2, 1860, the Excelsiors of South Brooklyn played at Albany's Washington Parade Grounds in baseball's first known road game. That day, the Excelsiors defeated the Champion club of Albany 24–6 behind pitcher Jim Creighton.

The Brooklyn club was to continue this first "road trip" by a "professional" team across New York State. When it was all said and done, the Excelsiors had visited Troy, beating the Victorys on July 3 at **Weir's Course** by a score of 13–7. Traveling to Niagara Falls, they polished off the Niagaras nine 50–19. Rochester followed, with two local teams—Flour City and the Live Oaks—losing to the Excelsiors 21–1 and 27–9, respectively. It was then back east to Newburgh, where, on their way home to Brooklyn, the Excelsiors notched up one more victory, scoring 59 runs to 14.

Outside of the short-term wins, the Brooklyners' trip helped encourage the spread of baseball to the upstate, especially using the rules pioneered in that city.

FMI: Johnson, *Ballparks Database*; Evanosky and Kos, *Lost Ballparks*; Johnson, *Ballparks Database*; Ross and Dyte, "The Washington Park Wall"; Ross and Dyte, "Washington Park"; Richard A. Puff, "The First to Take It on the Road," *The Empire State of Base Ball*; "Zachary Taylor Davis"; Benson, *Ballparks of North America*.

RIVERSIDE PARK (I)

Location: then called Bonacker Island, Greenbush, now Rensselaer, on the east side of the Hudson River (more information in the section on Troy)

Dimensions: unknown

Home Team(s): Albany Club; Troy Trojans/National League; and Albany/ New York State League

Built/In Operation: possibly in use as early as 1859/1859, 1880 through 1882, 1890, and 1901

Seats/Capacity: unknown

Fun Facts: Between 1880 and 1882, the Troy Trojans played six National League games at Riverside (I). During one of those contests, on September 10, 1881, Roger Connor hit the first "grand slam" in major league baseball for Troy. It happened in the bottom of the ninth inning. Playing Worcester, Connor's hit brought the Trojans from behind to win the game by a score of 8–7. Upon the Troy franchise's expiration in 1882, Roger Connor was signed by the New York Gothams, soon to be renamed the Giants.

FMI: Grondahl, "Baseball's First Grand Slam Produces a Rensselaer Hero"; Grondahl, "Historian Finds First Grand Slam in MLB History—in Rensselaer"; Fiesthumel, *Pent-Ups*; Richard A. Puff, "Albany Baseball: 130 Years Old and Still Going Strong," in *The Empire State of Base Ball*; David Pietrusza, "Upstate New York's Ballparks," in Puff, *The Empire State of Base Ball*; Jim Overmyer, "City of Diamond Heros," in Puff, *Troy's Baseball Heritage*; Richard A. Puff, "Haymakers and Daisycutters," in *Troy's Baseball Heritage*; Benson, *Ballparks of North America*.

RIVERSIDE PARK (II)

Location: Broadway and Quay Street, Herkimer Street and Westerlo Street

Dimensions: unknown

Home Team(s): Troy Haymakers/National League; and Albany/New York State League

Built/In Operation: 1860s/1880 through 1882, 1885, and 1899 through 1900

Seats: Capacity: unknown

Fun Facts: With a large wooden grandstand, Riverside Park (II) was in use for much of the late 19th and early 20th centuries. The Troy Haymakers played parts of their schedule at Riverside (II), while Albany's New York State League franchise utilized the park for a portion of the 1885 and 1899 through 1900 seasons.

FMI: David Pietrusza, "Upstate New York's Ballparks, in Puff, *The Empire State of Base Ball*; *Buffalo Morning Express*, July 23, 1885; "The Albany Club," *Democrat and Chronicle*, May 11, 1899.

SKATING PARK BASEBALL GROUNDS

> The new ground will soon be one of the best in the state; and the association intends to make ample accommodation for the ladies who shall attend the matches.
>
> —*Albany Evening Journal*, June 6, 1865

Location: unknown

Dimensions: unknown

Home Team(s): Knickerbocker Club; National Club; and Eckford Club

Built/In Operation: 1865

Seats/Capacity: unknown

Fun Facts: Skating Park opened in Albany with members from the Knickerbocker, National, and Eckford clubs playing in the first game.

FMI: unknown

UNKNOWN NAME

Location: unknown

Dimensions: unknown

Home Team(s): Albany Senators/International Association, Eastern Association, New York State League, Hudson River League, and Eastern League

Built/In Operation: 1879 through 1881, 1885 through 1886, 1888, and 1890 through 1896

Seats/Capacity: unknown

Fun Facts: Between 1879 and 1896, Albany's baseball promoters attempted to field a professional squad in at least five different leagues. None survived a whole season. At least one probably disbanded before even playing a single game, and another moved after a period of poor attendance to Ontario.

FMI: Richard Puff, "Albany Baseball: 130 Years Old and Still Going Strong," in *The Empire State of Base Ball*; John Pardon and Jerry Jackson, "New York State Ball Clubs," in Puff, *The Empire State of Base Ball*; Keetz, *"Doff Your Caps to the Champions!"*

CHADWICK PARK

> Chadwick Park at Albany was stripped of its antique grandstand and yesterday the work of putting up the steel framework for the new stand was begun. The Albany grounds are to be largely modeled after the . . . Utica Athletic Field as this is regarded as one of the most complete to be found anywhere.
>
> —*Wilkes-Barre Record*, March 23, 1910

Location: Broadway, Menands, NY

Dimensions: unknown

Home Team(s): Albany Senators/New York State League and Eastern League; Albany Champions/New York State League; and Troy Trojans, Washerwomen, and Collarmakers/New York State League

Built/In Operation: 1899 through 1916, and 1920 through 1927

Seats/Capacity: 4,000

Fun Facts: Chadwick Park, according to an official history of Menands, New York, was named for Henry Chadwick, "an early . . . baseball enthusiast." I've been unable to figure out if this was a local resident or the more famous *Brooklyn Eagle* sports reporter and baseball pioneer with this name.

There is newspaper reportage seemingly indicating a "new" ballpark for 1902. However, the article does not specify what improvements were "new," nor if the field was a complete substitution. It's unclear if, because two years later a new grandstand was again installed, temporary seating was utilized from 1910–1911, or, if the grandstand was replaced in 1910 and *again* in 1912.

FMI: Richard A. Puff, "Albany Baseball: 130 Years Old and Still Going Strong," in *The Empire State of Base Ball*; John Pardon and Jerry Jackson, "New York State Ball Clubs," in Puff, *The Empire State of Base Ball*; Keetz, *"Doff Your Caps to the Champions!"*; Benson, *Ballparks of North America*; *Post-Star*, October 31, 1917; *Democrat and Chronicle*, August 23, 1903; Menand, *History of Menands*; "Albany Shut Cleveland Out," *Buffalo Times*, September 14, 1903; "Rain at Albany," *Buffalo Courier*, May 26, 1904; *Buffalo Courier*, May 8, 1905; *Democrat and Chronicle*, July 7, 1905; *Post-Star*, May 14, 1906; *Buffalo Courier*, September 17, 1906; *Press and Sun-Bulletin*, March 24, 1908; *Star-Gazette*, May 14, 1908; "Mack May Play with Troy Team," *Star-Gazette*, March 3, 1909; *Star-Gazette*, February 7, 1912; "Eastern League Parks—Hawkins Stadium," *Star-Gazette*, January 11, 1953.

HAWKINS STADIUM

One of the many photographs made by General Electric to document and promote their newly installed lighting systems at area ballparks. Hawkins Stadium, 1950. Courtesy miSci/Museum of Innovation and Science, Schenectady, New York.

Location: Broadway, Menands

Dimensions: left 300', center 422', right 352'

Home Team(s): Albany Senators/Eastern League, International League, and New York-Penn League

Built/In Operation: 1927 through 1928/1928 through 1959. Demolished at the end of 1960. The site is now the location for state government offices at Mid-City Plaza.

Seats/Capacity: 8,300 to 10,000/13,500

Fun Facts: In 1927, construction was begun on a new facility for the Albany Senators. The site was identical to **Chadwick Park**, although the orientation of the ballfield was changed about 90 degrees.

The rebuilt park was designed by civil engineer Gustavus W. Thompson of Melrose, New York. Thompson, born in Baltimore, Maryland, was best known in baseball circles for his association with Branch Rickey. Thompson had designed stadiums for Rickey's St. Louis Cardinals affiliates the Rochester Red Wings, the Houston Buffs, and the Columbus Red Birds, among others (see **Red Wing Stadium**). The eventual cost for the steel and concrete ballpark was $240,000 (a little over $3.5 million today). A year after opening, **Chadwick Park** became Hawkins Stadium, renamed for former team owner Michael J. Hawkins.

Notable contestants at Hawkins included several visits by Babe Ruth. The earliest, in 1929, was with a barnstorming organization. Ruth hit the farthest home run in the history of Albany baseball that day. On July 30, 1931, the Senators took on the New York Yankees and the Babe at Hawkins Stadium before 6,300 fans, and Ruth homered twice. His Yankees inflicted a similar rout during the 1934 season. And, in 1939, at the end of his playing career, Babe Ruth hit a two-run homer against Albany while a member of the Dodgers organization.

In August of 1952, Hawkins hosted a contest between the Capitol District All-Stars and the traveling Kansas City Monarchs. With Satchel Paige pitching three innings for Kansas City in the twilight for the Negro Leagues, the Monarchs shut out the All-Stars 5–0.

FMI: O'Reilly, *Charlie's Big Baseball Parks Page*; *Stats Crew*, "Hawkins Stadium"; Richard Puff, "Albany Baseball: 130 Years Old and Still Going Strong," in Puff, *The Empire State of Base Ball*; Benson, *Ballparks of North America*; "John P. Ryan Will Admitted by Surrogate" and "G. W. Thompson, 80, Builder of Baseball Parks, Dies," *Times Record,* January 12 and 6, 1965; "Monarchs Blank Albany, 5–0; Paige Fans Four," *New York Age,* August 15, 1942.

BLEECKER (ATHLETIC) STADIUM (ALSO USED BY COLONIE)

Location: Clinton Avenue and Ontario Street

Dimensions: all distances under 345'

Home Team(s): Albany Black Sox/Twilight League (semiprofessional); and Albany-Colonie A's/Eastern League

Built/In Operation: 1934/1935, 1937, and 1983

Seats/Capacity: 2,000

Fun Facts: Bleecker Stadium was a municipal facility possibly constructed by the WPA (Works Progress Administration of the New Deal) over the site of the Bleecker Reservoir. Originally an arena for professional football, Bleecker was also used for amateur, school, and professional sports such as track and boxing. The first mention in print of baseball at Bleecker Stadium was in August of 1935. At that time, the (Black) State Porters took on the Albany Black Sox. The Sox were again using Bleecker two years later, when they contested with the visiting semiprofessional Kingston Colonials.

In the spring of 1936, Johnny Evers (a member of the double-play combination "Tinkers-to-Evers-to-Chance" and a participant in the "Merkle" play) was appointed by Mayor John Boyd Thacher II to run the Bleecker Athletic Stadium. Evers had been raised in Troy, and obviously had some affection for the area. Before running Bleecker Stadium, he had returned to the area for a job with the Albany Senators. Johnny Evers quit the Senators, where he had been the business manager and a scout, after the 1935 season to open a local sporting goods store. Concurrent to supervising Bleecker, Evers ran his retail business until the early 1940s, when a stroke ended his involvement.

The stadium was used by the military during World War II, and, in 1961, lights were installed. The only season Bleecker Stadium was utilized for professional baseball occurred during 1983, when the Colonie A's new facility was under construction. The team moved out of Bleecker in July.

FMI: O'Reilly, *Charlie's Big Baseball Parks Page*; Benson, *Ballparks of North America*; *New York Age*, August 24, 1935; "Colonials Miscue Nine Times,"

Kingston Daily Freeman, July 27, 1937; "Evers Made Boss of City Stadium," *Brooklyn Daily Eagle*, April 11, 1936; "Evers Overcome by Smoke" and "Famous Member of Infield Group," *Times Record*, April 5, 1943, and March 28, 1947.

AMSTERDAM
(WHOSE HISTORY IS INTERTWINED WITH GLOVERSVILLE/JOHNSTOWN)

UNKNOWN NAME

Location: unknown

Dimensions: unknown

Home Team(s): Amsterdam Carpet Tacks and Red Stockings/New York State League

Built/In Operation: 1894 through 1895

Seats/Capacity: unknown

Fun Facts: Amsterdam's State League franchise won the pennant their first year of play, and disbanded the next season in early July of 1895.

FMI: John Pardon and Jerry Jackson, "New York State Ball Clubs," in Puff, *The Empire State of Base Ball*; Pietrusza, *Baseball's Canadian-American League*; "New York State League," *Bullpen*; *Democrat and Chronicle*, July 12, 1895.

GUY PARK

Location: Guy Park Avenue

Dimensions: unknown

Home Team(s): Johnstown, Amsterdam and Gloversville Jags and Hyphens/ New York State League

Built/In Operation: 1882/1902 through 1905. Demolished.

Seats/Capacity: unknown

Fun Facts: Guy Park was originally a picnic ground built on the location of a Revolutionary War–era home.

FMI: *Stats Crew*, "Guy Park"; *Stats Crew*, "1903 Amsterdam-Johnstown-Gloversville Hyphens Roster"; "Amsterdam-Gloversville-Johnstown Hyphens," *Bullpen*; "Amsterdam, NY," *Bullpen*; *Buffalo Morning Express*, September 2, 1882.

CRESCENT PARK/JOLLYLAND/ MOHAWK MILLS PARK/SHUTTLEWORTH PARK

One of the many photographs made around 1940 by General Electric to document and promote their newly installed lighting systems at area ballparks. Mohawk Mills Park, August 1940. Courtesy miSci/Museum of Innovation and Science, Schenectady, New York.

Location: 65 Crescent Avenue

Dimensions: left 279', center 406', right 309'

Home Team(s): Amsterdam Empires (semiprofessional); Chappie Johnson's Stars (Negro Leagues); and Amsterdam Rugmakers/Can-Am League

Built/In Operation: 1914/1924 through 1925, 1938 through 1942, and 1946 through 1951

Seats/Capacity: 4,000

Fun Facts: Crescent Park was incorporated at the end of 1913. The original amusement facility included a dance hall, shooting gallery, theater, miniature railroad, and a "lake" for boating and bathing. The first baseball game at the park was in 1914 between the local Empires and the Philadelphia Colored Giants.

From the end of 1924 through the early parts of 1925's schedule, Chappie Johnson based his team at Jollyland. When the weather got warm in June, causing attendance to dip, Johnson moved some of his games to Saratoga and Glens Falls.

In the early 1930s, the property was purchased by Mohawk Mills, who closed the midway and changed its name to Mohawk Mills Park. However, music by dance bands continued at the pavilion. During the summer of 1937, both Ozzie Nelson (later a star of television's *Ozzie and Harriet* show) and Artie Shaw appeared with their respective orchestras. Bookings by swing bands continued into the early 1940s.

After the arrival of the Rugmakers in the lead up to World War II, a 16-foot green fence was added and improvements made to the playing surface. The enclosure was extended another 10 feet into left field to compensate for a shortened foul line. A flagpole was located in the fair territory of center field. Additionally, a new $600 scoreboard was funded with concessions fees. Lights from GE in Schenectady were introduced in 1940 at a cost of $10,000.

In early July of 1942, the park, including the 900-seat grandstand, some of the fencing, and the concession area, burned in what was determined to be an act of arson. It was quickly rebuilt a week later, with 200 additional seats, to accommodate a previously scheduled July game with the visiting New York Yankees.

The Yanks management must have liked what they saw, as, after the war, the Rugmakers became a Yankee affiliate. Amsterdam would develop players for the Bronx Bombers, and, in return, the American League franchise guaranteed the Rugmakers a yearly stipend along with their cast-off uniforms. To commemorate the deal, in April of 1946, the grandstand at Mohawk was given a new roof. For 1950, the Yankees took the further step of purchasing the Amsterdam franchise outright, retaining ownership for two seasons.

After 20 more years of semiprofessional baseball, Mohawk Mills sold the field to the city in 1964 for one dollar. Amsterdam renamed the ballpark Shuttleworth in honor of team owner, and son of Mohawk Mills' proprietor, Herb Shuttleworth.

The city-run Shuttleworth Park was rebuilt with federal funding and is evocative of Mohawk Mills Park. The grandstand is still covered, and its "retro" box seating was originally located at Philadelphia's defunct Veterans Stadium. Currently, Shuttleworth hosts a collegiate summer wooden bat league team.

FMI: Pietrusza, *Baseball's Canadian-American League*; Perfect Game Collegiate Baseball League, "Ballparks of the PGCBL: Shuttleworth Park"; Keetz, *Class "C" Baseball*; Keetz, *They, Too, Were "Boys of Summer"*; Keetz, *The Mohawk Colored Giants of Schenectady*; *New York Times*, December 19, 1913; Baker, "Shuttleworth Park—Amsterdam Mohawks."

CATSKILL

UNKNOWN NAME

Location: unknown

Dimensions: unknown

Home Team(s): Catskill/Hudson River League

Built/In Operation: 1903

Seats/Capacity: unknown

Fun Facts: At the end of July, Catskill inherited Ossining's Hudson River League team. The area electric railway had built a brand-new ballpark accessible through their service, and hopes were high for the local franchise. Unfortunately, Catskill came in dead last in the league, with the magnificent record of 21 and 68 (only some of those loses were inherited from Ossining).

FMI: John Pardon and Jerry Jackson, "New York State Ball Clubs," in Puff, *The Empire State of Base Ball*; Luse, "The 1903 Hudson River League."

COBLESKILL

UNKNOWN NAME

Location: unknown

Dimensions: unknown

Home Team(s): Cobleskill Giants/New York State League

Built/In Operation: 1890

Seats/Capacity: unknown

Fun Facts: unknown

FMI: Fiesthumel, *"Pent-Ups"*; John Pardon and Jerry Jackson, "New York State Ball Clubs," in Puff, *The Empire State of Base Ball*; "New York State League," *Bullpen*.

COLONIE

HERITAGE PARK

Location: 780 Watervliet Road at Albany-Shaker Road west of the Albany Airport

Dimensions: left 325', center 380–401', right 335'

Home Team(s): Albany-Colonie A's and Yankees/Eastern League; and Albany-Colonie Diamond Dogs/Northeast League and Northern League

Built/In Operation: 1983/1983 through 2002. Dismantled in 2005, the remainder demolished in 2009.

Seats/Capacity: 5,000 to 6,000/14,000

Fun Facts: Eight miles northwest of the city sat the home of the Albany Yankees. When the major league Yanks sought to move their West Haven, Connecticut, franchise into the capital area, they bought a plot west of the airport and began the process of constructing a brand-new stadium. The local affiliate started the 1983 season at **Bleecker Stadium**, a municipal facility, while the building process, begun in March, proceeded behind schedule. There were further delays, as the local community of Shakers brought a suit to halt construction. Unfortunately for the Yankees, their stadium site was perilously close to the burial ground for the Shaker Village's founder, Mother Ann Lee. Construction resumed when the order settled with the baseballers.

The Albany-Colonie team had to vacate **Bleecker Stadium** by July 1, sending the locals on the road until Heritage Park was "usable" (but not quite finished!) for home games on July 20. In all, the Yankees spent $1.2 million (a little over $3 million today) constructing the Albany-Colonie field.

Heritage Park was typical of minor league facilities built at that time: very utilitarian and lacking amenities. Aluminum bleacher seating sat far back from the field of play along the first and third base lines, with some individual chairs placed in front of them. A brick structure containing the locker rooms was topped by a small, covered grandstand, with individual seats and a press box on top. The outfield wall was covered by advertisements.

Several generations of future New York pros played here, including squad mates Derek Jeter and Mariano Rivera. Unhappy with a lack of upgrades to Heritage after a 10-year residency, the Yankees moved out in 1994.

FMI: *digitalballparks.com* on Heritage Park; Yasinsac, "Heritage Park, Colonie, NY"; Richard A. Puff, "Albany Baseball: 130 Years Old and Still Going Strong," in *The Empire State of Base Ball*; Walsh and Murphy, *The Fields of New York*; Benson, *Ballparks of North America*; "Heritage Park," *Uncle Bob's Ballparks*; Walter, *Heritage Park, Colonie, New York* (photographs); *Stats Crew*, "Heritage Park"; Peter Turkel, "Hearing Set on Shaker Building Protest," *Journal News*, March 20, 1983.

FALLSBURG/MOUNTAINDALE

BAXTER STADIUM

Location: New Road north of Old Route 17

Dimensions: unknown

Home Team(s): Sullivan County Mountain Lions/Northeast League; and Catskill Cougars/North Atlantic League, and Northeast and Northern League

Built/In Operation: 1994/1995 through 1998, and 2000. Demolished around 2005, to be eventually replaced by a residential subdivision.

Seats/Capacity: 3,500 to 4,000

Fun Facts: At the end of 1994, this lot was cleared and a field was shaped for baseball. Bleachers were moved from Aqueduct Raceway, blue molded plastic seats installed behind home plate, and a manual scoreboard placed in the outfield. One of the team's owners was actor Bill Murray, himself a baseball lover. According to one source, the plan was to create a kind of "mini-Cooperstown," with a small museum added as a tourist attraction.

Named for Ruth Baxter (the first fan to purchase season tickets), this minimalist stadium (if you could even call it that) was (literally) in the middle of nowhere, which led to a total lack of attendance during its short existence.

Groups from summer camps in the surrounding Catskills, brought in to bolster turn out, would attempt to rally the home team by singing "Hava Nagila." Even though this North Atlantic member took the league championship in 1996, the last of the pros departed in 2000.

For a few years, a summer wooden bat team and local high schoolers commandeered the facility. However, they couldn't save Baxter. The land was too valuable to contain a ballfield, and was eventually cleared for residential housing.

FMI: O'Reilly, *Charlie's Big Baseball Parks Page*; *digitalballparks.com* on Baxter Field; Walsh and Murphy, *The Fields of New York*.

FLEISCHMANNS

MOUNTAIN ATHLETIC FIELD/CLUB GROUNDS

MAC (Mountain Athletic Club) Grounds, Fleischmanns, New York, as pictured in the *New York World*, August 20, 1899. Courtesy of the Fleischmanns Museum of Memories.

The diamond is at the base of the mountains and the field has been laid out with no sparing of expense.

—*New York Sun*, July 12, 1900, quoted in Thorn, "Mangled Forms"

Location: Main Street, now within Fleischmanns Park, Wagner and Ballpark Avenues

Dimensions: unknown

Home Team(s): Mountain Athletic Club

Built: 1895 through 1897/1897 through 1913
Seats/Capacity: 2,000 to 5,000

Fun Facts: Throughout baseball's early professional history in the 19th and the first part of the 20th century, local franchises were not the moneymakers that they later became. A team's existence was often subject to the whims of wealthy baseball-loving owners. One of the most marked examples of dilettantish behavior was probably the short-lived Federal League discussed elsewhere within these pages. A vanity project for wealthy baseball fans desiring a stake in a major-league team, once their ownership goals had been met, this outlaw league was disbanded.

Another glaring example of wealth driving the game was in the ballpark and organization bankrolled by the Fleischmann family. In the use of financial resources to assemble a winning franchise, George Steinbrenner, the owner of the New York Yankees from 1973 through 2007, had nothing on the Fleischmanns.

Mountain Athletic Field was built by Austrian-Jewish yeast merchant Charles F. Fleischmann for use by his sons Julius and Max, themselves baseball players. The Fleischmann clan had originally purchased land in the Catskills around 1883, eventually building an enclave of five summer homes in this area known for its Jewish settlements.

The application for historic status of the field, along with John Thorn's essay "Mangled Forms," provides much of the information used for this entry. The historic designation submission dates Charles Fleischmann's acquisition of what became Mountain Athletic Field to 1894. After spending thousands of dollars on boulder removal and field preparation, a diamond and wooden grandstand behind home plate, along with a clubhouse and landscaping, were constructed. The 1897 season appears to have been the first for Julius Fleischmann's baseball team. During August, the Athletic Club squad dropped two games to the Cuban X Giants (Negro Leagues).

Initially, Julius and his family envisioned the field and team as a hobby. The Fleischmann siblings utilized Mountain Athletic Field as an outlet for Julius and Max Fleischmann's love of baseball, as well as to entertain family and friends. However, by the summer of 1899, Julius made the decision to assemble a winning franchise, and, toward that end, began hiring top-flight talent to stock the squad. Reds' center fielder James Wear "Bug" Holliday, from Fleischmann's hometown of Cincinnati, and New York Giants' pitcher Tom Colcolough were just two of the "ringers" that propelled Fleischmann's club to a championship schedule. For 1900, the team included three future Chicago White Stockings: pitchers Guy Harris "Doc" White and Nick Altrock joined slugger George "Whitey" Rohe. Fellow Cincinnatian Miller Huggins, who went on to fame as manager with the New York Yankees, was added at second base.

Why would these professionals forsake larger markets for this Podunk New York town? The answer was simple: money. Julius Fleischmann was able to lure talent away from the major and minor leagues by paying players $150 per month, as good or better than most professional organizations. Additionally, Fleischmann's boys were housed in first-class hotels. Visiting clubs were also treated well financially, reimbursed as much as $150 per game regardless of the small crowds attending the ballpark.

Just before the start of the 1901 season, the club grounds flooded, sustaining about $1,000 worth of damage. Fortunately, this didn't prevent Fleischmann's pros from winning the local championship for that season, echoed in their 1902 record of 20 wins and 4 losses. Following that year's schedule, the Mountain Athletic Field was rebuilt with increased seating. The original Cuban Giants (Negro Leagues) came in August of 1903, splitting two games with the team.

For the 1904 season, Julius Fleischmann initially decided to bring his unaffiliated squad into the professional Hudson River League. However, the town of Hudson, a league member, was miffed with Fleischmann. The owners of the Hudson squad alleged that Julius had "loaned" his best players to league member Kingston the previous season, who then went on to take the top honors. Ultimately, Fleischmann found the Hudson River League's terms unacceptable and chose to remain independent.

Midway through the second decade of the 20th century, the Fleischmann brothers, having moved into active roles with the family business, lost interest in their small-town club. Instead, they were content with ownership stakes in major league franchises such as Cincinnati and Philadelphia.

Following that loss of attention, in May of 1914, Julius Fleischmann accepted the sum of one dollar from the municipality, and turned the Mountain Athletic Field over to the Village of Fleischmanns. His terms included naming the resulting public park for his family, and maintaining the property for free use by area residents. By the 1940s, the original grandstand had disappeared. Julius Fleischmann's Field was added to the National Registry of Historic Places in 2020.

FMI: John Pardon and Jerry Jackson, "New York State Ball Clubs," in Puff, *The Empire State of Base Ball*; "Northern New York League," Wikipedia; Lang, "Mountain Athletic Club at Fleischmanns Park Gains Historic Designation"; "Mountain Athletic Club, 1895–1914"; *Pine Hill Sentinel*, July 17, 1897; *Pine Hill Sentinel*, August 28, 1897; *New York Sun*, July 12, 1900; Thorn, "Mangled Forms"; McKenna, "Mountain Athletic Club"; Shenk, "5 Catchers Who Left a Mark on the Phillies"; *Catskill Mountain News*, July 31, 1903; *Hobart Independent*, June 27, 1903; *Yonkers Herald*, February 19, 1904; *Poughkeepsie Eagle-News*, March 8, 1904; *Poughkeepsie Eagle-News*, April 2, 1904.

GLENS FALLS

LEAGUE PARK/WASHINGTON COUNTY FAIRGROUNDS

Location: unknown

Dimensions: unknown

Home Team(s): Glens Falls and Saratoga Springs Tri-County/Hudson River League

Built/In Operation: 1906

Seats/Capacity: unknown

Fun Facts: In the late 1800s, the fairgrounds were home to bicycle racing. For 1906, weekday ballgames were played here by a team shared with Saratoga Springs. Plans that year called for improving the grandstand and grounds, with added bleacher seating, a shifted diamond, and longer foul lines.

FMI: John Pardon and Jerry Jackson, "New York State Ball Clubs," in Puff, *The Empire State of Base Ball*; *Buffalo Courier*, April 5, 1906; *Post-Star*, April 20, 1906; *Post-Star*, May 2, 1906; "League Park," *Post-Star*, May 14, 1906.

RECREATION FIELD

Location: unknown

Dimensions: unknown

Home Team(s): Chappie Johnson's Stars

Built/In Operation: a few games in 1925

Seats/Capacity: unknown

Fun Facts: unknown

FMI: "Chappie Johnson and Bozzi Address Ball Convocation at Hotel," *Post-Star*, March 13, 1925.

EAST FIELD

Location: 175 Dix Avenue

Dimensions: left 315', center 380', right 330'

Home Team(s): Glens Falls White Sox and Tigers/Eastern League; Glens Falls Redbirds/New York-Penn League; and Adirondack Lumberjacks/Northeast and Northern League

Built/In Operation: 1980/1980 through 1988, 1993, and 1995 through 2002

Seats/Capacity: 8,000 to 12,000

Fun Facts: East Field was obviously designed for football, as the placement for the preponderance of bleachers in the outfield (added in 1983) dominate the baseball diamond. An uncovered grandstand filled with red and blue seats sits behind home plate, and a wooden press box tops the bleachers in center field. The concrete concourse above the grandstand features team and box offices, with concession stands refurbished in 1983. The video scoreboard, topped with "East Field" in white letters, can be seen above the eight-foot fence in left field. Lights facilitate night games, and the bullpens are on the field.

Players who ascended to the majors from here include John Smoltz. The Adirondack Lumberjacks took the Northeast League championship in 1995 and the Northern League pennant five years later. Currently part of a recreation center, East Field hosts an amateur wooden bat team in the summer.

FMI: O'Reilly, *Charlie's Big Baseball Parks Page*; Perfect Game Collegiate Baseball League, "Ballparks of the PGCBL: Shuttleworth Park"; Walsh and Murphy, *The Fields of New York*; Benson, *Ballparks of North America*; "A New East Field," *Post-Star*, April 16, 1983.

GLOVERSVILLE/JOHNSTOWN
(WHOSE HISTORY IS INTERTWINED WITH AMSTERDAM)

JOHNSTOWN FAIR GROUNDS/FULTON COUNTY-JOHNSTOWN FAIRGROUNDS

Location: Johnstown

Dimensions: unknown

Home Team(s): Gloversville and Johnstown/New York State League; Johnstown Buckskins/New York State League; Gloversville Glovers/New York State League; and Johnstown, Amsterdam, and Gloversville Jags/ New York State League

Built/In Operation: 1837/1890, 1894 through 1896, 1898, 1903, and 1905. The fair went bust in 1910, and the fairgrounds was divided into building lots.

Seats/Capacity: unknown

Fun Facts: The Fairgrounds, with a track for horse racing and spectator seating, seems to date to the 19th century. Over the course of several seasons, the JAGS played some of their games at the Grounds. These included an opening day contest in 1903, as well as hosting the Yonkers franchise of the Hudson River League two years later. The New York State League teams of this period seemed to have been cursed, as the league disbanded early in both 1894 and 1895.

FMI: *Democrat and Chronicle*, May 14, 1903; *Yonkers Herald*, May 2, 1905; John Pardon and Jerry Jackson, "New York State Ball Clubs," in Puff, *The*

Empire State of Base Ball; "Johnstown, NY," *Bullpen*; *Berkshire Eagle*, May 24, 1894; Older, "Rise and Fall of the Fulton County Fair"; *Star-Gazette*, July 5, 1895.

PARKHURST FIELD/JOHNSTOWN-AMSTERDAM-GLOVERSVILLE PARK/A., J. & G. BASEBALL PARK

"Johnstown Fairgrounds-Baseball," aka Johnstown-Amsterdam-Gloversville Park. Courtesy of the Parkhurst Field Foundation.

Location: Harrison Street, between the towns of Gloversville and Johnston

Dimensions: unknown

Home Team(s): Johnstown, Amsterdam, and Gloversville Jags/New York State League

Built/In Operation: 1906/1906 through 1908. Original structures demolished, still in use as a ballfield.

Seats/Capacity: 1,500

Fun Facts: Located an hour from Cooperstown, site of the National Baseball Hall of Fame and Museum, it isn't surprising that residents of Amsterdam, Johnstown, and Gloversville take their baseball history very seriously. Abundant pride is exhibited when fans in the greater tri-cities lay claim to their place in the game's genealogy.

Since the 1890 season, the three cities have, either individually or collectively, peripatetically fielded teams under various guises for the eight-member Independent New York State League. The team name while playing at A., J. & G. Field—the Jags—obviously refers to the initials of the three municipalities that supported and shared the franchise.

The Jags of the New York State League begun play during the 1902 season when their home field was Amsterdam's **Guy Park**. After two seasons, with the nine finishing dead last in the league, the team finally began to attract more talented ballplayers. In 1904, the Jags played .500 ball, for a fourth place league finish. This was obviously a vast improvement over their performance during their two inaugural seasons. Finally, in 1905, the squad ascended to the top of the State League, capturing a championship for the first time under the Jags moniker. It appears their win commanded the attention of local promoters for the national pastime, who soon sought to build a brand-new shrine to the sport to house their local proteges.

What eventually became Parkhurst Field was originally owned and operated by the F., J. & G. (Fonda, Johnstown, and Gloversville) Railroad. After leasing six acres on Harrison Street between the towns of Gloversville and Johnstown, the Railroad hired Gloversville architect and civil engineer Frederick Lacy Comstock to design the stadium's grandstand and fields. Comstock had graduated from Columbia University in 1896. Frederick Comstock previously designed a local hotel, remodeled homes, and built factories, including those making gloves, both locally and elsewhere in New York State.

Comstock's ballpark plans called for a 40-by-60-foot, one-story frame clubhouse with a projecting roof to cover the porch. His exterior design mimicked the look of the grandstand, which stood northwest of the clubhouse structure. The house's interior imitated the layout, although scaled down, of dressing rooms with lockers and baths utilized in the facilities of the National League during this period. The separate areas for the home and visiting squads were divided by a large entry hall. The field itself boasted the only grass diamond in the league at that time (the others were of dirt), laid out so that, during games, the sun would not shine directly in the eyes of the outfielders, a complaint from previous local ballparks.

Gloversville native Sam Lucas was brought in by the E. A. Satterlee construction company to help in overseeing the execution of Comstock's vision. Lucas went on to supervise field construction for the **Polo Grounds (V)** in New York City, as well as at Pittsburgh's Forbes Field. The railway topped off the fan experience by building a station stop just beyond the park's left-field wall. At the completion of all the work, the F., J. & G. had invested $3,088 (around $90,000 today).

What became known as A., J. & G. Field opened for play on July 12, 1906. The local nine won that first contest. Although seating capacity appears to have been 1,500, period newspaper coverage lists attendance at well above that number.

The Jags played two full seasons and one partial schedule in their new ballpark. In 1906, the year A., J. & G. opened, the team slipped to fifth place in New York State League, winning just half of their contests. The following year, the local nine did even worse. For 1907, with a record of just 39 wins and 95 loses, the Jags captured last place.

By 1908, the Railroad had enough. The final nail in the coffin for local baseball at A., J. & G. Field was the prohibition of Sunday baseball by local "blue laws." The team relocated to Elmira, and again finished last in the league. This ended the Jags association with the F., J. & G., and the Railroad's support for local professional baseball.

During June of 1908, the last season for pro baseball at the park, M. Sexton Northrup, a "senior member" of Johnstown's Northrup Glove Manufacturing (who made regular gloves, not sporting goods), died at a game from a heart attack. According to the *Leader-Herald* newspaper:

> Gloversville and Johnstown were the heartland of the American glove making industry [upon incorporation in 1853, the town was so named due to its preeminence in glove manufacturing], and it was a natural extension for [sporting] equipment manufacturing companies to arise in this area as they had access to a significant supply of quality leather materials and an ample work force already skilled in the processes needed to produce the required finished goods.

With the rise in the use of proper baseball gloves after the turn into the 20th century, the area around Gloversville became a manufacturing hub for sporting goods equipment. Eventually, area producers supplied most major league players, incorporating the athlete's suggestions into their designs and making important innovations in glove technology.

These manufacturers included the J. A. Peach Company. Founded by former Gloversville glove cutter John Peach in 1898, the concern made baseball gloves and other sporting goods. John Peach's main achievement was the development of a fielder's glove with a removable/adjustable padded lining. This attracted the attention of other manufacturers, resulting in Peach's operation evolving in 1906 into a satellite of Consolidated Sporting Goods, whose main office was in Philadelphia, Pennsylvania. Consolidated built an additional Gloversville factory that was also under Peach's management. Eventually, the line included 110 styles of fielder's gloves, 15 infielder's varieties, and 20 versions of catcher's mitts. Peach/Consolidated gloves were endorsed by the preeminent players of that time, including Ty Cobb, Honus Wagner, Christy Mathewson, Walter Johnson, Tris Speaker, John McGraw, and Connie Mack.

Consolidated went out of business in 1912, and Peach sold out to Ralph E. Bradford the following year. In 1914, Bradford experienced a fire, and no records exist of the company after that point. John Peach operated in several other states, but seems to have abandoned Gloversville as a manufacturing location.

After the Peach/Consolidated/Bradford departure from Gloversville, Ken-Wel Sporting Goods became the predominate baseball mitt maker of Fulton County. Ken-Wel relocated in 1927 to Utica, New York, staying in business at that location until 1960. Nearby Johnstown, another sponsor for the local ball team, hosted Michael Denkert and Company. Founded in 1909, the sporting goods maker finally closed in 1983.

The cities and towns of New York State were popular stops during the first decades of the 20th century for the many barnstorming teams of major league, Negro Leagues, and even female players. These encompassed various future inductees into the Baseball Hall of Fame, among them pitcher Cy Young, Honus Wagner, and Edd Roush. Another notable who participated in games as a member of the opposing team in this formative period was Archibald Wright "Moonlight" Graham. Graham was the real-life ballplayer who served as the basis for a character in W. P. Kinsella's novel *Shoeless Joe*. The book later provided the blueprint for the movie, *Field of Dreams*. Some of the Negro League teams that "exhibited" at Parkhurst included the Cuban Giants, Brooklyn Royal Giants, Philadelphia Colored Giants, and the Independent Havana Red Sox. In 1914, the female travel team, the New York Bloomer Girls, played against the locals. Both the Detroit Clowns and House of David squads appeared in 1931 to take on local nonprofessional teams in exhibition contests.

In 1918, the lease on A., J. & G. Park passed from the Railroad to the Parkhurst family, and the field gained a new moniker. After the loss of the New York League, the family hosted local semiprofessional fraternal baseball squads, industrial league ball, and "barnstorming" travel teams.

Beginning in 1955, the Parkhurst family allowed little league squads to play at the park. Today, A., J. & G. Field is claimed by the locals as one of the oldest extant baseball diamonds in existence. A nonprofit foundation was formed in 2014 to preserve and revitalize the remaining field and present events on its grounds.

FMI: *digitalballparks.com* on Glover Park; Parkhurst Field Foundation; Wager, "Year of the (Baseball) Glove—J. A. Peach Company"; Wager, "Year of the (Baseball) Glove—M. Denkert & Company"; City of Gloversville. "Parkhurst Field"; Wager, "Year of the (Baseball) Glove—Ken-Wel Sporting Goods"; "Moonlight Graham," Wikipedia; "New York State League," *Bullpen*; David Pietrusza, "Upstate New York's Ballparks," in Puff, *The Empire State of Base Ball*.

UNKNOWN NAME

Location: unknown

Dimensions: unknown

Home Team(s): Johnstown, Gloversville, and Amsterdam (separate teams)/ Eastern Association; and Johnston and Gloversville/New York-Penn League

Built/In Operation: 1909, 1926 through 1927

Seats/Capacity: unknown

Fun Facts: The Eastern Association of 1909 only lasted eleven days, due to a lack of capital and fans.

FMI: John Pardon and Jerry Jackson, "New York State Ball Clubs," in Puff, *The Empire State of Base Ball*; "Johnstown, NY," *Bullpen*; "New League Goes Up," *Star-Gazette*, June 10, 1909.

FULTON-HAMILTON (COUNTY) FAIRGROUNDS/
BERKSHIRE PARK/GLOVERS' PARK

Glovers' Park, Gloversville, August 1940. One of the many photographs made around 1940 by General Electric to document and promote their newly installed lighting systems at area ballparks. Courtesy miSci/Museum of Innovation and Science, Schenectady, New York.

Location: Gloversville-Johnstown

Dimensions: left 330', center 405', right 333'

Home Team(s): Gloversville and Johnstown Glovers/Can-Am League

Built/In Operation: 1937/1937 through 1942, and 1946 through 1951. Demolished in the mid-1960s, and replaced with the Nichols Plaza Shopping Center. The lighting towers were finally removed ten years later.

Seats/Capacity: 2,000 to 3,000

Fun Facts: The fairgrounds hosted baseball by 1898 and horse racing the following year. In preparation for the 1937 professional season, a new diamond was placed in front of the preexisting grandstand, and the field was fenced. During this inaugural run in the Can-Am League, the team occasionally played home games at Coessens Park in nearby Amsterdam.

The following year, additional improvements included a new fence and upgrades to the grandstands and field. Lights were installed in 1940, but could not stem the park's deterioration. In 1942, the Glovers became affiliated with the St. Louis Browns before minor league baseball was suspended for the remainder of World War II. Glovers' Park was renovated in 1948, with a new scoreboard added in 1950.

FMI: *digitalballparks.com* on Glover Park; David Pietrusza, "Upstate New York's Ballparks," in Puff, *The Empire State of Base Ball*; Pietrusza, *Baseball's Canadian-American League*; Benson, *Ballparks of North America*.

HAVERSTRAW

UNKNOWN NAME

Location: unknown

Dimensions: unknown

Home Team(s): Haverstraw/Hudson River League

Built/In Operation: 1888

Seats/Capacity: unknown

Fun Facts: The league disbanded in early June of 1888.

FMI: John Pardon and Jerry Jackson, "New York State Ball Clubs," in Puff, *The Empire State of Base Ball*.

HUDSON

UNKNOWN NAME

Location: unknown

Dimensions: unknown

Home Team(s): Hudson/New York State League; and Hudson Marines/ Hudson River League

Built/In Operation: 1885, and 1903 through 1907

Seats/Capacity: unknown

Fun Facts: The Hudson Marines took the pennant for the River League in 1905. The league disbanded toward the end of June in 1907.

FMI: John Pardon and Jerry Jackson, "New York State Ball Clubs," in Puff, *The Empire State of Base Ball*; *Stats Crew*, "1903 Hudson River League"; *Stats Crew*, "Hudson Marines Franchise History (1903–1907)"; *Sun*, June 24, 1907.

KINGSTON

DONOVAN FIELD

Location: unknown

Dimensions: unknown

Home Team(s): Kingston Leaders; Kingston Colonials/Hudson River League; and Kingston Patriarchs and Colonels/New York State League

Built/In Operation: 1879 through 1883, 1886, 1888, and 1894

Seats/Capacity: unknown

Fun Facts: The Kingston Leaders were named for (and sponsored by) an area newspaper. Like other nearby locales, various Kingston teams of the late 19th century closed due to financial problems. The 1888 Hudson River League collapsed in early June and the 1894 State League disbanded by early July, although the Colonels vowed to finish their season with exhibition games.

FMI: Thorn, "When Baseball Was Big in Kingston"; John Pardon and Jerry Jackson, "New York State Ball Clubs," in Puff, *The Empire State of Base Ball*; *Stats Crew*, "1903 Kingston Colonials Statistics"; Thorn, "Baseball's First All-Star Game"; *Freeland Tribune*, July 16, 1894.

KINGSTON DRIVING PARK

Location: opposite Kingston Union Railroad Station, North Manor Avenue

Dimensions: unknown

Home Team(s): Kingston Colonials/Hudson River League

Built/In Operation: 1903/1903 through 1907

Seats/Capacity: unknown

Fun Facts: The first fall horse races were advertised for this Driving Park in 1872. The Colonials came in 1903, taking on the barnstorming Rube Foster and his X-Giants (Negro Leagues), as well as the "Sioux Indians" (see Elmira and Schenectady) in exhibition games. Foster, who went on the create the Negro National League, squeaked by Kingston with a score of 3–2. The Indians brought along their own portable lights to play an early night contest, which they lost to the local nine. That year, the Colonials finished first in the Hudson River League.

By 1907, however, the league and the team was in financial trouble. Kingston's franchise disbanded at the end of May; the Hudson River League went out of business by the third week of June.

FMI: *Sun*, June 24, 1907; *Poughkeepsie Eagle-News*, October 15, 1872; *New York Times*, October 16, 1872; *Stats Crew*, "1903 Kingston Colonials Statistics"; Thorn, "Remember the Old Hudson River League?"

ATHLETIC GROUNDS/PARK

Location: Cornell Street

Dimensions: unknown

Home Team(s): Kingston Colonials/Eastern Association and New York-New Jersey League

Built/In Operation: 1909, and 1913

Seats/Capacity: unknown

Fun Facts: The 1909 Eastern Association only lasted 11 days, as the league disbanded in early June. On the other hand, the 1913 season went basically as planned. As an added incentive, all ballparks in the league had an outfield sign sporting the image of a bull. With shades of **Ebbets Field**, if any player hit a ball into the sign, they would earn $50.

FMI: *Kingston Daily Freeman*, October 22, 1943; *Stats Crew*, "Athletic Park."

KINGSTON MUNICIPAL STADIUM/ROBERT DIETZ MEMORIAL STADIUM

Location: Grandma Brown Place

Dimensions: deep right field

Home Team(s): Kingston Dodgers/North Atlantic League; and Kingston Hubs and Colonials/Colonial League (semiprofessional) and Can-Am League

Built/In Operation: 1939/1947 through 1951

Seats/Capacity: 1,500 to 2,100/6,500

Fun Facts: In 1939, with help from the WPA (Works Progress Administration), Kingston Municipal Stadium was erected on the site of the old fair grounds. The preceding wooden ballpark had burnt down in the 1930s. The first games began on July 22. As with many instances cited elsewhere within this guide, the park opened for play before being fully finished.

At first, the brick and concrete facility hosted semiprofessional baseball, with the Colonials taking on the Mohawk Giants (Negro Leagues) under the lights on August 2. After World War II, the Brooklyn Dodgers moved their Walden affiliate, the Hummingbirds, to Kingston for one year. After clinching the pennant in 1947, the Dodgers went elsewhere. Professional baseball was attempted again in 1951, but, as before, didn't stay in Kingston. In 1954, Municipal Stadium was renamed for Staff Sgt. Robert Dietz, a local war hero and Medal of Honor winner who had perished in the conflict. The city transferred the park to the Kingston Board of Education in 1989.

FMI: O'Reilly, *Charlie's Big Baseball Parks Page*; *digitalballparks.com* on Dietz Memorial Stadium; Pietrusza, *Baseball's Canadian-American League*; Benson, *Ballparks of North America*; "Border League (1946–1951)," *Fun While It Lasted*; "Yerkes Gains Club Backing," *Poughkeepsie Eagle-News*, February 27, 1939; "Stadium Receives Its Official Name," *Kingston Daily Freeman*, March 8, 1939.

MIDDLETOWN

UNKNOWN NAME

Location: unknown

Dimensions: unknown

Home Team(s): Wallkills Base Ball Club and Lone Stars

Built/In Operation: 1866 through 1870s, 1874 through 1877, and 1880 through 1888

Seats/Capacity: 1,500

Fun Facts: An article in the *New York Sun* from the spring of 1888, reprinted by baseball historian Bob Mayer, mentioned that when the local Wallkill Base Ball Association was sold, improvements to the baseball park included a new grandstand, with a relocated original one used as a "free" seating section.

FMI: John Pardon and Jerry Jackson, "New York State Ball Clubs," in Puff, *The Empire State of Base Ball*; *Stats Crew*, "1913 New York-New Jersey League"; Mayer, "The Asylum Base Ball Club"; Stats Crew, "Watts Field"; "Watts Memorial Park, Middletown, New York," *BaseballparkReviews.com*; *Middletown Times-Press*, March 13, 1918; *Sun*, April 22, 1888.

MAPLE HILL PARK

Location: West Main and County Road 78

Dimensions: unknown

Home Team(s): Middletown/Eastern Association; and Middletown Asylums and Middies/New York-New Jersey League and Atlantic League

Built/In Operation: 1909, and 1913 through 1914

Seats/Capacity: unknown

Fun Facts: The 1909 Eastern Association only lasted eleven days, as the league disbanded in early June. On the other hand, the 1913 season went basically as planned. As an added incentive, all ballparks in the league had an outfield sign sporting the image of a bull. With shades of **Ebbets Field**, if any player hit a ball into the sign, they would earn $50.

FMI: John Pardon and Jerry Jackson, "New York State Ball Clubs," in Puff, *The Empire State of Base Ball*; *Stats Crew*, "1913 New York-New Jersey League"; Mayer, "The Asylum Base Ball Club"; *Stats Crew*, "Watts Field"; "Watts Memorial Park, Middletown, New York," *BaseballparkReviews.com*; *Middletown Times-Press*, March 13, 1918.

NEWBURGH

SOUTH AND JOHNSTON STREETS

Location: South and Johnston Streets

Dimensions: unknown

Home Team(s): Newburgh Newburghs; Newburgh Hudson Rivers; and Newburgh/Hudson River League

Built/In Operation: 1856 through 1860, 1859 through 1868, 1873, and 1886 through 1887

Seats/Capacity: unknown

Fun Facts: The Newburghs original grounds boasted a clubhouse and home plate under a willow tree on the south end of the property. On the other hand, the Hudson Rivers utilized a clubhouse with eight sides. During the Civil War and afterwards, the Newburgh squad often played the best of the New York City-area teams, including the Brooklyn Resolutes, Stars, and Enterprise Club, along with the New York Mutuals and the Empire State Club. This encompassed both home games in Newburgh and sojourns to the Big Apple.

FMI: "Newburgh, NY," *Bullpen*; Peter Morris, "Hudson Rivers of Newburgh," in Morris et al., *Base Ball Pioneers, 1850–1870*; protoball.org, "Club of Newburgh."

WEST END PARK/DRIVING PARK

Location: 401 Washington Street

Dimensions: unknown

Home Team(s): Newburgh Hillsides, Taylor-Mades, Hill Climbers, and Hillies/Hudson River League; Newburgh Colts/Eastern-National Association; Newburgh Dutchmen and Hilltoppers/New York-New Jersey League; and Newburgh Hillclimbers/Atlantic League

Built/In Operation: 1903 through 1907, 1909, and 1913 through 1914

Seats/Capacity: 4,000

Fun Facts: Newburgh Driving Park existed as early as the fall of 1899, according to newspaper accounts of horse racing, which continued at least through 1909. High school football was played here in 1904, and amateur baseball through 1910.

In 1907, the season lasted until the third week of June, when the league folded. The schedule was even shorter in 1909, lasting all of 11 days. However, the Colts did come in first! During 1913, Newburgh lost home contests to the Royal Giants (Negro Leagues) as well as the Chicago Cubs. As an added incentive, all ballparks in the league had an outfield sign sporting the image of a bull. With shades of **Ebbets Field**, if any player hit a ball into the sign, they would earn $50.

In 1916–1917, the property passed from Mrs. F. Delano Hitch, one of Franklin Roosevelt's aunts, to the city (see **Delano-Hitch Stadium**).

FMI: John Pardon and Jerry Jackson, "New York State Ball Clubs," in Puff, *The Empire State of Base Ball*; Luse, "The 1903 Hudson River League"; *Stats Crew*, "1903 Hudson River League"; *Stats Crew*, "1903 Newburgh Taylor-Mades Statistics"; "Newburgh, NY," *Bullpen*; *Stats Crew*, "1909 Newburgh Roster"; *Post-Star*, May 19, 1906; *Poughkeepsie Eagle-News*, March 20, 1905; *Democrat and Chronicle*, January 24, 1907; *Sun*, June 24, 1907.

DELANO-HITCH STADIUM/RECREATION PARK/DRIVING PARK

Crab grass in the outfield. A manual scoreboard. Minuscule crowds. Welcome to Newburgh's Delano Hitch Stadium, the weakest of the Atlantic League's four facilities. Not much has changed since [1927]. The wooden bleachers along [the] first- and third-base line appear old and shaky, and the outfield grass has the look of a golf course rough. "The field is the worst in the league," said Somerset catcher Jorge Morales.

—Jeff Schuler, "First Year Won't Be Easy," *Morning Call*, April 2, 1997

Location: 401 Washington Street.

Dimensions: left 390', center 425', right 390'

Home Team(s): Newburgh Hummingbirds/North Atlantic League; Newburgh Night Hawks/Northeast League; Newburgh Black Diamonds/Atlantic League; and Newburgh Newts/North Country League

Built/In Operation: 1926/1946, 1995 through 1996, 1998, and 2015

Seats/Capacity: 3,100 to 3,500

Fun Facts: Originally a "driving park" (i.e., horse racing track) was located on this site. The land was donated to the city by Annie Delano Hitch, aunt to President Franklin D. Roosevelt, in 1916.

The Newburgh Hummingbirds began their 1946 season at Recreation Park. However, the lack of a fully fenced facility hampered their ability to collect admission fees from the fans. This deficiency, combined with poor weather and attendance, led to a failure to pay the rent and install lighting. Finally, the untimely death of the Hummingbirds' president resulted in the team's decamping for Walden after only a couple of weeks.

Fifty years later, fan discomfort with a deteriorated downtown Newburgh where Delano-Hitch was located eroded support for the baseball team. An attempt was made to spruce up the Park in 1996 with new chair-style seating installed in the grandstand. However, this wasn't enough to keep a team playing for 1997.

According to Michael Bosi of the *Poughkeepsie Journal*:

> The city, [stated the team owner, had] promised new concession stands, team offices, locker rooms and a scoreboard along with 500 additional seats and a fence surrounding Delano Hitch Stadium when he purchased the team prior to the 1996 season from its former owner, who reportedly ran up more than $100,000 in debts.
>
> A city spokesman said the improvements have been held up by complications over a matching grant from the state [a budget revision rescinded a state grant for stadium renovations]. ("Financial Woes in Newburgh," August 8, 1995)

Several more attempts were made at bringing a professional franchise back to Delano-Hitch Stadium. The 1998 Black Diamonds were only in Newburgh as a stopgap while their new facility in Easton, Pennsylvania, was being constructed. The team and their league both viewed the stadium as below par and were looking for a new facility, out of reach for Newburgh's government.

FMI: O'Reilly, *Charlie's Big Baseball Parks Page*; digitalballparks.com on Delano Hitch Stadium; Jerry Carino, "Newburgh's Home Stadium Is Certainly No Field of Dreams," *Courier-News*, July 26, 1998.

NYACK

"DOC" BERNARD STADIUM/
CLARKSTOWN COUNTRY CLUB SPORTS CENTRE

The Giants may brag of ["Irish"] Meusel and the Yanks boast of Babe Ruth, but up in the rugged hills of Rockland County the bustling little town of Nyack has a champion who outshines them all—a baserunner incomparable, a batter indomitable, a pitcher undefeatable. Who is this paragon of the baseball field, this [hero from J. M. Barrie's play] Admirable Crichton of the diamond? None other than our old friend of the Loving Guru of the Mystic Tantriks—Oom the Omnipotent himself—known . . . as Pierre Bernard.

—"Oom the Omnipotent," *Daily News*, September 26, 1922

Location: Waldron Avenue and Main Street, now Route 59 near Exit 11 on the New York State Thruway

Dimensions: unknown

Home Team(s): Nyack Nighthawks (semiprofessional) and New York Black Yankees

Built/In Operation: 1932 through 1933/1933 through 1936

Seats/Capacity: 8,500

Fun Facts: New York State seems to incubate groups of alternative thinkers, like the Mormons and the Shakers. Some were even baseball fans. (Well, the Shakers, not so much. See Colonie.) One of these individuals was "Doctor" Pierre A. "Oom" (his self-applied moniker) Bernard.

Bernard, rather than a board-certified medical practitioner, was a self-proclaimed healer preaching an "alternative" lifestyle. You might be surprised to learn that Pierre Bernard is credited with bringing the practice of hatha yoga to the United States, where he was its biggest promoter. The Doc also ran for a time what might have been labeled in the 1960s a "free love" cult.

Doc Bernard was a supporter (and player) of local baseball. Regardless of his love for the game, like another nonmedical "doctor," John R. Binkley, who utilized radio and country music to push his supposed treatments, Bernard liked the publicity he gained from hosting sporting events. However, just as the Fleischmanns developed their Mountain Athletic Club, Doc Bernard, at least for a period of time, had the financial resources to build a dandy of a baseball enterprise.

Writers that have attempted to spin the yarn of Pierre Bernard's organization often confuse his multiple ballfields with each other. As best I can figure from the available information, the Doctor started holding amateur matches on a small diamond located at his Country Club property between North Midland Avenue and the Hudson River (now the location of the Nyack Field Club). Bernard had initially planned to premiere a team at an event in 1919. Unfortunately, Sunday "blue laws" prevented this from happening, as local law enforcement shut the game down before it had even begun.

Three years later, to circumvent the authorities, Pierre Bernard built a second field on the Bradley property in South Nyack. Here, Bernard's Nyack Nighthawks took on other semipro squads, as well as barnstormers such as the House of David. Games continued throughout the 1924 season, after which Yogi Bernard withdrew his support for the local franchise.

Semiprofessional play resumed at the South Nyack field in the summer of 1932. Pierre Bernard had decided to take a chance on night baseball, and, along with 750 new seats, 6 poles of lights were added to the facility (this predated the major leagues by several years). Fortunately, the illumination for night contests was somewhat disguised from local authorities by the surrounding greenery. However, accounts claimed that you still could see them at Sing Sing Correctional Facility, 12 miles north and across the Hudson River.

Doc Bernard's penultimate stadium was constructed on 11 acres in Central Nyack known locally as the Brush estate. Beginning work in March of 1933, 1,800 cases of dynamite and elephants owned by Bernard were used to level and clear the property. At a cost of $75,000 ($1.5 million today), the brand-new ballpark seated 8,500, with parking for 3,000 automobiles. Steel towers constructed by Rockland Power and Light held the lighting for night games, begun soon after Bernard's field opened in June of 1933.

Unfortunately, in the depths of the depression, Doc Bernard's team couldn't draw an audience. After several seasons, baseball at "Doc" Bernard Stadium was ended midway through 1936, when the ballfield was converted to a dog-racing track.

FMI: John Pardon and Jerry Jackson, "New York State Ball Clubs," in Puff, *The Empire State of Base Ball*; Burrell, "Historic McCallman [*sic*] Field"; *digitalballparks.com* on McCallman Field; Schultz, "A True Nyack Character . . . Pierre Bernard"; "The Colorful History of the Clarkstown Country Club"; Leiner, "Rockland Baseball Has Roots in Nyack"; advertisements, *Journal News*, August 16, 1933; "Radio Stars to Appear at Opening of Sports Center for Night Ball Season," *Journal-News*, May 24, 1934; Hays, "Nyack People and Places: The Baseball Game of the Century"; "Oom Forfeits Sunday Ball Game," *New York Tribune*, August 8, 1921; Batson, "Nyack Sketch Log: Nyack Field Club"; Love, *The Great Oom*.

NYACK HIGH SCHOOL FIELD/MACCALMAN FIELD

Location: 5th Avenue and North Midland Avenue

Dimensions: unknown

Home Team(s): Nyack Rocklands (aka "Rockies")/North Atlantic League

Built/In Operation: 1937/1946 through 1948

Seats/Capacity: 3,500

Fun Facts: Built by the WPA (Works Progress Administration), with its concrete and wood bleachers, this high school field was designed for football. As Doc Bernard was friendly with superintendent of schools Kenneth MacCalman (for whom the stadium was eventually named), Bernard supplied his stadium lights for this new school facility after the demise of **Bernard Stadium**.

When the North Atlantic League franchise named for Rockland County played at MacCalman Field, it was regarded, in the words of writer James F. Leiner, "as the worst in the league." Players complained about the inadequacy of the lights, prompting the Rockies' move to Pennsylvania in 1949.

FMI: John Pardon and Jerry Jackson, "New York State Ball Clubs," in Puff, *The Empire State of Base Ball*; Burrell, "Historic McCallman [*sic*] Field"; *digitalballparks.com* on McCallman [*sic*] Field; Schultz, "A True Nyack Character . . . Pierre Bernard"; "The Colorful History of the Clarkstown Country Club"; Leiner, "Rockland Baseball Has Roots in Nyack"; *Journal News*, August 16, 1933; "Radio Stars To Appear At Opening Of Sports Center For Night Ball Season," *Journal-News*, May 24, 1934; Hays, "Nyack People and Places: The Baseball Game of the Century."

OSSINING

UNKNOWN NAME

Location: unknown

Dimensions: unknown

Home Team(s): Ossining/Hudson River League

Built/In Operation: 1903

Seats/Capacity: unknown

Fun Facts: The team moved during the season to Catskill.

FMI: John Pardon and Jerry Jackson, "New York State Ball Clubs," in Puff, *The Empire State of Base Ball*; Luse, "The 1903 Hudson River League."

PEEKSKILL

MIDWAY OVAL/PARK

Location: Middletown

Dimensions: unknown

Home Team(s): Peekskill/Hudson River League; and Peekskill/Atlantic League

Built/In Operation: 1888, 1903, and 1905

Seats/Capacity: unknown

Fun Facts: It appears that the 1888 season only lasted one month. In 1903, after playing independently and losing money, Peekskill joined the Hudson River League in August.

FMI: *Yonkers Herald*, May 6 and July 29, 1905; Steven J. Stark, "Field Days," *Daily Item*, April 5, 1993.

PEEKSKILL STADIUM

Location: South Street and Welcher Avenue

Dimensions: unknown

Home Team(s): Peekskill Highlanders/North Atlantic League; and Poughkeepsie Giants/Colonial League

Built/In Operation: 1946 through 1949. "Dismantled" in September 1957. The property now contains a shopping district. The current Peekskill Stadium is in a different location.

Seats/Capacity: 3,700

Fun Facts: The Highlanders had affiliations with the New York Giants and the St. Louis Browns, taking the North Atlantic League pennant in both 1946 and 1948. Since the Peekskill and Poughkeepsie franchises shared an owner, the 1947 Poughkeepsie Giants started the season at Peekskill Stadium, moving to their new ballpark in June.

On August 23, 1947, singer Paul Robeson staged a peaceful concert at the stadium, overcoming opposition by the local American Legion because of his affiliation with the Communist Party. Two years later, however, in town for another appearance, Robeson and Woody Guthrie, along with Pete Seeger and his family, were greeted with life-threatening violence in what has been labeled the "Peekskill Riots."

After baseball left Peekskill, the facility hosted stock car racing through the 1950s. Peekskill Stadium was "dismantled" in September of 1957. The lights were first sold to the Cold Springs Little League, and then, several months later, acquired by the Beacon Braves of the NY-NJ League. The stadium's steel grandstands were moved to the Orange County Fairgrounds.

FMI: John Pardon and Jerry Jackson, "New York State Ball Clubs," in Puff, *The Empire State of Base Ball*; Luse, "The 1903 Hudson River League"; *Stats Crew*, "Peekskill Franchise History (1888–1905)"; "Legion Post Opposes Support for Robeson," *Daily Item*, August 19, 1947; "Coaches Go to Court," *Poughkeepsie Journal*, October 6, 1957, January 19, 1958.

PLATTSBURGH

UNKNOWN NAME

Location: unknown

Dimensions: unknown

Home Team(s): Plattsburgh/Eastern International League

Built/In Operation: 1886, 1895 through 1896

Seats/Capacity: unknown

Fun Facts: unknown

FMI: Richard A. Puff, "Albany Baseball: 130 Years Old and Still Going Strong," in *The Empire State of Base Ball*; John Pardon and Jerry Jackson,

"New York State Ball Clubs," in Puff, *The Empire State of Base Ball*; Hayner, "Plattsburgh's Old Ball Game"; Aubrey, "Baseball at Clinton Park."

CLINTON PARK

The only extant photograph of Clinton Park, shown here during the first years of the 20th century. From the collections of Clinton County Historical Association.

Location: off current US Route 9 on the shores of Lake Champlain east of the Plattsburgh airport

Dimensions: unknown

Home Team(s): Plattsburgh Burghers/Northern New York League and Northern League; Plattsburgh/Independent Northern League; and Laconia and Plattsburgh Brewers/New Hampshire State League and Vermont State League

Built/In Operation: 1900/1901 through 1907. The park closed in 1916.

Seats/Capacity: 3,000

Fun Facts: At the end of the 19th century, Clinton Park hosted local amateur and industrial league baseball teams, as well as theatrical performances on a portable stage placed atop the field. The Burghers of the Northern New York League took first in 1901. At the start of the 1907 season, the New Hampshire League immediately disintegrated, and Laconia transferred to the new Vermont State League, moving in the process to Plattsburgh.

FMI: Richard A. Puff, "Albany Baseball: 130 Years Old and Still Going Strong," in *The Empire State of Base Ball*; John Pardon and Jerry Jackson, "New York State Ball Clubs," in Puff, *The Empire State of Base Ball*; Hayner, "Plattsburgh's Old Ball Game"; Aubrey, "Baseball at Clinton Park."

POUGHKEEPSIE

HUDSON RIVER DRIVING PARK

Location: unknown

Dimensions: unknown

Home Team(s): Poughkeepsie Bridge Citys/New York State League

Built/In Operation: 1874/1894

Seats/Capacity: unknown

Fun Facts: Originally used for horse racing, this driving park was purchased by brewer and racing aficionado Jacob Ruppert, Sr., around 1890.

The State League disbanded in early July of 1894, but the Bridge Citys continued playing until season's end. After this one attempt at fielding a professional squad, Hudson River Driving Park was utilized until the 1920s for agricultural fairs and other events.

Jacob's namesake son inherited the park upon his father's death in 1915. Of course, Colonel Ruppert, Jr., by that time owned the New York Yankees.

FMI: "1894 New York State League," *Baseball Reference*; *Freeland Tribune*, July 16, 1894.

RIVERVIEW PARK (I)

Location: 4 Liberty Street

Dimensions: unknown

Home Team(s): Poughkeepsie Giants-Colts/Hudson River League; Pough-keepsie Students/Eastern Association; Poughkeepsie Honey Bugs/New York-New Jersey League and Atlantic League; and Long Branch Cubans (Negro Leagues)/New York-New Jersey League and Atlantic League

Built/In Operation: 1886, 1888, 1903 through 1907, 1909, 1913 through 1914, and 1916. Demolished by 1947.

Seats/Capacity: 1,700

Fun Facts: Riverview Park (I) hosted Poughkeepsie's earliest professional team, who took the Hudson River League pennant in 1886. Just two years later, after four of its member clubs collapsed in early June, the league disbanded.

Before the 1903 season, Riverview (I) was rebuilt. The diamond was rotated 180 degrees, an enclosure added, and a new grandstand constructed. The Poughkeepsie club of the 20th century's Hudson River League won the pennant in 1904 and again in 1907, although (once again), the league disbanded in June. In a now familiar pattern, the Eastern Association of 1909 also went out in June, after playing only 11 games.

In 1913, Poughkeepsie hosted two barnstorming organizations. The Royal Giants cut a wide swath through New York State, besting squads in Middletown, Newburgh, Elmira, and Binghamton. The Long Branch (New Jersey) Cubans, after visiting in 1913, would soon move to Poughkeepsie, replacing the Honey Bugs as the home team at Riverview Park (I).

More travel teams visited in 1930, including one from the House of David. In 1937, the Pittsburgh Crawfords played the Nashville Elites (Negro Leagues) here under portable lights. That same year, the WPA (Works Progress Administration) added bleachers and painted the fencing as well as the buildings in the ballpark.

FMI: O'Reilly, *Charlie's Big Baseball Parks Page*; *digitalballparks.com* on Stitzel Field; John Pardon and Jerry Jackson, "New York State Ball Clubs," in Puff, *The Empire State of Base*; Stats Crew, "1907 Poughkeepsie Colts Statistics"; "Crawfords Play Elites at Riverview Tuesday," *Poughkeepsie Eagle-News*, August 14, 1937; *Poughkeepsie Eagle-News*, April 28 and May 5, 1903; *Sun*, June 24, 1907; "Royal Giants to Play Here Today," *Pough-keepsie Eagle-News*, May 17, 1913; "1700 Fans See Danbury Defeat Locals," *Poughkeepsie Eagle-News*, May 27, 1913; "Cubans to Quit the Bridge City," *Middletown Times-Press*, September 7, 1916; "Dr. Henriquez Outlines Plans for the Season" and "Cubans Arrive in New York," *Poughkeepsie Eagle-News*, March 30 and April 5, 1916.

RIVERVIEW PARK (II)/FRED STITZEL FIELD

One of the many photographs made by General Electric to document and promote their newly installed lighting systems at area ballparks. This very basic facility at Riverview Park (II) was shot during April of 1948. Courtesy miSci/Museum of Innovation and Science, Schenectady, New York.

Location: east of Lincoln Avenue and south of Montgomery Street in Eastman Park

Dimensions: (as of 1990) left 334', center 423', right 372'

Home Team(s): Poughkeepsie Giants and Chiefs/Colonial League

Built/In Operation: 1947/1947 through 1950

Seats/Capacity: 1,700 to 2,500/4,500 to 5,500

Fun Facts: The last professional franchise to call Poughkeepsie home began their 1947 season in Peekskill, moving for night games to Memorial Field behind the W. W. Smith school on Church Street, and, finally, to Riverview Field (II) on July 17. The Colonial League folded in mid-July of 1950, and professional baseball left Poughkeepsie for good. In 1971, the field was renamed for Fred W. Stitzel, a founding member and later president of the local recreation commission.

FMI: O'Reilly, *Charlie's Big Baseball Parks Page*; *digitalballparks.com* on Stitzel Filed; John Pardon and Jerry Jackson, "New York State Ball Clubs," in Puff, *The Empire State of Base Ball*; *Stats Crew*, "1907 Poughkeepsie Colts Statistics"; "Crawfords Play Elites at Riverview Tuesday," *Poughkeepsie Eagle-News*, August 14, 1937; "Colonial League to Open Tomorrow Night," *Poughkeepsie Journal*, May 6, 1947; "Giants to Use Peekskill Park Tomorrow" and "Riverview Park Lights," *Poughkeepsie Journal*, June 9 and 24, 1947, and July 17, 1976; *Poughkeepsie Journal*, July 17, 1976.

ROUSES POINT

UNKNOWN NAME

Location: unknown

Dimensions: unknown

Home Team(s): Rouses Point/Eastern International League

Built/In Operation: 1895

Seats/Capacity: unknown

Fun Facts: unknown

FMI: unknown

SARATOGA SPRINGS

SOUTH BROADWAY BASEBALL GROUNDS

Location: South Broadway

Dimensions: unknown

Home Team(s): Saratoga Springs Tri-County/Hudson River League

Built/In Operation: 1886, and 1906

Seats/Capacity: unknown

Fun Facts: In anticipation of professional baseball, grandstands, a board fence, and other improvements were made to the baseball grounds in 1885. The Hudson River franchise left the league in early August of 1886.

Sharing the 1906 team with Glens Falls, only Sunday games were played here during that season.

FMI: John Pardon and Jerry Jackson, "New York State Ball Clubs," in Puff, *The Empire State of Base Ball*; Stats Crew, "Glens Falls-Saratoga Springs Franchise History (1906)"; September 4, 1885, *Post-Star*.

RECREATION FIELD

Location: unknown

Dimensions: unknown

Home Team(s): Chappie Johnson's Stars (Negro Leagues)

Built/In Operation: 1925 through 1926

Seats/Capacity: unknown

Fun Facts: The city fathers appear to have had a high tolerance for Sunday baseball by both the locals and patrons of this resort town. Beginning in July of 1925, Johnson's Stars (Negro Leagues) played summer Sabbath contests in Saratoga.

FMI: unknown

SAUGERTIES

TOWN DRIVING PARK/CANTINE FIELD

Location: Washington Avenue Extension

Dimensions: unknown

Home Team(s): Saugerties/Hudson River League

Built/In Operation: 1889/1903 through 1905

Seats/Capacity: unknown

Fun Facts: For their third season in Saugerties, the Hudson River League team moved midseason to Pittsfield, Massachusetts. In 1937, the WPA (Works Progress Administration) completed their remake for the city of the field, turning home plate 180 degrees and renaming the ballpark for the original owners of the site, the Cantine family.

FMI: John Pardon and Jerry Jackson, "New York State Ball Clubs," in Puff, *The Empire State of Base Ball*; *Stats Crew*, "1905 Saugerties/Pittsfield Hillies Statistics"; Village of Saugerties, "Cantine Veterans Memorial Complex (aka Cantine Field)"; Thorn, "Remember the Old Hudson River League?"

SCHENECTADY

ALERT GROUNDS

Location: Front Street near the Mohawk River

Home Team(s): Mohawks, Alerts, Pastimes, and Ancient Cities

Dimensions: unknown

Built/In Operation: 1860, and 1869 through 1870

Seats/Capacity: unknown

Fun Facts: unknown

FMI: Keetz, *The Mohawk Colored Giants of Schenectady*.

DRIVING PARK/COUNTY FAIRGROUNDS/RACING PARK

I am perfectly satisfied that Schenectady could support a baseball team. It is one of the most live, wide awake cities in the state. There seems to be plenty of money in circulation and the town is full of men who are admirers of the national game.

—John H. Farrell, president, New York State League, *Daily Union*, February 1899, quoted in Keetz, *1899: Schenectady's First Complete Season*

Schenectady has gone baseball crazy.

—quoting the local newspaper, Keetz, *"Doff Your Caps to the Champions!"*

Location: Hamilton Hill, near downtown

Dimensions: unknown

Home Team(s): Schenectady Dorps, Electrics, and Frog Alley Bunch/New York State League

Built/In Operation: 1894 through 1895, and 1899 through 1900

Seats/Capacity: 2,000

Fun Facts: Driving Park was in use for horse racing as early as 1867. Local baseball began here by the turn-of-the-twentieth-century.

The first "professional" game in the Electric City was an exhibition contest between the locals and the visiting New York Giants. However, the New York State League only lasted about two months, disbanding before the season could be completed. This pattern was repeated in 1895, when the league was dead by early July.

The first full season for professional ball here was in 1899, when the locals finished dead last in the revived New York State League. A record of 29 wins and 77 loses was perhaps a reflection of the frequent management and ownership changes that challenged the stability of the squad. At the end of April/beginning of May that year, the bleachers were enlarged, the grandstand was redone, and the field reconditioned for play. Unfortunately, there was a lack of a press booth, and the field stayed uneven throughout the season. "Blue laws" prevented Sunday baseball in Schenectady during 1899.

FMI: "The Early Years of Professional Baseball in Schenectady"; Keetz, "Baseball in Schenectady"; John Pardon and Jerry Jackson, "New York State Ball Clubs," in Puff, *The Empire State of Base Ball*; David Pietrusza, "Upstate New York's Ballparks," in Puff, *The Empire State of Base Ball*; Keetz, *1899: Schenectady's First Complete Season*; "1894 New York State League," *Baseball Reference*.

ISLAND PARK/COLUMBUS PARK

The overflow crowd captured in this photograph around the beginning of the 20th century was standing around the outer boundary of the outfield at Schenectady's Island Park. Courtesy miSci/Museum of Innovation and Science, Schenectady, New York.

Professional ball in any city is one of the characteristics of a live, progressive people and is a desirable acquisition to any place, and of the best means of advertising a town. It furnishes an animating entertainment to people who are bored by the hot summer months. . . . It relieves you of that tired and weary feeling and puts you in good humor with yourself.

—*Evening Star*, between the 1899 and 1900 baseball seasons

Location: Van Slyck Island (later named Iroquois Island) in the Mohawk River

Dimensions: unknown

Home Team(s): Schenectady Electricians and Frog Alleys/New York State League and Eastern Association; and Mohawk Colored Giants (Negro Leagues)

Built/In Operation: 1901/1901 through 1904, 1909, and 1913 through 1914. Demolished in 1925.

Seats/Capacity: 2,000 to 2,800/5,661

Fun Facts: During the first years of the 20th century, Schenectady was the location for the headquarters and manufacturing facility of General Electric. The fortunes of the city and GE were so intertwined that Schenectady's nickname was "the Electric City." So strong was General Electric's influence that even the local ball team was designated the Electricians.

For the 1901 season, Schenectady professional baseball moved their New York State League team from **Driving Park** to Island Park in the Mohawk River. The new facility boasted two sections of covered seating flanking the infield and nonshielded bleachers along the right and left field lines in the outfield. Island Park's grandstand box seats contained 1,000 fans; base line bleachers another 1,000. An additional 800 bleacher seats were added in early June of 1913.

During those early years at the Van Slyck Island facility, the ballfield lacked an outfield fence. The absence of a full enclosure couldn't have aided in the collection of admission, nor in keeping out unpaid spectators, or players chasing aggressively hit baseballs. A contemporary photograph shows many viewers surrounding the outfield at a particularly popular game. The park had been leased from the owners, the Hudson River Power and Transmission Company, with the franchise responsible for additions/improvements to the grandstands and bleachers.

For the Electricians' first year at Island Park, the squad won 65 and lost 50 games to finish fifth in the league. The following season of 1902, even though they only played .500 ball, Schenectady again grabbed fifth place in the New York State League.

The team's peak for their early period at Island Park occurred in 1903, the only year the team went by the "Frog Alleys" moniker. For all of you nonlocals, "Frog Alley" was the name given long ago to Schenectady's Washington Avenue south of State Street. Frogs used to show up in that area after flooding by the Mohawk River. Another possible source for the team's name might have come from the Binnekill Creek, which was called by some the Frog Alley River. Van Slyck Island, the location for Island Park, was situated near the confluence of the Binnekill and the Mohawk.

One of the season's highlights was an early night game. Utilizing portable lights, the squad played an exhibition contest against the barnstorming "Sioux Indians." The Schenectady nine won the five-inning contest by a score of 11–3. Another highlight, although not entirely positive, took place on May 25. On that date, the entire squad was arrested for violating the local "blue laws" by attempting to play baseball on a Sunday. The jury acquitted team captain Ellis and the entire team was discharged, the Rochester *Democrat and Chronicle* newspaper reported. From that date onward, Island Park fans were asked to be quiet during Sunday games as not to draw the attention of the ministerial association fighting against baseball on the Sabbath. Clearly buoyed by their acquittal, later on the day of their court case, the Frog Alleys took to the field, coming back in the ninth inning to beat Albany. However, the battle hadn't concluded, as on a later date, the clergy had two Island Park ticket agents arrested.

Populated with seasoned, imported players, the Frog Alleys filled their ballpark for its final games of the season. In the 1903 home stretch, Schenectady managed to eke out victory, beating Troy by one and a half games, and winning the State League championship. Unfortunately, the team's owners still managed to lose money, a trend that terminated the organization just one year later. Partway through the 1904 schedule, the team decamped for Scranton, Pennsylvania. After one more attempt in 1909 at fielding a squad, with the franchise only lasting until June 1, pro ball departed Schenectady.

Four years elapsed before baseball returned to Island Stadium. In 1913, the ballpark became the venue for the best-known assemblage to have played on the island: the Mohawk Colored Giants.

According to historian Frank Keetz, newspaper accounts of Black teams in Schenectady date to 1870, when a tournament was locally held.

"There were four clubs from abroad at the baseball tournament yesterday," wrote the *Daily Union*:

> The first prize, a gold ball valued at $50 was won by the "Heavy Hitters" of Canajoharie. The second prize, a silver ball valued at $25 was won by the "Hannibals" of Troy. The third prize was not played for but was presented to the "Pastimes" of this city.

The two remaining teams in the competition were the "Bachelors" of Albany and the "Wide Awakes" of Johnstown.

Baseball scholar David Pietrusza wrote that the 1913 Mohawks were preceded in Schenectady by another assemblage of Black athletes, a 1908 team that played alongside the Asphalt Giants. The 1913 competitors were recruited from around the country by General Electric employee Bill Wernecke. Wernecke, who was white, obtained a lease for Island Park, but couldn't interest any Anglo teams or players in his franchise. Therefore, Bill Wernecke turned to recruiting Black baseballers.

Wernecke may or may not have had knowledge of the precedent for local Black players and teams. However, with a local Black population of only .003 percent, the team organizer must have believed that these baseballers could also appeal to a white audience of fans.

Schenectady's 1913 Mohawk Colored Giants featured such Black stars as pitchers Frank "The Red Ant" Wickware, William "Dizzy" Dismukes, "Smoky Joe" Williams, and George "the Georgia Rabbit" Ball; pitcher-catcher Harry Buckner; catchers Chappie Johnson, Speck Webster, and Big Bill Smith; first basemen Pete Booker and LeRoy Grant; manager-utility player Phil Bradley; third basemen Jesse Braggs and Johnny Pugh; and outfielders Jude Gans, Blainey Hall, Ashby Dunbar, and Smokey Edwards. Supposedly, Bill Wernecke paid full-time salaries to attract these quality players for his part-time squad. Although they lacked a league affiliation, the Giants still were an extremely popular local aggregation.

Because all these athletes had experience on high-profile Negro League teams, the usual style of play prevailed. As has been noted by other historians, the Negro Leagues not only offered up high-level competition, but were entertaining as well. As an example, Giants ace hurler Frank Wickware used a trick also utilized by Satchel Paige, bringing in his outfielders and then proceeding to strike out the opposing squad's last batter.

Like other teams of the period, the Giants had to contend with area "blue laws" prohibiting Sunday contests. Rather than utilize a ballpark outside of city limits, Wernecke aped a method used by New York City's

Lincoln Giants. Fans were admitted to the park without an admission charge. In the case of the Lincoln Giants, those allowed were then obligated to purchase a program booklet. The Mohawk Giants also experimented with both a charge to attend a pregame concert and a toll to cross the pontoon bridge joining Island Park to the mainland.

On October 5, 1913, this first incarnation of the Mohawk Giants most famously took on a barnstorming group of major league (white) all-stars led by Washington Senators pitcher Walter Johnson. Seven thousand fans, three and a half times the normal capacity for Island Park, crossed the bridge connecting Schenectady to the ballfield that day. Frank Wickware was slated to pitch the game against Johnson's barnstormers. A massive game delay was caused by the Giants refusing to play without their salaries, which had gone unpaid all season. Once that matter was resolved, the game proceeded. Regrettably, the exceedingly late start time resulted in a truncated contest, which was called at dusk. The Mohawk Giants, by the way, were declared the winners by a score of 1–0. The Giants finished the 1913 season with an impressive record of 52 wins, 22 loses, and two ties. Unfortunately, Bill Wernecke was finished underwriting the team.

Between the end of the 1913 and 1920, Island Park fell into complete disrepair. When the semiprofessional Knights of Columbus team took over the facility, Island was renamed (not surprisingly) Columbus Park. From 1920 to 1923, the Knights rebuilt the bleachers and grandstand, as well as renovating the bridge to the mainland. The semipro Knights often played traveling teams. In 1921, for example, the Brooklyn Robins (also known as the National League Dodgers) visited Columbus Park.

In 1924, George "Chappie" Johnson revived professional Black baseball in Schenectady by organizing a team and renting out Columbus Park for their rare "home" games. However, in early August, after a disagreement about the price between Johnson and the Knights, Chappie moved his team to Amsterdam.

Today, with the island joined to the mainland by landfill, the site contains a parking lot for Schenectady County Community College.

During the period when Island Park was in use for baseball, John H. Grady and George Howell opened a sporting-related manufactory in town. After 1910, the pair focused on producing baseballs, eventually winning endorsement from the Pacific Coast League and the American Association, among other circuits.

FMI: "The Mohawk Colored Giants of Schenectady"; "Original 1913 Mohawk Giants Team"; "The Early Years of Professional Baseball in

Schenectady"; *Stats Crew*, "Island Park"; Keetz, "Baseball in Schenectady"; Mahoney, "Schenectady Baseball History: The Mohawk Giants"; Schenectady County Historical Society, "Laura Brown Slide Collection"; Martin and Martin, "The Mohawk Colored Giants of Schenectady," in *The Negro Leagues in New Jersey*; Barnes, "Frog Alley Brewing under Development in Schenectady"; Hagerty, "This Day in History: An Entire Team Gets Arrested for Playing on Sunday"; Yankeebiscuitfan, "Minor League history: Eastern Association"; Keetz, *"Doff Your Caps to the Champions!"*; Keetz, *The Mohawk Colored Giants of Schenectady*.

MOHAWK PARK/ELECTRIC CITY PARK

Location: at the end of Broadway trolley line, just outside of Schenectady city limits in Rotterdam, New York

Dimensions: left 276', center 366', right 280'

Home Team(s): Mohawk Colored Giants

Built/In Operation: 1914/1914 through 1915

Seats/Capacity: 1,500

Fun Facts: The Mohawk Giants staggered on under various managers for the first part of the 1914 season. Finally, local businessman Samuel R. Flansburgh bought the team, and built the Giants their own stadium. Moving in the spring to the newly constructed Mohawk Park in Electric City Park just outside the Schenectady city limits, midway through their schedule, the Giants folded. One of the causes appears to be the continuing player prosecutions for Sunday baseball. For the following season, the Mohawk Giants disbanded after only three games.

FMI: Ashwill, "Schenectady Mohawk Giants/Mohawk Park," *Agate Type*, February 20, 2012; David Pietrusza, "Upstate New York's Ballparks," in *Puff, The Empire State of Base Ball*; Keetz, *The Mohawk Colored Giants of Schenectady*.

CENTRAL PARK

Location: 500 Iroquois Way

Dimensions: unknown

Home Team(s): Mohawk Giants/Eastern New York State League and City Twilight League; and Schenectady Blue Jays/Can-Am League

Built/In Operation: 1929/1929 through 1943, and 1946

Seats/Capacity: 1,850/5,000 to 15,000

Fun Facts: Named for the more famous location in New York City, Schenectady's park lacked fencing. Seating as well was limited, so most spectators stood or sat along the sidelines or on the land surrounding the field. No admission could be charged, so a collection would be taken to pay the players (this was the Depression after all). Sometimes, portable lights were brought in for night games. The best-known player on the revived Mohawk Giants was "Buck" Ewing, for whom the current diamond on this site is named. The Blue Jays of the Canadian-American League played half of their 1946 schedule here while their new ballpark, **McNearney Stadium**, was being constructed.

FMI: Mahoney, "Schenectady Baseball History: The Mohawk Giants"; *The Mohawk Giants: Schenectady and the Negro Leagues* (video); "The Mohawk Colored Giants of Schenectady"; David Pietrusza, "Upstate New York's Ballparks," in Puff, *The Empire State of Base Ball*; Keetz, *Class "C" Baseball*; Keetz, *The Mohawk Colored Giants of Schenectady*.

MCNEARNEY STADIUM/SCHENECTADY STADIUM

> [McNearney Stadium] was as good a facility as most in the minors and certainly better than other Canadian-American League Parks.
>
> —Frank Keetz

Location: Jackson Avenue

Dimensions: left 320', center 390', right 320'

Home Team(s): Schenectady Blue Jays/Can-Am League and Eastern League

Built/In Operation: 1946/1946 through 1957. The interior was demolished or sold-off in 1958 and replaced with a golf course.

Seats/Capacity: 4,550 to 6,300

Fun Facts: After World War II, professional baseball experienced a boom period of expansion. Locally, Schenectady's beer barons the McNearney brothers purchased a franchise in the Can-Am League. They also invested nearly $250,000 (almost $3.5 million today) to build their proteges a brand-new ballpark.

While the constructors were attempting to procure steel and concrete for the stadium's structure (in short supply following World War II), the Blue Jays began their freshman season at **Central Park**. When McNearney Stadium opened on July 13, 1946, it was only partially completed. Eventually, the 43-acre stadium site included an octagonal diamond à la **Ebbets Field**, a large amount of parking, and (unusual for the area) an electronic scoreboard. The wooden walls of the outfield rose 12 feet and were covered with advertisements.

McNearney Stadium also had a unique entry system. Subway-esque turnstiles took silver dollars acquired at a ticketing kiosk, thus eliminating the need for ticket takers. Ultimately, the entrance turnstiles were switched to tokens.

As with many area fields, Schenectady's General Electric supplied the lighting for night games. In fact, rumor has it that GE liked to test out new lighting systems at McNearney.

The brewery boys even built a 125-seat restaurant (open from 1952 to 1957). Extending the length of the third base grandstand and replacing seven rows of seats, its bank of windows faced the field, allowing patrons to enjoy a sit-down meal while viewing the action. No wonder McNearney Stadium was considered to be one of the nicer facilities in the area.

For their first 12 years in the league, the Blue Jays were associated with the Philadelphia Phillies. In 1947, Schenectady took first in their division, as well as winning the postseason playoffs. The grandstand was covered in 1948, the year pitcher Tommy Lasorda, then a member of the Phillies' organization, spent the season with the Jays. Of course, Lasorda went on to manage the Dodgers, but that was yet to come.

In 1951, the infield was raised four inches to facilitate drainage, and reseeded. New concession stands were constructed at the termination of the first and third baselines and the rest rooms and clubhouses were also upgraded. McNearney became Schenectady Stadium, and the team moved to the Eastern League. Three years later, the Phillies saw improvements made to the grandstand with new seating and a relocated scoreboard and concessions. The whole park as well received a repaint.

The parent team often visited for exhibition games. Also stopping by were barnstorming Negro Leaguers, including Satchel Paige and the Philadelphia Stars, as well as the Indianapolis Clowns facing the Birmingham Black Barons. The Blue Jays took the Eastern League pennant in 1956.

Two seasons later, pro baseball had moved elsewhere. Rather than court another franchise, the stadium's owner decided that golf would be more profitable. Therefore, after selling off the grandstand, bleachers, and lights, as well as removing the outfield fencing, a nine-hole course was installed within the walls of what had been a baseball facility. Making Schenectady Stadium one of the strangest ballpark conversions of all time.

FMI: Wilkin, "Local Baseball Teams Date Back to 1800s"; *digitalballparks. com* on McNearney Stadium; Keetz, "Baseball in Schenectady"; Pietrusza, *Minor Miracles*; David Pietrusza, "Upstate New York's Ballparks," in Puff, *The Empire State of Base Ball*; Pietrusza, *Baseball's Canadian-American League*; Keetz, *Class "C" Baseball*; Keetz, *They, Too, Were "Boys of Summer"*; Benson, *Ballparks of North America*; newspapers.com; *Berkshire Eagle*, April 16, 1946; *Berkshire Eagle*, July 9, 1946; "Schenectady Park Boasts Restaurant," *Elmira Advertiser*, February 7, 1953; "Satchel Paige in Dorp Exhibition," *Times Record*, July 6, 1950.

TROY/LANSINGBURGH

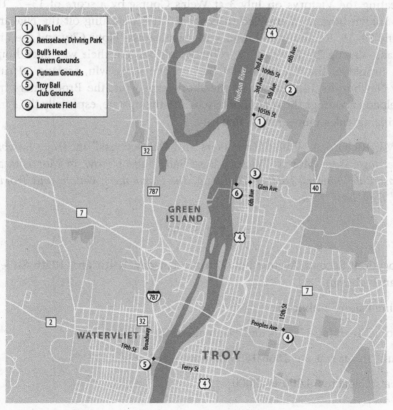

Map 10. Troy Ballparks.

WEIR'S COURSE

Location: John Weir's Hotel, Lansingburgh Road

Dimensions: unknown

Home Team(s): Troy Victorys

Built/In Operation: 1859/1859 through 1860

Seats/Capacity: 400 to 500

Fun Facts: On July 2, 1860, the Excelsiors of South Brooklyn played at Albany's **Washington Parade Grounds** in baseball's first known travel game. That day, the Excelsiors defeated the Champion club of Albany 24–6 behind the pitching of early star Jim Creighton.

When it was all said and done, the Excelsiors had visited Troy, beating the Victorys on July 3 at Weir's Course by a score of 13–7. The Brooklyn boys then traveled to Niagara Falls, polishing off the Niagaras nine 50–19. Rochester followed, with two teams—Flour City and the Live Oaks—losing 21–1 and 27–9 to the Excelsiors. On their way back home to Brooklyn, the Excelsiors notched up one more win, scoring 59 runs to Newburgh's 14. Outside of the short-term wins, the Brooklyners trip helped encourage the spread of baseball to the upstate, especially the game utilizing rules pioneered in that city.

FMI: Richard A. Puff, "Haymakers and Daisycutters," in *Troy's Baseball Heritage*; Peter Morris, "Victory Base Ball Club of Troy," in Morris et al., *Base Ball Pioneers, 1850–1870*; Laing, *The Haymakers, Unions and Trojans of Troy, New York.*

VAIL'S LOT

Location: Second Avenue between present-day 104th and 105th Streets, Lansingburgh

Dimensions: unknown

Home Team(s): Unions and Haymakers

Built/In Operation: 1866/1866 through 1867, and 1877

Seats/Capacity: 4,000 to 5,000

Fun Facts: According to early baseball historians Michael Benson, Peter Morris, and Jeffrey Michael Laing, Vail's Lot was the home for the Unions-Haymakers for 1866 through 1867. Their contests drew crowds upwards of 5,000 fans. Games also used the Village Green, between 112th and 113th Streets, north of what was then Twelfth Street near Third Avenue, in Lansingburgh.

FMI: Benson, *Ballparks of North America*; Peter Morris, "Unions of Lansingburgh," in Morris et al., *Base Ball Pioneers, 1850–1870*; Laing, *The Haymakers, Unions and Trojans of Troy, New York*; Warren F. Broderick, "Haymakers' Bats Brought Fame," *Troy Record*, August 23, 1969.

RENSSELAER DRIVING PARK

Location: bordered by what is now 110th Street and 108th Street, Fifth and Ninth Avenues, Lansingburgh, New York.

Dimensions: unknown

Home Team(s): Victorys; Unions of Lansingburgh and Troy Haymakers/ National Association; National Club of Albany; and National Club of Troy

Built/In Operation: 1867/1868 through 1869, and 1879. The driving park closed right after World War I, when local streets were extended through the facility and the land was divided into building lots. Currently, the former location of the Rensselaer Driving Park hosts the Rensselaer Park School, built in 1975 and opened for the 1975–1976 school year.

Seats/Capacity: 2,000/4,000

Fun Facts: This Driving Park, a 42-acre horse facility, was formally incorporated, according to local newspapers, in the spring of 1868. However, baseball had already been contested here the previous fall. At that time, the mayor of Troy, along with his club, the Troy Victory, sponsored a tournament. The second day, the Unions beat the Cohoes, the Victory triumphed over the Granville Eureka, and the Albany Live Oaks played the Lansingburgh Griswolds. A total of $1,350 in prizes were awarded.

The Union Baseball Club had been formed thru the 1861 merger of the Troy Priams and the National Club of Lansingburgh. The Unions appear to have temporarily disbanded for the Civil War.

During this same time, confusing the matter somewhat, there also existed a "Van Rensselaer Skating Park," which was utilized as well for baseball. The *Buffalo Courier* writes that the facility included

> a skating rink and two base ball grounds . . . contained within the track; about these are seats in three tiers, with capacity for seating 2,000 persons. The grand stand is 100 by 60 feet, and will seat some two thousand. This stand is complete in all its arrangements and fixtures, and cost $5,000. (June 27, 1868)

The "Haymakers" nickname had been earned by the Unions during a road trip in August of 1866. The squad, reorganized the previous year, had traveled downstate to engage local New York City–area teams. When the Troy squad met the Atlantics of Brooklyn on the **Capitoline Grounds**, they lost 46–11, which was expected. After the loss, the Brooklyn fans dubbed the out-of-towners "Haymakers" because they were perceived as unsophisticated rubes. The very next day, however, the Troy/Lansingburgh squad proved the Atlantics rooters wrong by beating the Mutual Club 15–13 on the Elysian Athletic Field.

Preceding their 1868 schedule, the Lansingburgh Unions challenged the Albany National Club to a baseball game on skates. For the 1868 season, the Unions played the New York Mutuals here at their home park, winning by a score of 22–12. A week later, the Unions-Haymakers versus the Brooklyn Atlantics contest was called on account of rain.

In 1869, the powerhouse Cincinnati Red Stockings, an early professional assemblage, visited Lansingburgh and barely topped the Haymakers 32–30. Later that season, a rematch was scheduled in the Queen City. Controversial rulings by the official provided by the Reds finished the game in favor of the hometown squad. The New Yorkers barely escaped intact from the resulting disputes. Match-ups between the two teams planned to immediately follow the first contest had to be canceled, and, later that night, to guarantee their safety, the Troy/Lansingburgh players snuck across the Ohio River into Kentucky. The National Association later ruled the official had illegally ended the game in Cincinnati's favor and declared a tie.

Half way through the 1872 season, the Haymakers ran out of funds and disbanded. Rensselaer Driving Park continued to be used for horse and bicycle racing through the end of the 19th century.

Just south of the former location of Rensselaer Park is the Troy baseball monument. Residing in Knickerbacker Park, the monument honors Troy players for their contributions to professional baseball.

FMI: Thomas M. Blair, "A Reminder of Troy's Proud Baseball History," in Puff, *Troy's Baseball Heritage*; Richard A. Puff, "Haymakers and Daisycutters," in Puff, *Troy's Baseball Heritage*; Kim, "When Troy Was a Major-League City"; Puff, *The Empire State of Base Ball*; Atlantic Base Ball Club; Benson, *Ballparks of North America*; Peter Morris, "Unions of Lansingburgh," in Morris et al., *Base Ball Pioneers, 1850–1870*; Laing, *The Haymakers, Unions and Trojans of Troy, New York*; Warren F. Broderick, "Haymakers' Bats Brought Fame," *Troy Record*, August 23, 1969; *Buffalo Commercial*, April 28, 1879; *Brooklyn Union*, April 9, 1869; "Base Ball Tournament at Troy," *Burlington Times*, October 5, 1867; "National Base-Ball Tournament," *Rutland Weekly Herald*, October 17, 1867; "The Base Ball Tournament," *Buffalo Commercial*, October 17, 1867; *Chicago Evening Post*, August 5, 1868; *Brooklyn Union*, August 12, 1868; "Memories of Rensselaer Park," *Time Record*, July 27, 1964; "Base Ball on Skates," *Baltimore Sun*, February 10, 1868.

BULL'S HEAD TAVERN GROUNDS

This photograph was taken of the Bull's Head Tavern Grounds by James Irving during an 1870 game. Courtesy of the New York State Museum, Albany, New York.

Location: Batestown, Second, Sixth and Glenn Avenues

Dimensions: unknown

Home Team(s): Troy Haymakers/National Association

Built/In Operation: 1869/1869 through 1872

Seats/Capacity: unknown

Fun Facts: Possibly used in conjunction with, or, instead of, **Rensselaer Driving Park**.

FMI: Richard A. Puff, "Haymakers and Daisycutters," in *Troy's Baseball Heritage*; Benson, *Ballparks of North America*; Peter Morris, "Unions of Lansingburgh," in Morris et al., *Base Ball Pioneers, 1850–1870*; Laing, *The Haymakers, Unions and Trojans of Troy, New York*.

HAYMAKERS' GROUNDS

Location: Center Island in the Hudson River, Lansingburgh. The site is just south of Troy-Green Island Bridge (more information in the section on Albany)

Dimensions: unknown

Home Team(s): Troy Haymakers/National Association and League Alliance; Troy Trojans and Citys/National League; and Putnam Base Ball Club of Troy

Built/In Operation: 1871/1871 through 1872, 1877, and 1879 through 1881. Sold by the owners in the off-season between the fall of 1881 and the winter/spring of 1882. Demolished.

Seats/Capacity: 2,500

Fun Facts: In 1871, Lipman Pike was the playing manager for the Troy nine. Pike was the earliest documented Jewish player in the major leagues. One of his troupe, Esteban "Steve" Bellan of Cuba, was the first Latin/Hispanic athlete in professional baseball.

The National Association of 1871–1872 was the original fully pro league, and the Haymakers played against squads from much larger cities. These included the Boston Red Stockings, Philadelphia Athletics, New York Mutuals, Washington Olympics, and Cleveland's Forest City. This version of the Troy Trojans only made it through one and a half seasons, departing baseball in early August of 1872.

After several years of amateur ball, one last professional season was played at these grounds. The 1881 schedule ended in a rainstorm, when the September 27 contest against the Chicago White Stockings was witnessed by 12 fans, the smallest ever to attend a big-league ball game.

FMI: Healey, "Troy Baseball Monument"; Richard A. Puff, "Albany Baseball: 130 Years Old and Still Going Strong," in *The Empire State of Base Ball*; Richard A. Puff, "Haymakers and Daisycutters," in *Troy's Baseball Heritage*; Peter Morris, "Unions of Lansingburgh," in Morris et al., *Base Ball Pioneers, 1850–1870*; Laing, *The Haymakers, Unions and Trojans of Troy, New York*; Helander, "The League Alliance"; Batesel, *Players and Teams of the National Association, 1871–1875*.

PUTNAM GROUNDS

Location: Peoples Avenue and 15th Street

Dimensions: unknown

Home Team(s): Troy Citys and Trojans/National League; and Troy Putnams

Built/In Operation: 1879, and 1882

Seats/Capacity: unknown

Fun Facts: unknown

FMI: "Troy Trojans Attendance, Stadiums, and Park Factors," *Baseball Reference*; Laing, *The Haymakers, Unions and Trojans of Troy, New York*.

TROY BALL CLUB GROUNDS/WEST TROY GROUNDS

The grounds themselves were excellent and the turf diamond was one
of the best in the country, but the location was not a fortunate one.

—*Troy Daily Times*, September 22, 1908, quoted in Laing, *The
Haymakers, Unions and Trojans of Troy, New York*

Location: 19th Street at the southwest intersection with the Delaware and Hudson railroad tracks, across the Hudson River from Troy, West Troy, now Watervliet, New York

Dimensions: unknown

Home Team(s): Troy Trojans/National League, Hudson River League, and International Association; and Troy Trojans and Washerwomen/Eastern League

Built/In Operation: 1882/1885 through 1886, 1888, and 1890 through 1896

Seats/Capacity: 800/5,000

Fun Facts: Between the 1881 and 1882 schedules, the heads of the National League decided to change the way players on member teams dressed. In the past, of course (and since that time), each team had coordinated outfits worn by all their players to distinguish them from the opposite squad. However, in their infinite wisdom, the league redesigned uniforms across all teams to match a player's position. Therefore, deemed the executives, from that point forward, all catchers would wear scarlet, all pitchers dress in light blue, first basemen wear red and white, and so on. Only stocking colors were shared by a whole team (as an example, Troy was issued green socks). Not surprisingly, this barely lasted a few games before everyone went back to dressing as before. In a sport that's seen its share of stupid ideas, I hesitate to call the uniforms prescribed by league management for the 1882 season as one of the top boneheaded decisions for all time. However, whoever came up with this concept certainly had more important concerns to address.

The last game played at the West Troy Grounds by Troy's National League franchise was on August 27 against Cleveland, who shut out the Trojans 3–0. The error-committing ball handlers were labeled "Ferguson's Fumblers" in the local press after their manager, Bob Ferguson. By that time, the other league members badly wanted them out to replace Troy with a higher-earning/attended big city franchise.

For 1890, with African-American pitcher George Stovey briefly on the squad during their first year in the league, Troy took first place.

FMI: Johnson, *Ballparks Database*; Richard A. Puff, "Haymakers and Daisycutters," in *Troy's Baseball Heritage*; Dave Walsh, "The Last Major League Season," in Puff, *Troy's Baseball Heritage*; Helander, "The League Alliance"; Benson, *Ballparks of North America*; Laing, *The Haymakers, Unions and Trojans of Troy, New York*; "May Be Played Over," *Buffalo Courier*, September 18, 1891; *Sunday Leader*, July 15, 1894; *Nebraska State Journal*, February 2, 1886; "The West Troy Baseball Grounds Leased," *Wilkes-Barre News*, November 16, 1887.

LAUREATE FIELD

Location: northwest of River Street at the end of Turner's Lane (now Glen Avenue)

Dimensions: unknown

Home Team(s): Troy Trojans/Eastern Association; and Troy Trojans, Washerwomen, and Collarmakers/New York State League

Built/In Operation: 1890/1891, 1902 through 1904, and 1910 through 1916. Acquired by the Army Corp of Engineers and demolished in 1962.

Seats/Capacity: 3,000

Fun Facts: Long before this site contained a baseball field, a Civil War army camp was located on the property, which sits on the banks of the Hudson River. After the Laureate Boat Club was founded in 1866, this land was purchased and, between 1870 and 1871, a clubhouse built. The ballfield followed about 20 years later, with wooden extensions over the Hudson adding to the outfield. In 1891, the Troy Trojans relocated to Laureate Field after the grandstand at the **West Troy Grounds** was destroyed by fire.

Playing on the river bank sometimes brought added excitement to the games. When the Syracuse Stars were contesting Troy at Laureate, Stars right fielder Frank "Wildfire" Schulte chased a fly ball over an 18-inch-high wire outfield fence. After making the catch, Schulte slid down the embankment into the Hudson River. Of course, the fans went crazy, and Frank Schulte soon was called to the Chicago Cubs. Another common occurrence also involved Schulte, as, later the same game, he hit a home run into the river.

In 1913, issues with the location provoked management to search for new grounds, or, at least, make improvements to the current facility. The last year for the Troy pros playing at Laureate Field, 1916, the season ended midway when the franchise was sold and moved to Pennsylvania.

From the late 1910s through the early 1950s, Laureate Field was used for amateur football and baseball, circuses and carnivals. In 1952, the field was acquired by the city of Troy for a playground. The property eventually went to the Army Corp of Engineers and was demolished in 1962.

FMI: John Pardon and Jerry Jackson, "New York State Ball Clubs," *The Empire State of Base Ball*; Richard A. Puff, "Haymakers and Daisycutters," in *Troy's Baseball Heritage*; Helander, "The League Alliance"; Laing, *The Haymakers, Unions and Trojans of Troy, New York*; "The Laureate Boat Club"; *Democrat and Chronicle*, May 15, 1891; Pietrusza, *Minor Miracles*; Fiesthumel, *"Pent-Ups"*; Bob Fusco, "Army Engineers Acquire Laureate Field," *Troy Record*, January 19, 1962; "Schultz May Set Home-Run Record," *Press and Sun-Bulletin*, September 28, 1911; "May Secure Troy," *Buffalo Morning Express*, November 17, 1912; "Hank Ramsey Is at Work on the Troy Team," *Star-Gazette*, February 6, 1913.

WALDEN

BRADLEY PARK

Location: Albany Street, west of NY 208, on the Wallkill River

Dimensions: unknown

Home Team(s): Walden Hummingbirds and Keen Kutters/North Atlantic League (more information in the section on Newburgh)

Built/In Operation: 1946

Seats/Capacity: 1,000

Fun Facts: The Hummingbirds of the North Atlantic League began their season at **Delano-Hitch Stadium/Recreation Park** as Bradley was being readied. Even though there was a preexisting amateur baseball diamond located in Bradley Park as early as 1932, the field was barely functional when the Birds played their first home game on June 10, 1946. The lights weren't fully operational and new bleachers wouldn't appear until June 20.

From the beginning, professional baseball seemed like a poor idea for Walden. The Hummingbirds franchise passed through several hands, and, toward the end of the summer, the team was renamed the Keen Kutters after a local knife factory. Finishing dead last in the league and failing to draw fans, the franchise moved to Kingston.

FMI: John Pardon and Jerry Jackson, "New York State Ball Clubs," in Puff, *The Empire State of Base Ball*; O'Reilly, *Charlie's Big Baseball Parks Page*; "Walden Keen Kutters," *Bullpen*; Stats Crew, "1946 Newburgh Hummingbirds/Walden Keen Kutters Roster"; "Rocklands Spoil Walden Opener," *Journal News*, June 11, 1946; "New Bleachers Set Up," *Middletown Times Herald*, June 21, 1946.

References

"1894 New York State League." *Baseball Reference*. https://www.baseball-reference.com/register/league.cgi?id=bc22ba3d.

"1900 Northern New York League." *Baseball Reference*. https://www.baseball-reference.com/register/league.cgi?id=3a03962d;%20newspapers.com.

"1918 Havana Red Sox." http://negroleagues.bravehost.com/adm.html.

"1955 World Series: Brooklyn Dodgers over New York Yankees (4–3)." *Baseball Reference*. https://www.baseball-reference.com/postseason/1955_WS.shtml.

"70 Years of Jamestown Pro Baseball to Be Celebrated." *The Post-Journal*, August 18, 2009. https://www.chautauquasportshalloffame.org/70yearsb.php.

Alberts, Hana R. "Remembering New York's Historic Baseball Stadiums, in Photos." *Curbed*, July 2, 2013. https://ny.curbed.com/2013/7/2/10224418/remembering-new-yorks-historic-baseball-stadiums-in-photos.

Anapolis, Nick. "Robinson Debuts Five Days after Signing with Dodgers." National Baseball Hall of Fame. https://baseballhall.org/discover/inside-pitch/robinson-signs-first-big-league-contract.

Anderson, Randy. "JCB Journal: 1940." *Jamestown Gazette*. https://jamestowngazette.com/jcb-journal-1940/.

"And Now, the New York Female Giants: (Briefly) A League of Their Own." *Bowery Boys*, June 4, 2015. https://www.boweryboyshistory.com/tag/lenox-oval.

Ashwill, Gary. *Agate Type*. https://agatetype.typepad.com/agate_type/.

Astifan, Priscilla. "1877—Rochester's First Year of Professional Baseball." *Rochester History* 64, no. 4 (2002): 3–23. https://rochesterbaseballhistory.files.wordpress.com/2012/04/part-5-2002.pdf.

———. "Baseball in the Nineteenth Century." *Rochester History* 52, no. 3 (1990): 2–24. https://rochesterbaseballhistory.files.wordpress.com/2012/04/part-1-1990.pdf.

———. "Baseball in the Nineteenth Century, Part Two." *Rochester History* 62, no. 2 (2000): 1–23. https://rochesterbaseballhistory.files.wordpress.com/2012/04/part-2-2000.pdf.

———. "The Dawn of Acknowledged Professionalism and Its Impact on Rochester Baseball." *Rochester History* 63, no. 1 (2001): 1–23. https://rochesterbaseballhistory.files.wordpress.com/2012/04/part-3-2001.pdf.

———. "Rochester's Last Two Seasons of Amateur Baseball." *Rochester History* 63, no. 2 (2001): 1–23. https://rochesterbaseballhistory.files.wordpress.com/2012/04/part-4-2001.pdf.

Atlantic Base Ball Club. https://brooklynatlantics.org.

Aubrey, Mark. "Baseball at Clinton Park." *Mark's Ephemera*, June 23, 2011. https://marksephemera.blogspot.com/2011/06/baseball-at-clinton-park.html.

Baker, Paul. "Shuttleworth Park—Amsterdam Mohawks." *Stadium Journey*, August 10, 2020. https://www.stadiumjourney.com/stadiums/shuttleworth-par-amsterdam-mohawks.

Barnes, Steve. "Frog Alley Brewing under Development in Schenectady." *Times-Union*, August 28, 2018. https://blog.timesunion.com/tablehopping/60210/frog-alley-brewing-under-development-in-schenectady/.

Barthel, Thomas. *Baseball's Peerless Semipros: The Brooklyn Bushwicks of Dexter Park*. Haworth, NJ: St. Johann Press, 2009.

Batesel, Paul. *Players and Teams of the National Association, 1871–1875*. Jefferson, NC: McFarland, 2012.

Batson, Bill. "Nyack Sketch Log: Nyack Field Club." *Nyack News and Views*, July 3, 2018. https://nyacknewsandviews.com/2018/07/nyack-field-club/.

Baxter, Elizabeth, and Persis Yates Boyesen. *Historic Ogdensburg*. Ogdensburg, NY: Ryan Press, 1995. https://www.ogdensburg.org/DocumentCenter/View/92/Historic-Ogdensburg-brochure?bidId=.

Bennett, Byron. "Buffalo Base Ball Park and Offermann Stadium." *Deadball Baseball*, January 28, 2015. https://deadballbaseball.com/2015/01/buffalo-base-ball-park-and-offermann-stadium/.

———. "Charlie Ebbets's Field." *Deadball Baseball*, January 17, 2013. https://deadballbaseball.com/2013/01/charlie-ebbetss-field/.

———. "Dutch Damaschke Field in Oneonta NY." *Deadball Baseball*, August 6, 2015. https://deadballbaseball.com/2015/08/dutch-damaschke-field-in-oneonta-ny/.

———. "Hilltop Park and the Church of Baseball." *Deadball Baseball*, December 17, 2010. https://deadballbaseball.com/2010/12/hilltop-park-and-the-church-of-baseball/.

———. "The Rockpile—Buffalo's War Memorial Stadium." *Deadball Baseball*, January 30, 2015. https://deadballbaseball.com/2015/01/the-rockpile-buffalos-war-memorial-stadium/.

———. "Shea Stadium's Ghost in the Shadow of Citi Field." *Deadball Baseball*, October 17, 2011. https://deadballbaseball.com/2011/10/shea-stadiums-ghost-in-the-shadow-of-citi-field/.

———. "There Once Was a Ballpark—Rochester's Silver Stadium/Red Wing Stadium." *Deadball Baseball*, September 24, 2014. https://deadballbaseball.com/2014/09/there-once-was-a-ballpark-rochesters-silver-stadium-red-wing-stadium/.

Benson, Michael. *Ballparks of North America: A Comprehensive Historical Encyclopedia of Baseball Grounds, Yards, and Stadiums, 1845 to 1988*. Jefferson, NC: McFarland, 1989.

Berowski, Freddy. "Baseball on Staten Island." https://nynpa.com/docs/nie/baseball/StatenIsland.pdf.

Bielewicz, Paul J. *Hallowed Grounds: A Look at Rochester's Ballparks*. https://rochesterbaseballhistory.files.wordpress.com/2013/09/bielewicz-rochester-ballparks-9-30-13.pdf.

———. *Hallowed Grounds: The Baseball Grounds of Rochester*. Rochester Baseball Historical Society. https://rochesterbaseballhistory.files.wordpress.com/2017/04/bielewicz-hallowed-grounds-04-01-17.pdf.

"Border League (1946–1951)." *Fun While It Lasted*. https://funwhileitlasted.net/border-league-baseball-1946-1951/.

Botero, Julia. "It Took Almost 20 Years, but Pro Baseball Is Finally Back in Watertown." NCPR, June 3, 2015. https://www.northcountrypublicradio.org/news/story/28558/20150603/it-took-almost-20-years-but-pro-baseball-is-finally-back-in-watertown.

Boyce, Janet. Photo of Island Park sign. June 2017. Embedded in Google Maps. https://www.google.com/maps/uv?pb=!1s0x89d21d9a4850aee1%3A0x7638401df4e9cec8!3m1!7e115!4shttps%3A%2F%2Flh5.googleusercontent.com%2Fp%2FAF1QipNPGvO254YZj5JjCO7qZCi2VkJZenhNRFKV6U5i%3Dw426-h320-k-no!5stullar%20field%2C%20wellsville%2C%20ny%20-%20Google%20Search!15zQ2dJZ0FRPT0&imagekey=!1e10!2sAF1QipM71Og3VPc4Tvlq4A9phssaIsBC-BbViu0yE-Mr&hl=en&sa=X&ved=2ahUKEwiW9tz5u7PwAhUI2qwKHWc7CkgQoiowCnoECBQQAw.

"Bradner Stadium, Olean, New York." *RochesterAreaBallparks.com*. http://www.frontiernet.net/~rochballparks2/olean/olean.htm.

Brancato, Tony. "Researching Rochester's Live Oak Baseball Club of the 19th Century" [lecture]. Ryan Brecker, YouTube, posted May 18, 2017. https://www.youtube.com/watch?v=4YQtHhtqJf0.

Brewster, William H. *That Lively Railroad Town: Waverly, New York, and the Making of Modern Baseball, 1899–1901*. Eugene, OR: Luminare, 2020.

———. *The Workingman's Game: Waverly, New York, the Twin Tiers and the Making of Modern Baseball, 1887–1898*. Eugene, OR: Luminare, 2019.

"The Brooklyn Bushwicks and Dexter Park." *The Brooklyn Trolley Blogger*, February 13, 2017. https://thebrooklyntrolleyblogger.blogspot.com/2017/02/the-brooklyn-bushwicks-and-dexter-park.html.

"Brooklyn Dodgers Team History." *Sports Team History*. https://sportsteamhistory.com/brooklyn-dodgers.

Bullpen. https://www.baseball-reference.com/bullpen/Main_Page. Search in *Bullpen* rather than in entire *Baseball Reference* site.

Burk, Bill. "The Babe." Chautauqua Sports Hall of Fame. https://www.chautauquasportshalloffame.org/billburk2015b.php.

Burrell, Bryan. "Historic McCallman Field." *Patch*, posted October 16, 2013. https://patch.com/new-york/nyack/historic-mccallman-field.

"Canadian-American League (1936–1951)." *Fun While It Lasted*. https://funwhileitlasted.net/canadian-american-league-baseball-1936-1951/.

Casway, Jerrold. "July 24, 1860: The First Enclosed Ballpark." Society for American Baseball Research. https://sabr.org/gamesproj/game/july-24-1860-the-first-enclosed-ballpark/.

"The Chautauqua Community." http://freepages.rootsweb.com/~howardlake/history/amusement7/celoron.html.

Chautauqua Sports Hall of Fame. "Old Baseball Ticket Discovered." https://www.chautauquasportshalloffame.org/2019/wp-content/uploads/2019/05/42016.pdf.

Chemung County Historical Society. "Baseball." https://cchsonlineexhibits.wixsite.com/gildedage/baseball.

Cichon, Steve. "From 1880 to Today: Hamlin Driving Park, Buffalo's Famed Horse Track." *The Buffalo News*, October 24, 2018, and August 3, 2020. https://buffalonews.com/news/local/history/from-1880-to-today-hamlin-driving-park-buffalos-famed-horse-track/article_4221b4d3-4490-5538-a376-edfb5307fc04.html.

———. "From 1880 to Today: West Side Home of the National League Buffalo Bisons." *The Buffalo News*, May 1, 2019. https://buffalonews.com/news/local/history/from-1880-to-today-west-side-home-of-the-national-league-buffalo-bisons/article_e5f5f89a-e5ae-5e86-91da-99c52805dfbc.html.

———. "Torn-Down Tuesday: Federal League Park, Buffalo's Last Major League Ballpark." *The Buffalo News*, August 11, 2020. https://buffalonews.com/news/local/history/torn-down-tuesday-federal-league-park-buffalo-s-last-major-league-ballpark/article_96400988-db52-11ea-9fd3-03becabd223c.html.

City of Gloversville. "Parkhurst Field." http://www.cityofgloversville.com/tag/history/.

City of Little Falls. "Veterans Memorial Park." http://www.cityoflittlefalls.net/index.cfm?section=parks-recreation&page=veteran-s-memorial-park.

Cody, Daniel. "500 Norton Street: A Rochester Destination." Rochester Public Library. https://rochistory.wordpress.com/2020/09/10/.

Cohen, Marvin A., and Michael J. McCann. *Baseball in Broome County*. Charleston, SC: Arcadia, 2003.

"The Colorful History of the Clarkstown Country Club." *Palisades Newsletter*, May 2016. http://palisadesny.com/people/colorful-history-clarkstown-country-club/.

"Comstock, C. B. (1874–1932): Projects." *Philadelphia Architects and Buildings*. https://www.philadelphiabuildings.org/pab/app/ar_display_projects.cfm/63635.

Costello, Rory. "Dyckman Oval (New York)." Society for American Baseball Research. https://sabr.org/bioproj/park/dyckman-oval-new-york/.

————. "Shea Stadium (New York)." Society for American Baseball Research. https://sabr.org/bioproj/park/shea-stadium-new-york/.

Croyle, Jonathan. "Throwback Thursday: Syracuse Chiefs Left Homeless after Big Mac Burns." *Syracuse.com*, May 12, 2016. https://www.syracuse.com/vintage/2016/05/throwback_thursday_big_mac_bur.html.

"Dachshunds, Dog Wagons and Other Important Elements of Hot Dog History." National Hot Dog and Sausage Council. https://www.hot-dog.org/culture/hot-dog-history.

Delaney, James, Jr. "The 1887 Binghamton Bingos." Society for American Baseball Research. https://sabr.org/journal/article/the-1887-binghamton-bingos/.

Dereszewski, John. "The Bushwick Ridgewood Border Was Once Home to a Majorly Important Baseball Field." *Bushwick Daily*, August 16, 2017. https://bushwickdaily.com/community/4877-bushwick-ridgewood-wallace-field/.

digitalballparks.com. Baxter Field. https://digitalballparks.com/CanAm/Baxter1.html.

————. Bay Street Ball Grounds. https://digitalballparks.com/International/BayStreet1.html.

————. Colonial League. https://digitalballparks.com/Colonial/Stitzel6.html.

————. Corning Memorial Stadium. https://digitalballparks.com/NYPenn/Corning1.html.

————. Damaschke Field. https://digitalballparks.com/NYPenn/Damaschke1.html.

————. Delano Hitch Stadium. https://digitalballparks.com/Atlantic/DelanoHitch1.html.

————. Dietz Memorial Stadium. https://digitalballparks.com/Colonial/Dietz1.html.

————. Duffy Fairgrounds. https://digitalballparks.com/NYPenn/Watertown_640_1.html.

————. Dunn Field (II). https://digitalballparks.com/Eastern/Elmira1.html.

————. Dwyer Stadium (I). https://digitalballparks.com/NYPenn/Dwyer1.html.

————. Falcon Park (I). https://digitalballparks.com/NYPenn/Falcon1.html.

————. Glover Park. https://digitalballparks.com/CanAm/Glover1.html.

————. Heritage Park. https://digitalballparks.com/Eastern/Albany1.html.

————. Johnson Field. https://digitalballparks.com/Eastern/JohnsonCity1.html.

————. MacArthur Stadium. https://digitalballparks.com/International/MacArthur1.html.

————. McCallman Field. https://digitalballparks.com/Colonial/Nyack1.html.

————. McConnell Field. https://digitalballparks.com/Eastern/McConnell1.html.

————. McNearney Stadium. https://digitalballparks.com/Eastern/McNearney1.html.

————. New York-Penn League. https://digitalballparks.com/NYPenn/Dwyer_640_2.html.

————. Offerman Stadium. https://digitalballparks.com/AmerAssoc/Rockpile10.html.

———. Silver Stadium. https://digitalballparks.com/International/Silver1.html.

———. Stitzel Field. https://digitalballparks.com/Colonial/Stitzel1.html.

———. Veterans Park. https://digitalballparks.com/NYPenn/LittleFalls1.html.

"The Dyckman Oval." *My Inwood*, December 12, 2012. https://myinwood.net/the-dyckman-oval/.

"The Early Years of Professional Baseball in Schenectady." Grems-Doolittle Library Collections, April 9, 2014. http://gremsdoolittlelibrary.blogspot.com/2014/04/the-early-years-of-professional.html.

"Ebbets Field." *Ballparks, by Munsey and Suppes*. https://ballparks.com/baseball/national/ebbets.htm.

"Ebbets Field Scoreboard." *The Schaefer Story*, January 7, 2010. https://theschaeferstory.wordpress.com/2010/01/07/what-is-this-blog/.

Eberth, John T. "History of Bradner Stadium: Baseball Craze." *Olean Times Herald*, August 3, 2008. https://www.oleantimesherald.com/news/history-of-bradner-stadium-baseball-craze/article_9f1b5584-3150-5514-9e8a-75cf383870f6.html.

Evanosky, Dennis, and Eric J. Kos. *Lost Ballparks*. London: Pavilion, 2017.

Evershed, Floyd J. *A Farewell to Silver*. [Rochester, NY?]: self-published, 1995.

"The Famous Lenox Oval in Harlem NY 1911–1930's." *Harlem World*, October 28, 2016. https://www.harlemworldmagazine.com/famous-lenox-oval-harlem-ny-1911-1930s/.

"The Federal League Ballparks." http://www.toyou.com/fl/ballparks/index.html.

"Federal League Park (Buffalo)." *curveinthedirt.com*, October 16, 2017. https://curveinthedirt.com/2017/10/16/federal-league-park-buf/.

Fiesthumel, Scott. *"Pent-Ups": Minor League Baseball in Utica NY, 1878–1892*. [Utica, NY]: self-published, 1995

Fox, Austin M. "Louise Blanchard Bethune: Buffalo Feminist and America's First Woman Architect." *Buffalo Architecture and History*. https://buffaloah.com/a/archs/beth/bethfox.html.

Freyer, John, and Mark Rucker. *Peverelly's National Game*. Charleston, SC: Arcadia, 2005.

Friedlander, Brett, and Robert Reising. *Chasing Moonlight: The True story of Field of Dreams' Doc Graham*. Winston-Salem, NC: John F. Blair, 2009.

Gershman, Michael. *Diamonds: The Evolution of the Ballpark*. Boston: Houghton Mifflin, 1993.

Gilbert, Thomas W. *How Baseball Happened: Outrageous Lies Exposed! The True Story Revealed*. Boston: Godine, 2020.

Gleason Works. "This Is Our Story." http://www.gleason150.com/the-gleason-works.

Goldman, Mark. "Buffalo's Historic Neighborhoods: Hamlin Park." *Buffalo Architecture and History*. https://buffaloah.com/h/hamln/hamlin.html.

Grondahl, Paul. "Baseball's First Grand Slam Produces a Rensselaer Hero." *Times-Union*, September 17, 2019. https://www.timesunion.com/news/article/Baseball-s-first-grand-slam-produces-a-Rensselaer-14445886.php.

————. "Historian Finds First Grand Slam in MLB History—in Rensselaer." *Times-Union*, March 19, 2019.

Growing Up in Tonawanda. "Tonawanda Driving Park." Facebook, September 8, 2018. https://www.facebook.com/groups/53152993737/permalink/10156 853624873738/.

Hagerty, Tim. "This Day in History: An Entire Team Gets Arrested for Playing on Sunday." *Sporting News*, May 25, 2016. https://www.sportingnews.com/ us/mlb/news/this-date-history-schenectady-frog-alleys-baseball-blue-laws-sunday-arrested/1swktjq0tkkiz13bu487b3kens.

Hall, Paul. "Dunn Field Municipal Stadium—Elmira, New York." *Little Ballparks*. https://littleballparks.com/dunn-field-municipal-stadium-elmira-new-york/.

Hare, James. "Elmira History: 'Demon of the Skies' Wowed Elmirans." *Star-Gazette*, December 23, 2014. https://www.stargazette.com/story/news/local/ twin-tiers-roots/2014/12/23/elmira-history-lincoln-beachey/20830927/.

Hayner, Ryan. "Plattsburgh's Old Ball Game." *Press-Republican*, August 22, 2011. https://www.pressrepublican.com/sports/local_sports/plattsburghs-old-ball-game/article_9ace4056-3f85-5bda-92e3-b983a7146cb3.html.

Hays, Mike. "Nyack People and Places: The Baseball Game of the Century." *Nyack News and Views*, May 17, 2018. https://nyacknewsandviews.com/2018/05/ nyack-people-places-baseball/.

Healey, Paul. "Federal League Park." *Project Ballpark*. http://www.projectballpark. org/history/fl/buffalo.html.

————. "St. George Cricket Grounds." *Project Ballpark*. http://www.projectballpark. org/history/nl/alt/george.html.

————. "Troy Baseball Monument." *Project Ballpark*. http://www.projectballpark. org/other/troymount.html.

————. "Union Grounds." *Project Ballpark*. http://www.projectballpark.org/history/ nl/union.html.

Helander, Brock. "The League Alliance." Society for American Baseball Research. https://sabr.org/bioproj/topic/the-league-alliance/.

"Heritage Park." *Uncle Bob's Ballparks*. https://unclebobsballparks17.tripod.com/ heritagepark/.

Higgs, Norma. "What's in a Name? The History of Sugar Street." *Niagara Gazette*, September 10, 2018. https://www.niagara-gazette.com/opinion/higgs-whats-in-a-name-the-history-of-sugar-street/article_dcb55974-28d9-53ab-b1a5-666a52 c4a038.html.

"Hilltop Park." *Ballparks, by Munsey and Suppes*. https://ballparks.com/baseball/ american/hilltp.htm.

"Hilltop Park Historical Analysis." *Baseball Almanac*. https://www.baseball-almanac. com/stadium/st_hill.shtml.

"History" [Richardson-Bates House]. Oswego County Historical Society. https:// www.rbhousemuseum.org/history/.

Hogan, Lawrence D. "The Negro Leagues Discovered an Oasis at Yankee Stadium." *New York Times*, February 12, 2011. https://www.nytimes.com/2011/02/13/sports/baseball/13stadium.html.

"House for V. F. Whitmore, Esq., Rochester, NY, 1889, Otto Block." St. Croix Architecture. https://www.pinterest.ca/pin/house-for-v-f-whitmore-esq-news--822821794396595758/.

Hyde, Frank. "A Look Back at the Jamestown Falcons." *The Post-Journal*, 1949. http://www.milb.com/gen/articles/printer_friendly/clubs/t489/y2009/m08/d18/c6483428.jsp.

Ilion Free Public Library. "Chismore Pk. View from N. Ilion." Facebook post, March 19, 2020. https://www.facebook.com/ilionfpl/photos/exacta-trifecta-and-daily-double-wagering-anyone-then-go-to-chismore-park-in-ili/2738094722905867/.

"Ilion Recreation and Sports." From *The Centennial Book: Ilion 1852–1952*. https://herkimer.nygenweb.net/ilion/ilionsports.html.

"Iroquois Trail League." *Fandom*. https://baseball.fandom.com/wiki/Iroquois_Trail_League.

James, Nelson. "Ballparks, Scoreboards and Signage: History at Two Baseball Parks." *signs.com*, May 15, 2013. https://www.signs.com/blog/ballparks-scoreboards-and-signage-history-at-two-baseball-parks/.

Johnson, Kevin D. *Ballparks Database*. https://www.seamheads.com/ballparks/index.php.

Kaplan, Dave. "10 Black Baseball Sites in NYC." *Untapped New York*. https://untappedcities.com/2021/02/18/black-baseball-sites-nyc/.

Karpinski, David. "Havana Red Sox at Parkhurst." Parkhurst Field Foundation. http://www.parkhurstfield.org/havana-red-sox-at-parkhurst/.

Keenan, Jimmy. "September 7, 1929: Havana's Luis E. Tiant Knocked Out in Baltimore Exhibition Game." Society for American Baseball Research. https://sabr.org/gamesproj/game/september-7-1929-havanas-luis-e-tiant-knocked-out-in-baltimore-exhibition-game/.

Keetz, Frank. *1899, Schenectady's First Complete Season: An Exciting Factual Account of an Amazing Baseball Season*. Schenectady, NY: self-published, 1980.

———. "Baseball in Schenectady." *Schenectady County Historical Society Newsletter*, September–October 2009. https://schenectadyhistorical.org/admin/wp-content/uploads/2013/08/SEPT-OCT-2009.pdf.

———. *Class "C" Baseball: A Case Study of the Schenectady Blue Jays in the Canadian-American League, 1946–1950*. Schenectady, NY: self-published, 1988.

———. *"Doff Your Caps to the Champions!" Schenectady: A Case Study of a Minor League Baseball Franchise in 1903*. Schenectady, NY: self-published, 1984.

———. *The Mohawk Colored Giants of Schenectady*. Schenectady, NY: self-published, 1999.

————. *They, Too, Were "Boys of Summer": A Case Study of the Schenectady Blue Jays in the Eastern League, 1951–1957*. Schenectady, NY: self-published, 1993.

Kim, Ray. "When Troy Was a Major-League City." http://www.empireone.net/~musicman/troyball.html.

King, Norm. "May 24, 1935: Reds Fans See the Lights in First Night Game in MLB History." https://sabr.org/gamesproj/game/may-24-1935-reds-fans-see-the-lights-in-first-night-game-in-mlb-history/.

Kissel, Tony. "The Pumpkin and Cabbage Tournament of 1866." https://www.tonykisselbaseball.com/articles.

Krutz, David. "Early Baseball in Little Falls and the Little Falls Baseball Association." Little Falls Historical Society Museum. https://littlefallshistoricalsociety.org/museum-exhibit/early-base-ball-in-little-falls/.

Laing, Jeffrey Michael. *The Haymakers, Unions and Trojans of Troy, New York: Big-Time Baseball in the Collar City, 1860–1883*. Jefferson, NC: McFarland, 2015.

Lamb, Bill. "Hilltop Park (New York)." Society for American Baseball Research. https://sabr.org/bioproj/park/hilltop-park-new-york/.

————. "Metropolitan Park (New York)." Society for American Baseball Research. https://sabr.org/bioproj/park/metropolitan-park-new-york/.

————. "Ridgewood Park (New York)." Society for American Baseball Research. https://sabr.org/bioproj/park/ridgewood-park-ny/.

"Landmarking: Wonder Bread Factory." *Buffalo Rising*, September 7, 2018. https://www.buffalorising.com/2018/09/landmarking-wonder-bread-factory/.

Lang, Max. "Mountain Athletic Club at Fleischmanns Park Gains Historic Designation." *The Daily Star*, November 18, 2020. https://www.thedailystar.com/sports/local_sports/mountain-athletic-club-at-fleischmanns-park-gains-historic-designation/article_8da500f0-f098-5882-9ff4-dfb52c77d273.html.

Langendorfer, Paul. *Baseball in Buffalo: Images of Baseball*. Charleston, SC: Arcadia, 2017

"The Laureate Boat Club." Lansingburgh Historical Society. https://www.lansingburghhistoricalsociety.org/laureate-boat-club.

Leiner, James F. "Rockland Baseball Has Roots in Nyack." *Patch*, June 15, 2011. https://patch.com/new-york/nyack/bp--professional-baseball-in-rockland-country-started-in-nyack.

Leland, Jacob. "Black Baseball: Giants, Giants Split Doubleheader at Ebbets Field." *New York 1920s: 100 Years Ago Today, When We Became Modern*, July 17, 2020. https://www.ny1920.com/jul-17.

LeMoine, Bob. "February 4, 1861: Brooklyn Atlantics Win a Baseball Game on Ice." Society for American Baseball Research. https://sabr.org/gamesproj/game/february-4-1861-brooklyn-atlantics-win-a-baseball-game-on-ice/.

Linnabery, Ann Marie. "Niagara Discoveries: The Screwball Club." *Lockport Union-Sun and Journal*, January 26, 2019. https://www.lockportjournal.com/news/

lifestyles/niagara-discoveries-the-screwball-club/article_aecde00b-14eb-58
ee-8c30-942e8656c18f.html.

Linnabery, Ann Marie, and Jim Boles. "Over the Hill: A Brief History of Outwater
Park." *Lockport Union-Sun and Journal*, September 17, 2020. https://www.
lockportjournal.com/news/lifestyles/over-the-hill-a-brief-history-of-out-
water-park/article_50f3b1a2-5e23-5e5c-a798-9b7d090192a4.html.

Lippman, David. *List of New York's Baseball Sites*. Society for American Baseball Research, Casey Stengel Chapter–New York City. http://sabrnyc.org/
NYBaseballSites.pdf.

"Look Back: Photo Gallery of Bleecker St. in Utica." *Observer-Dispatch*, July
3, 2013. https://www.uticaod.com/picture-gallery/news/local/2013/07/04/
look-back-photo-gallery-of/509753007/.

Los Angeles Dodgers. "Ballparks: 1862–Present." https://www.mlb.com/dodgers/
history/ballparks.

"The Lost Baseball Stadium That Became a Supermarket Parking Lot." *Untapped
New York*. https://untappedcities.com/2019/10/08/dexter-park-the-lost-base-
ball-stadium-that-became-a-supermarket-parking-lot/.

Love, Robert. *The Great Oom: The Improbable Birth of Yoga in America*. New
York: Viking, 2010.

Luse, Vern. "The 1903 Hudson River League." Society for American Baseball
Research, Research Journals Archive. http://research.sabr.org/journals/1903-
hudson-river-league.

MacAlpine, Rich. "The Penn Yan Colored Giants (the 1925 Season)." *Yates Past*,
September 2007. Yates County History Center. http://www.yatespast.org/
articles/coloredgiants.html

———. "The Penn Yan Cuban Giants (1924)." *Yates Past*, July 2007. Yates County
History Center. http://www.yatespast.org/articles/cubangiants.html.

"Madison Square Park: Where Baseball Was Born." *Ephemeral New York*. https://
ephemeralnewyork.wordpress.com/2012/07/23/madison-square-park-where-
baseball-was-born/.

Maggiore, Jim, and Michael J. McCann. *Celebrating 100 Years of Baseball in Greater
Binghamton*. Vestal, NY: self-published, 2014.

Mahoney, Ryan. "Schenectady Baseball History: The Mohawk Giants." *New York
Almanack*, March 6, 2013. https://www.newyorkalmanack.com/2013/03/
schenectady-baseball-history-the-mohawk-giants/.

Mandelaro, Jim, and Scott Pitoniak. *Silver Seasons: The Story of the Rochester Red
Wings*. Syracuse, NY: Syracuse University Press, 1996.

Martin, Alfred M., and Alfred T. Martin. "The Mohawk Colored Giants of Schenectady." In *The Negro Leagues in New Jersey: A History*. Jefferson, NC:
McFarland, 2008.

"The Marvin House." *The Chautauqua County Historic Structures Database*. http://
app.chautauquacounty.com/hist_struct/Jamestown/12WestFifthStreetJames-
town.html.

Mayer, Bob. "The Asylum Base Ball Club: The Great Reunion Game, September 29, 1905." Society for American Baseball Research. https://sabr.org/journal/article/the-asylum-base-ball-club-the-great-reunion-game-september-29-1905/.

McCarthy, William E. *Rochester Diamond Echoes*. [Rochester, NY]: self-published, 1949.

McGreal, Jim. "Colonial League a Trail Blazer in 1947 Debut." Society for American Baseball Research. http://research.sabr.org/journals/stamford-team-fielded-six-black-players.

McKenna, Brian. "Mountain Athletic Club." *Glimpses into Baseball History*, June 13, 2011. https://bit.ly/2zqUS3w.

Mele, Andrew Paul. "Staten Island Memories: When the Mets Called the Island Home." *silive.com*, August 18, 2013. https://www.silive.com/memories_column/2013/08/staten_island_memories_when_the_mets_called_the_island_home.html.

Menand, Howard. *History of Menands*. https://villageofmenands.com/wp-content/uploads/2016/06/Menands-History-by-Howard-Menand-1974-anniversary-book.pdf.

Messenger, Robert. " 'Ilion Is Remington and Remington Is Ilion': An End to Typewriter Ties with New York Village?" *ozTypewriter*, November 3, 2020. https://oztypewriter.blogspot.com/2020/11/ilion-is-remington-and-remington-is.html.

"The Mohawk Colored Giants of Schenectady." *All over Albany*, February 13, 2015. http://alloveralbany.com/archive/2015/02/13/the-mohawk-colored-giants-of-schenectady.

The Mohawk Giants: Schenectady and the Negro Leagues. WMHT. Video. https://www.wmht.org/mohawk/.

Morin, Dave. "William Henry Baldwin." *The Yankee Volunteer: A Virtual Archive of Civil War Likenesses*. https://dmorinsite.wordpress.com/officer-2nd-lieutenant-unidentified/.

Morris, Peter, William J. Ryczek, Jan Finkel, Leonard Levin, and Richard Malatzky, eds. *Base Ball Founders: The Clubs, Players, and Cities of the Northeast That Established the Game*. Jefferson, NC: McFarland, 2013.

———, eds. *Base Ball Pioneers, 1850–1870: The Clubs and Players Who Spread the Sport Nationwide*. Jefferson, NC: McFarland, 2012.

Morry, Emily. "Tonight There's Gonna Be a Jailbreak: Crime and Punishment at the Western House of Refuge." Rochester Public Library. https://rochistory.wordpress.com/2019/12/30/tonight-theres-gonna-be-a-jailbreak-crime-and-punishment-at-the-western-house-of-refuge/.

"Mountain Athletic Club, 1895–1914." Mountain Athletic Club Vintage Base Ball. https://www.macvintagebaseball.org/macbaseballhistory1895-1914.

Nemec, David. "Jay Faatz." Society for American Baseball Research. https://sabr.org/bioproj/person/jay-faatz/.

New Century Atlas of Herkimer County, New York. Philadelphia: Century Map, 1906.

New York Mets. "Citi Field." https://www.mlb.com/mets/ballpark.

Nielsen, Euell A. "The Lincoln Giants (1911–1930)." *Black Past*, December 31, 2020. https://www.blackpast.org/african-american-history/the-lincoln-giants-1911-1930/.

Nightingale, Van. "The Unknowable Superstar (Part 3)." Guest blog, May 3, 2017. Ars Longa Art Cards. http://arslongaartcards.com/guest-blog/.

"Northern New York League." *Fandom*. https://baseball.fandom.com/wiki/Northern_New_York_League.

Older, Patricia. "Rise and fall of the Fulton County Fair." *Leader-Herald*, September 4, 2017. https://leaderherald.com/gloversville-local-news-johnstown-local-news/local-news/2017/09/rise-and-fall-of-the-fulton-county-fair/.

O'Reilly, Charles. *Charlie's Big Baseball Parks Page*. https://www.charliesballparks.com/stadiums.htm.

"Original 1913 Mohawk Giants Team." New York Heritage, Digital Collections. https://cdm16694.contentdm.oclc.org/digital/collection/p16694coll45/id/236/.

Outlaw League Executives. Photograph, 1912. Bain New Service photograph collection, Library of Congress. https://www.loc.gov/item/2014690252/.

Overfield, James H., ed. *The Seasons of Buffalo Baseball, 1857–2020*. Grand Island, NY: Billoni Associates, 2020

Parkhurst Field Foundation. https://www.parkhurstfield.org/.

Perfect Game Collegiate Baseball League. "Ballparks of the PGCBL: Colburn Park." https://pgcbl.com/news/index.html?article_id=432.

———. "Ballparks of the PGCBL: Damaschke Field." https://pgcbl.com/news/index.html?article_id=4.

———. "Ballparks of the PGCBL: Duffy Fairgrounds." https://pgcbl.com/news/index.html?article_id=439.

———. "Ballparks of the PGCBL: Shuttleworth Park." http://pgcbl.com/news/index.html?article_id=487.

Pietrusza, David. *Baseball's Canadian-American League*. Jefferson, NC: McFarland, 1990.

———. *Minor Miracles: The Legend and Lure of Minor League Baseball*. South Bend, IN: Diamond Communications, 1995.

Pitoniak, Scott. *Baseball in Rochester*. Charleston, SC: Arcadia, 2003.

———. "Gem of Local Baseball History Found." Negro League Baseball Players Association, February 26, 2006. http://www.nlbpa.com/news/febuary-26-2006.

———. "Vintage Baseball League Evokes the 19th-Century Game." AARP, September 18, 2020. https://www.aarp.org/home-family/friends-family/info-2020/vintage-baseball-leagues.html.

protoball.org. "Club of Newburgh." https://protoball.org/Club_of_Newburgh.

———. Fields in New York index page. https://protoball.org/Fields_in_NY.

Pousson, Eli. "Ward Baking Company Building." *Explore Baltimore Heritage.* https://explore.baltimoreheritage.org/items/show/292.

"Professional Baseball in Port Chester, New York: Historical Records." http://www.luckyshow.org/baseball/PortChester.htm.

Puff, Richard A., ed. *The Empire State of Base Ball: A Look at the Game in Upstate New York.* Albany, NY: Society for American Baseball Research, 1989.

———, ed. *Troy's Baseball Heritage.* Troy, NY: Committee to Preserve Troy's Baseball Heritage, 1992.

Puma, Mike. "The History of Hamlin Park, Part IV: Hamlin's Driving Park and the Home Builders." *Buffalo Rising*, August 21, 2013. https://www.buffalorising.com/2013/08/the-history-of-hamlin-park-part-iv-hamlins-driving-park-and-the-home-builders/.

"Randall's Island Park." New York City Department of Parks and Recreation. https://www.nycgovparks.org/parks/randalls-island/highlights/6515.

Revel, Layton. *Early Pioneers of the Negro Leagues: Nat Strong.* Center for Negro League Baseball Research, 2016. http://www.cnlbr.org/Portals/0/EP/Nat%20Strong%202018-04.pdf.

Riggs, Jim. "Jamestown Played a Role in Black Baseball History." *The Post-Journal*, July 6, 2019. https://www.post-journal.com/sports/local-sports/2019/07/jamestown-played-a-role-in-black-baseball-history/.

"The Rise of the Cubans." *Harlem Baseball.* https://harlembaseball.weebly.com/the-rise-of-the-cubans.html.

Robertson, Stephen. "Harlem and Baseball in the 1920s." *Digital Harlem Blog*, July 27, 2011. https://drstephenrobertson.com/digitalharlemblog/maps/baseball-1920s-harlem/.

Robinson, Sandy. "The Magic of Allen Park." *The Post-Journal*, March 25, 2018. https://www.post-journal.com/life/arts-entertainment/2018/03/the-magic-of-allen-park/.

Rochester Baseball Historical Society. "Research Projects." https://rochesterbaseballhistory.org/research-projects/.

Roe, Dawn. "Meet Some of Auburn's Earliest Baseball Players." *Citizen*, November 24, 2013. https://auburnpub.com/columnists/dawn_roe/meet-some-of-auburns-earliest-baseball-players/article_c532937e-af9c-5685-ac57-43317b1669f3.html.

"Roots of Local Baseball." *Observer*, April 9, 2015. https://www.observertoday.com/sports/local-sports/2015/04/roots-of-local-baseball/.

Ross, Andrew, and David Dyte. "The Brooklyn Bandits." *BrooklynBallParks.com.* http://www.covehurst.net/ddyte/brooklyn/bandits.html.

———. "Brooklyn's Ancient Ball Fields." *BrooklynBallParks.com.* http://www.covehurst.net/ddyte/brooklyn/ancient.html.

———. "Brooklyn's Semipro Fields." *BrooklynBallParks.com.* http://www.covehurst.net/ddyte/brooklyn/semipro_parks.html.

———. "The Capitoline Grounds." *BrooklynBallParks.com*. http://www.brooklyn-ballparks.com/.

———. "Dexter Park." *BrooklynBallParks.com*. http://www.covehurst.net/ddyte/brooklyn/dexter.html.

———. "Eastern Park." *BrooklynBallParks.com*. http://www.covehurst.net/ddyte/brooklyn/eastern_park.html.

———. "Ebbets Field." *BrooklynBallParks.com*. http://www.brooklynballparks.com.

———. "The Parks of Maspeth." *BrooklynBallParks.com*. http://www.covehurst.net/ddyte/brooklyn/maspeth.html.

———. "Washington Park." *BrooklynBallParks.com*. http://www.covehurst.net/ddyte/brooklyn/washington_park.html.

———. "The Washington Park Wall." *BrooklynBallParks.com*. http://www.covehurst.net/ddyte/brooklyn/washwall.html.

"Russell Diethrick Park." *In the Ballparks*. https://www.intheballparks.com/pgcbl/diethrick.

Ryczek, Bill. "Baseball's First Enclosed Field, Brooklyn's Union Grounds." Society for American Baseball Research. https://sabr.org/latest/ryczek-baseballs-first-enclosed-field-brooklyns-union-grounds/.

Schenectady County Historical Society. "Laura Brown Slide Collection" [catalog]. https://schenectadyhistorical.org/admin/wp-content/uploads/2010/07/2006.2.16-Laura-Brown-Slide-Collection.pdf.

Schlapp, Ken. "Past Ballparks of New York City." *ballparksofbaseball.com*. http://www.ballparksofbaseball.com/kenschlapp/nyc_past_three.htm.

Schultz, John Patrick. "A True Nyack Character . . . Pierre Bernard." *At Home in Nyack*, September 3, 2010. https://athomeinnyack.wordpress.com/2010/09/03/a-true-nyack-character-pierre-bernard/.

Schwartz, Larry. "Hodges Sets NL Record with Four Home Runs." *ESPN Classic*, November 19, 2003. http://www.espn.com/classic/s/moment010831-hodges-four-HRs.html.

Seymour, Harold. *Baseball: The Early Years*. New York: Oxford University Press, 1960.

Shenk, Larry. "5 Catchers Who Left a Mark on the Phillies." MLB, news, November 4, 2015. https://www.mlb.com/news/phillies-top-catchers-in-franchise-history/c-156466686.

"Silver Stadium." Emporis. https://www.emporis.com/buildings/1395997/silver-stadium-rochester-ny-usa.

Simonson, Mark. "The Early Years: Local area benefactor Morris honored in 1936." *The Daily Star* (Oneonta), December 9, 2016. https://www.thedailystar.com/opinion/columns/backtracking-the-early-years-local-area-benefactor-morris-honored-in-1936/article_b2a455ca-5424-575a-b427-d21227ea96c4.html.

Spellen, Suzanne. "The Architect, the Baseball Stadium and a Really Bad Couple of Years." *Brownstoner*, June 25, 2015. https://www.brownstoner.com/history/walkabout-the-architect-the-baseball-stadium-and-a-really-bad-couple-of-years/.

———. "The Ward Bakery Company, the Snow-White Temple of Cleanliness." *Brownstoner*, April 7, 2015. https://www.brownstoner.com/history/walkabout-the-ward-bakery-company-the-snow-white-temple-of-cleanliness/.

Staten Island Cricket Club. "A Brief History." https://www.statenislandcc.org/history.

Stats Crew. "1888 Eastern International League." https://www.statscrew.com/minorbaseball/l-EINT/y-1888.

———. "1890 Jamestown Roster." https://www.statscrew.com/minorbaseball/roster/t-jj12216/y-1890.

———. "1890 Western New York League." https://www.statscrew.com/minorbaseball/l-WNYL/y-1890.

———. "1898 New York State League." https://www.statscrew.com/minorbaseball/l-NYSL/y-1898.

———. "1903 Amsterdam-Johnstown-Gloversville Hyphens Roster." https://www.statscrew.com/minorbaseball/roster/t-ah10138/y-1903.

———. "1903 Hudson River League." https://www.statscrew.com/minorbaseball/l-HUDR/y-1903.

———. "1903 Kingston Colonials Statistics." https://www.statscrew.com/minorbaseball/stats/t-kc12350/y-1903.

———. "1903 Newburgh Taylor-Mades Statistics." https://www.statscrew.com/minorbaseball/stats/t-nt13339/y-1903.

———. "1905 Empire State League Standings." https://www.statscrew.com/minorbaseball/standings/l-EMST/y-1905.

———. "1905 Saugerties/Pittsfield Hillies Statistics." https://www.statscrew.com/minorbaseball/stats/t-ss14442/y-1905.

———. "1906 Empire State League Standings." https://www.statscrew.com/minorbaseball/standings/l-EMST/y-1906.

———. "1907 Poughkeepsie Colts Statistics." https://www.statscrew.com/minorbaseball/stats/t-pc13914/y-1907.

———. "1907 Utica Pent-Ups Roster." https://www.statscrew.com/minorbaseball/roster/t-up15101/y-1907.

———. "1909 Newburgh Roster." https://www.statscrew.com/minorbaseball/roster/t-nn13332/y-1909.

———. "1913 New York-New Jersey League." https://www.statscrew.com/minorbaseball/l-ATLL3/y-1913.

———. "Ambrose McConnell Field." https://www.statscrew.com/venues/v-2784.

———. "Athletic Grounds." https://www.statscrew.com/venues/v-1971.

———. "Athletic Park." https://www.statscrew.com/venues/v-1335.

————. "Canisteo Franchise History (1890)." https://www.statscrew.com/minor baseball/t-cc10705.

————. "Canton Franchise History (1901)." https://www.statscrew.com/minor baseball/t-cc11707.

————. "Celeron Park." https://www.statscrew.com/venues/v-1254.

————. "Donovan Stadium." https://www.statscrew.com/venues/v-2785.

————. "Elmira Pioneers Franchise History (1895–2005)." https://www.statscrew. com/minorbaseball/t-ep11410.

————. "Empire Stadium." https://www.statscrew.com/venues/v-2152.

————. "Geneva Franchise History (1906–1907)." https://www.statscrew.com/ minorbaseball/t-gg11694.

————. "Glens Falls-Saratoga Springs Franchise History (1906)." https://www. statscrew.com/minorbaseball/t-gs11713.

————. "Guy Park." https://www.statscrew.com/venues/v-78.

————. "Hawkins Stadium." https://www.statscrew.com/venues/v-41.

————. "Heritage Park." https://www.statscrew.com/venues/v-43.

————. "Hudson Marines Franchise History (1903–1907)." https://www.statscrew. com/minorbaseball/t-hm12090.

————. "Ilion/Fulton Franchise History (1905–1907)." https://www.statscrew.com/ minorbaseball/t-ff11646.

————. "Island Park." https://www.statscrew.com/venues/v-2478.

————. "Johnson Field." https://www.statscrew.com/venues/v-261.

————. "Lyons Franchise History (1897–1907)." https://www.statscrew.com/ minorbaseball/t-ll12731.

————. "Malone Franchise History (1887–1902)." https://www.statscrew.com/ minorbaseball/t-mm12763.

————. "New York State League Team Rosters and Statistics"[a]. https://www. statscrew.com/minorbaseball/l-NYSL.

————. "New York State League Team Rosters and Statistics"[b]. https://www. statscrew.com/minorbaseball/l-IL.

————. "Niagara-Rhode Island Grounds." https://www.statscrew.com/venues/v-369.

————. "No Known Name." https://www.statscrew.com/venues/v-2033.

————. "Nu-Crume Park." https://www.statscrew.com/venues/v-1903.

————. "Otis Field." https://www.statscrew.com/venues/v-2005.

————. "Outwater Park." https://www.statscrew.com/venues/v-1490.

————. "Peekskill Franchise History (1888–1905)." https://www.statscrew.com/ minorbaseball/t-pp13691.

————. "Penn Yan Franchise History (1888–1906)." https://www.statscrew.com/ minorbaseball/t-py13706.

————. "Richardson Park." https://www.statscrew.com/venues/v-2003.

————. "Riverside Park." https://www.statscrew.com/venues/v-2303.

————. "Seward Avenue Park." https://www.statscrew.com/venues/v-146.

————. "Sports in Elmira, New York." https://www.statscrew.com/sports/places/m-4156267.

————. "Sports in Jamestown, New York." https://www.statscrew.com/sports/places/m-4157220.

————. "Sports in Olean, New York." https://www.statscrew.com/sports/places/m-4158419.

————. "Sports in Utica, New York." https://www.statscrew.com/sports/places/m-4159950.

————. "Syracuse Stars Franchise History (1877–1941)." https://www.statscrew.com/minorbaseball/t-ss14851.

————. "Tullar Field." https://www.statscrew.com/venues/v-2886.

————. "War Memorial Stadium." https://www.statscrew.com/venues/v-619.

————. "Watts Field." https://www.statscrew.com/venues/v-1681.

————. "Winter Park." https://www.statscrew.com/venues/v-1956.

"Syracuse Chiefs." *Fun While It Lasted*. https://funwhileitlasted.net/2019/10/27/1961-2018-syracuse-chiefs/.

Thorn, John. "The All-Star Game You Don't Know." *Our Game*, July 8, 2013. https://ourgame.mlblogs.com/the-all-star-game-you-dont-know-cf8082747852.

————. "Base Ball in Brooklyn, 1845 to 1870: The Best There Was." *Our Game*, August 20, 2012. https://ourgame.mlblogs.com/base-ball-in-brooklyn-1845-to-1870-the-best-there-was-89848ac1de40.

————. "Baseball's First All-Star Game." *Our Game*, July 9, 2012. https://ourgame.mlblogs.com/baseballs-first-all-star-game-4fcda47ecab2.

————. "Mangled Forms." *Our Game*, October 11, 2016. https://ourgame.mlblogs.com/mangled-forms-b7f73a2e40d9.

————. "Remember the Old Hudson River League?" *Thorn Pricks*, May 9, 2005. http://thornpricks.blogspot.com/2005/05/remember-old-hudson-river-league.html.

————. "Walt Whitman, Baseball Reporter: The Poet Worked the Beat." *Our Game*, April 25, 2016. https://ourgame.mlblogs.com/walt-whitman-baseball-reporter-973282e2ab58.

————. "When Baseball Was Big in Kingston." *Thorn Pricks*, May 25, 2006. http://thornpricks.blogspot.com/2006/05/when-baseball-was-big-in-kingston.html.

Thornley, Stew, ed. *The Polo Grounds*. Jefferson, NC: McFarland, 2019.

"Troy Trojans Attendance, Stadiums, and Park Factors." *Baseball Reference*. https://www.baseball-reference.com/teams/TRT/attend.shtml.

Village of Celoron. "Park History." http://www.celoronny.org/html/history.html.

Village of Saugerties. "Cantine Veterans Memorial Complex (a.k.a. Cantine Field)." https://villagesaugerties.digitaltowpath.org:10064/content/Parks/View/6.

Violanti, Anthony. *Miracle in Buffalo: How the Dream of Baseball Revived a City.* New York: St. Martin's, 1991.

Wager, Paul. "Year of the (Baseball) Glove—J. A. Peach Company." *Leader-Herald*, May 5, 2019. https://leaderherald.com/sports/local-sports/2019/05/upstate-n-y-sports-lore-year-of-the-baseball-glove-j-a-peach-company/.

———. "Year of the (Baseball) Glove—Ken-Wel Sporting Goods." *Leader-Herald*, May 12, 2019. https://leaderherald.com/sports/local-sports/2019/05/year-of-the-baseball-glove-ken-wel-sporting-goods/.

———. "Year of the (Baseball) Glove—M. Denkert & Company." *Leader-Herald*, May 26, 2019. https://leaderherald.com/sports/local-sports/2019/05/upstate-n-y-sports-lore-year-of-the-baseball-glove-m-denkert-company/.

"Walker Park." New York City Department of Parks and Recreation. https://www.nycgovparks.org/parks/walker-park/history.

Walsh, Bernard G., and Timothy P. Murphy. *The Fields of New York.* Bloomington, IN: AuthorHouse, 2015.

Walter, Jason. *Heritage Park, Colonie, New York.* Photographs. http://www.frontiernet.net/~rochballparks2/albany/heritage.htm.

"Watts Memorial Park, Middletown, New York." *BaseballparkReviews.com.* http://www.ballparkreviews.com/template2.php?in_name=Watts+Memorial+Park&in_city=Middletown&in_state=New%20York.

Weingardt, Richard G. "Frank Osborn: Nation's Pioneer Stadium Designer." *Structure*, March 2013. https://www.structuremag.org/?p=930.

"Western House of Refuge." *Lost Rochester.* Monroe County (NY) Library System. https://www.libraryweb.org/rochimag/architecture/LostRochester/WesternHouse/WesternHouse.htm.

"Western House of Refuge." *RocWiki.* https://rocwiki.org/Western_House_of_Refuge.

Whittemore, Bob. *Baseball Town: A Place Where Yankees Grow.* Manchester Center, VT: M. Jones, 1995.

"William C. Gray." *Biographies of Monroe County People.* https://mcnygenealogy.com/bios/biographies033.htm.

William G. Pomeroy Foundation. Richardson background. https://www.wgpfoundation.org/historic-markers/on-this-site/.

Wilkin, Jeff. "Local Baseball Teams Date Back to 1800s." *Daily Gazette*, March 30, 2015. https://dailygazette.com/2015/03/30/local-baseball-tea_wp/.

Worth, Richard. *Baseball Team Names: A Worldwide Dictionary, 1869–2011.* Jefferson, NC: McFarland, 2012.

Yankeebiscuitfan. "Minor League History: Eastern Association." *Dutch Baseball Hangout*, February 15, 2016. https://dutchbaseballhangout.blog/2016/02/15/minor-league-history-eastern-association/.

———. "Minor League History: Iron and Oil League." *Dutch Baseball Hangout*, April 18, 2017. https://dutchbaseballhangout.blog/2017/04/18/minor-league-history-iron-and-oil-league/.

Yasinsac, Rob. "Heritage Park, Colonie, NY." *Hudson Valley Ruins.* http://www. hudsonvalleyruins.org/yasinsac/albany/heritagepark.html.

"Yates County Fair." Freethought Trail. https://freethought-trail.org/trail-map/ location:yates-county-fair/.

"Yates County Fair—Once Attracted Carrie Nation and Billy Sunday." Yates County History Center. http://www.yatespast.org/articles/ycfair.html.

"Yonkers Police Historical Notes." https://www.yonkersny.gov/live/public-safety/ police-department/police-history/historical-notes.

"Zachary Taylor Davis." http://zacharytaylordavis.com/.

Zinn, John G. "Summer 1858: The Brooklyn-New York Baseball Rivalry Begins." Society for American Baseball Research. https://sabr.org/gamesproj/game/ summer-1858-the-brooklyn-new-york-baseball-rivalry-begins/.

Name Index

59th Street Sandlot/Recreation Park, 10, *41*, 58

Addison and Wellsville Strippers, 135, 136
Addison and Wellsville Tobacco Strippers, 79
Addison White Sox, 79
Adirondack Lumberjacks, 217–218
Aguilera, Rick, 154
Albany Black Sox, 206
Albany Champions, 203
Albany Cricket Grounds, 199–200
Albany Live Oaks, 255
Albany Senators, 202–203, 205, 206
Albany-Colonie A's, 206
Albany-Colonie A's and Yankees, 211–212
Albany-Colonie Diamond Dogs, 211
Albions (Brooklyn), 23
Alcoa (Aluminum Company of America), 156
Alcoa Field, 156
Alert Grounds (Schenectady), 244
Alerts (Little Falls), 153
Alerts (Schenectady), 244
Alerts Baseball Club (Rochester), 168–169
Alex T. Duffy Fairgrounds, 197–198

Allen Park, 127–128
Alou, Moises, 198
Altrock, Nick, 215
American Association, 23, 44, 45, 50, 62, 63, 65, 74, 123, 172, 175, 188
American League, 12, 27, 37, 39, 40, 48, 51, 52, 71, 85, 118
Amsterdam Carpet Tacks and Red Stockings, 207
Amsterdam Empires, 208–209
Amsterdam Rugmakers, 208–209
Ancient Cities (Schenectady), 244
Armory Park, 185–186
Asphalt Giants, 248
Athletic Association Grounds, 132–133
Athletic Field (Cortland), 143–144
Athletic Grounds/Park (Kingston), 227
Athletic Park/Nu-Crume Park (Niagara Falls), *105*, 130–131
Atlanta Black Crackers, 77
Atlantic Association, 63
Atlantic Base Ball Club of Brooklyn, 61
Atlantic Club (Brooklyn), 17, 20
Atlantic Grounds, *15*, 17
Atlantic League, 36, 68–70, 89, 90, 229, 230, 231, 240

Brooklyn Alerts, 16
Brooklyn Atlantics, 17, 23, 31, 33, 34, 62, 69, 107, 187, 192, 256
Brooklyn Atlantics, Edisons, Senors, and Invaders, 68
Brooklyn Brown Dodgers, 36, 40
Brooklyn Charter Oaks, 16
Brooklyn Chelseas, 33
Brooklyn Cyprus Hills, Dexters, and Bushwicks, 66
Brooklyn Eagles, 36, 40
Brooklyn Eckfords, 31, 161
Brooklyn Edisons, 36
Brooklyn Enterprise, 33
Brooklyn Esculapians, 16
Brooklyn Excelsiors, 16, 33, 106, 168
Brooklyn Farmers, 69
Brooklyn Gladiators, 63, 64, 65
Brooklyn Grays, Bridegrooms, Superbas, Trolley Dodgers, Robins, Nationals, and Dodgers, 23, 24, 25, 26, 31, 35, 36, 37, 38, 39, 40, 62, 63, 64, 71, 73, 77, 94, 134, 148, 205, 249, 252
Brooklyn Independent, 16
Brooklyn Marions, 18
Brooklyn Mohawk, 16–17
Brooklyn Murray Hills, 87
Brooklyn Mutuals, 20, 31, 33
Brooklyn Paramounts, 65
Brooklyn Pioneers, 36
Brooklyn Powhatans, 33
Brooklyn Ridgewoods, 28, 63, 64, 68–69, 70
Brooklyn Royal Giants, 66, 70, 97, 101, 190, 222
Brooklyn Royal-Cuban Giants, 63
Brooklyn Royals, 91
Brooklyn Stars, 16–17, 230
Brooklyn Tip Tops, 27–30
Brooklyn Typographicals, 16
Brooklyn Ward's Wonders, 35

Brooklyn Waverlys, 16
Brooklyn-Philadelphia Colored Giants, 83
Brooklyn, Penn Yan, and Cumberland (MD) Cuban Giants, 65, 164–165
Brotherhood-Players League, 35, 47, 112
Brown's Square, University Grounds, Franklin Square, 165–167
Buckner, Harry, 248
Buffalo Baseball League Grounds/City Baseball Park/Franklin Park/East Side Base Ball Grounds, 105, 112, 113–114, 115
Buffalo Bisons (the "little" Bisons), 113, 114
Buffalo Bisons, 109, 110, 111, 112, 113, 114, 115, 116, 117, 118, 119, 120, 121, 123, 124, 131
Buffalo Buffalos and Bisons, 109
Buffalo Buffeds, Blues, and Electrics, 117, 119
Buffalo Driving Park, 118
Buffalo Mutuals, 106
Buffalo Niagaras, 106–107, 117
Buffalo Niagaras and Cliftons, 106
Buffalo Niagaras and Eries, 105, 106
Buffalo Pan-Ams, 116
Buhner, Jay, 198
Bull's Head Tavern Grounds, 253, 257, 257–258
Bunning, Jim, 121
Burgor, Frank, 153
Burrows, William F., 110

Cammeyer, William, 31–32
Can-Am League, 95, 99, 100, 101, 139, 140, 156, 159, 162, 163, 183, 196, 197, 208, 224, 225, 228, 250, 251
Canandaigua Rustlers, 142
Capital City Club, 172

House of David, 12, 134, 152, 223, 234
Houston Buffs, 180, 205
Howard Street Grounds, 102, 103–104
Howell, George, 249
Hudson Marines, 225–226
Hudson River Driving Park, 239
Hudson River League, 75, 76, 202, 210, 215, 218, 225, 226, 227, 230, 235, 236, 240, 242, 243, 260
Hudson River Power and Transmission Company, 246
Huggins, Miller, 14, 215
Hundley, Todd, 154
Hussey, Ambrose William Jr., 28, 69
Hussey, Ambrose William Sr., 28, 64, 69, 70
Hyde Park Stadium/Sal Maglie Stadium, *105*, 123, 130, 131–132
Hyde, Charles B., 131

Ilion Clippers, 150
Ilion Independents, 150
Ilion Riflemen and Ilionites, 150, 151
Ilion Typewriters, 151
Independent Northern League, 238
Indianapolis Blues, 108
Indianapolis Clowns, 121, 191, 252
International Association, 80, 96, 108, 109, 113, 171, 172, 175, 187, 188, 193, 202, 260
International League, 80, 81, 84, 109, 110, 112, 119, 120, 123, 130, 131, 139, 161, 164, 172, 174, 178, 180, 181, 188, 190, 191, 193, 205, 237, 242
International League of Colored Baseball Clubs, 63
Interstate League, 23, 97, 124, 125, 133, 136
Interstate League Park, 133

Invincibles (Buffalo), 107
Iron and Oil League, 124, 125, 132
Ironsides (Brooklyn), 23
Island Park (Wellsville), 135–136
Island Park/Columbus Park (Schenectady), 54, 245–250
Ithaca Ithacas, 152

J.A. Peach Company, 222
James J. Fleming Field/Prescott Field, 77–78
Jamestown Falcons, 128, 129
Jamestown Hill Climbers and Dubois Miners, 124, 125
Jamestown Jaguars and Pirates, 124
Jamestown Lohrels, Rabbits, and Giants, 124, 125
Jamestown Municipal Stadium/College Stadium/Russell E. Diethrick, Jr., Park, 128–129
Jamestown Oseejays, 124, 125
Jamestown Tigers, Dodgers, Braves, Falcons, Expos, and Jammers, 128
Jasper Oval/Hebrew Orphan Asylum Oval, *42*, 57
Jersey City Jerseys, 63
Jersey City Skeeters, 63
Jeter, Derek, 212
Jewett, Josiah, 110
John J. Downing Stadium/Triborough Stadium/Randall's Island Stadium, *41*, 57–58
John Schwabl's Park/Forest Grove Park, *105*, 114, 115
Johnson Field, 83, *84*, 84–85
Johnson, Ban, 52
Johnson, Chappie, 209, 248, 249
Johnson, Charles Fred, 85
Johnson, George F., 83, 84–85
Johnson, Mark, 123
Johnson, Walter, 222, 249
Johnstown Buckskins, 218

Johnstown Fair Grounds/Fulton County-Johnstown Fairgrounds, 218–219
Johnstown, Amsterdam, and Gloversville Jags, 218, 219
Johnstown, Amsterdam, and Gloversville Jags and Hyphens, 207
Jones Square (Jones Square Park), *166*, 168–170, *169*
Jurrgens, Jair, 102

Kansas City Athletics, 85, 121
Kansas City Monarchs, 40, 205
Kansas City Royals, 88
Keeler, "Wee" Willie, 81
Kelly, Don, 102
Kelly, R. A., 127
Ken-Wel Sporting Goods, 222
Kingsbridge Athletics, 55, 56
Kingston Colonials, 206, 226–227
Kingston Dodgers, 228
Kingston Driving Park, 226–227
Kingston Hubs and Colonials, 228
Kingston Leaders, 226
Kingston Municipal Stadium/Robert Dietz Memorial Stadium, 227–228
Kingston Patriarchs and Colonels, 226
Kline, Steve, 198
Knickerbocker Club (Albany), 202
Koufax, Sandy, 16
Kranepool, Ed, 140

Laconia and Plattsburgh Brewers, 238–239
Lakeside Park, *186*, 187–188
Lansingburgh Griswolds, 255
Larson, Don, 14
Lasorda, Tommy, 252
Laureate Field, *253*, 261–262
Law and Order League of Irondequoit, 176, 177
Lawson, Alfred, 69

League Alliance, 33, 80, 138, 139, 145, 258
League Park (Cleveland), 13
League Park (I), 75–76
League Park (II)/Central Oval, 76–77
League Park/Washington County Fairgrounds, 216–217
Leiter, Al, 102
Lenox Oval, *42*, 53–54
Leone, Adele, 78
Levinson, Barry, 123
Lincoln (Niagara Falls), 168
Little Falls Mets, 154
Live Oak Club (Rochester), 165, 166, 167, 168, *169*, 169–170, 200, 254
Lockport Locks, 130
Lockport White Sox, Cubs, Socks, and Reds, 130
Lone Star Baseball Club (Rochester), 168
Lone Stars (Middletown), 228
Long Branch Cubans, 240
Long Island Athletic Club, 62
Long Island Club, 65
Long Island Cricket Club Grounds, *15*, 20
Louisville Reds, 108
Lucas, Sam, 221

MacArthur Stadium (aka "BIG MAC")/Municipal Stadium, *186*, 191–192
MacArthur, General Douglas, 142, 191
MacCalman, Kenneth, 235
Macedon Macedons, 138
Mack, Connie, 113, 222
Maddox, Elliot, 72
Madison Square Park, *41*, 41–43
Maglie, Sal, 131–132
Malone Hop Pickers, 155–156

Manor House Grounds/Eckford
  Grounds/Greenpoint Grounds, *15*,
  18–19
Mantle, Mickey, 14, 85
Maple Avenue (Driving) Park/
  Interstate Fair Grounds, 89–93
Maple City Park, 97
Maple City Stadium, 97
Maple Hill Park, 229
Martin, Father Harold J., 159
Marvin Park, 127
Marvin, R. P., 127
Massena Alcoas, 156
Massena Grays, 156
Mathewson, Christy, 49, 69, 222
Mattingly, Don, 102
Mays, Willie, 72
McCarthy, Joe, 113
McConnell, Ambrose, 196
McDonough, Joseph, 148
McGee, Willie, 102
McGraw, John, 13, 26, 132, 222
McGraw, Tug, 140
McKinley, President William, 116
McMahon brothers, 53, 54
McNearney Brothers, 251
McNearney Stadium/Schenectady
  Stadium, 251–253
Mellon, Dr. Don, 183
"Merkle" play, 179, 206
Merkle, Fred 69, 179
Metropolitan Park/East River Ball
  Park, *41*, 50–51
Meusel, Emil Frederick "Irish," 232
Meyerrose Park/Ridgewood Park (II),
  60, 64, 68–71
Meyerrose, Joseph, 68–70
Michael Denkert and Company, 222
Mid-Atlantic League, 130
Middle Atlantic League, 131
Middletown Asylums and Middies,
  229

Midway Oval/Park, 236
Milwaukee Braves, 85, 136
Milwaukee Brewers, 157
Minnesota Twins, 148, 191
Mohawk Club (Brooklyn), 21
Mohawk Colored Giants, 246,
  247–250
Mohawk Giants (Schenectady), 54,
  228, 250
Mohawk Park/Electric City Park,
  250
Mohawk Valley Diamond Dawgs,
  154
Mohawk Valley Landsharks, 154
Mohawks (Schenectady), 244
Molina, Jose, 14
Monitor Club (Brooklyn), 21, 31
Monroe County Fairgrounds, 170
Montreal Expos, 124
Morgan's Flats, 80, 81
Morris, Dr. Lewis Rutherford, 100
Moscoso, Guillermo, 102
Mosier, Charles, 118
Mountain Athletic Field/Club
  Grounds, *213*, 213–216, 233
Murnane, Charles F., 196
Murray, Bill, 212
Murray's Park/League Park, 183, 184
Musial, Stan, 181
Mussina, Mike, 181
Mutuals (Washington, DC), 170
Mutuals of New York City, 192

Nashville Elites/Elite Giants, 57, 240
National Association, 1, 2, 10, 31, 33,
  40, 171, 172, 255, 256, 258
National Association of (Professional)
  Base Ball Players, 17, 31, 172
National Club of Lansingburgh, 255
National Club of Troy, 255
National Club/National Club of
  Albany, 202, 255, 256

Pagliarulo, Mike, 102
Paige, Satchel, 205, 248, 252
Pal-Mac Aqueduct County Park, 163–164
Palmyra Mormons, 145, 163
Pan-American Stadium, *105*, *116*, 116
Parkhurst Field/Johnstown-Amsterdam-Gloversville Park/A., J. & G. Baseball Park, *219*, 219–223
Pastime Club (Brooklyn), 20
Pastimes (Little Falls), 153
Pastimes (Schenectady), 244, 248
Peach, John A., 222
Peacock, Oscar Henry, 171
Peekskill Highlanders, 236
Peekskill Stadium, 236–237, 241
Penn Yan Colored Giants, 164–165
Penn Yan Cuban Giants, 164–165
Penn Yan Grape Pickers, 142, 164
Pepitone, Joe, 140
Petite, Andy, 14
Philadelphia Athletics, 88, 113, 171, 184, 258
Philadelphia Colored Giants, 209, 222
Philadelphia Giants, 91
Philadelphia Phillies, 50, 121, 124, 134, 159, 184, 191, 196, 197, 252
Philadelphia Stars, 57, 134
Pike, Lipman, 258
Pittsburgh Crawfords, 57, 191, 240
Pittsburgh Pirates, 40, 97, 124, 128, 134, 148
Plattsburgh Burghers, 238–239
Polo Grounds (I+II), 32, 34, *41*, *43*, 43–45
Polo Grounds (III)/Manhattan Field, *42*, 45–46, 47, 50, 64, 74
Polo Grounds (IV)/Brotherhood Park, *42*, *46*, 46–47, 48, 52
Polo Grounds (V)/Brush Stadium, 13, 28, 30, 40, *42*, 46, 47–50, *48*, 52, 221

Pompez, Alessandro, 56
PONY League, 97, 124–125, 128–129, 130, 131, 136
PONY League and New York–Penn League, 88, 95, 133, 141
Port Chester Clippers, 58–59
Posada, Jorge, 102
Poughkeepsie Bridge Citys, 239
Poughkeepsie Giants, 236–237
Poughkeepsie Giants and Chiefs, 241
Poughkeepsie Giants-Colts, 240
Poughkeepsie Honey Bugs, 240
Poughkeepsie Students, 240
Powell, John "Boog," 181
Powers, Pat, 176
Pre Emption Park/Fairgrounds, 145–146
Pugh, Johnny, 248
Pulteney Street Grounds, 146
Putnam Base Ball Club of Troy, 258
Putnam Grounds (III), 18
Putnam Grounds (Troy), *253*, 259
Putnams (Brooklyn), 18, 19, 31, 32

Quade, Mike, 198
Queens County Grounds, *60*, 61–62, 65
Queens Park, 11, 58

Racing Park, 107–108
Recreation Field (Glens Falls), 217
Recreation Field (Saratoga Springs), 243
Red Wing Stadium/Silver Stadium, *166*, 176, *179*, 179–182, 205
Remington company, 150–151
Rensselaer Driving Park, *253*, 255–257, 258
Resolutes/Resolute Club (Brooklyn), 20, 31, 230
Rhymes, Will, 102
Richardson Field/Park, 161–162

Author Biography

Although Bob Carlin is the author of 10 books and over 130 articles about American fiddle, banjo, and string band music, he is also a passionate follower of minor league and "wooden bat" college league baseball. As Carlin travels the country giving musical performances and lectures and conducting research, he spends his off-hours at local baseball parks. He continues to research, perform, and otherwise champion the music of rural America. For more information, visit www.bobcarlinmusic.com or his Facebook page.